The New Narcissus in the Age of Reality Television

This book explores the emergence and encouragement of the new narcissus in our society and the ways in which this is portrayed in reality television. Through studies of well-known reality shows, including *Toddlers and Tiaras*, *Hoarders*, *Sister Wives*, *Catfish: The TV Show*, *Celebrity Rehab with Dr. Drew* and *The Real Housewives*, the author examines the combined effects of narcissism and consumerism, shedding light on the ways in which people are pushed to focus on their own biographies and self-promotion to the point of creating a false self within the individual and the development of a sense of dissatisfaction, dis-ease and unhappiness.

Applying Freud's concept of narcissism and tracing it through the work of key social theorists including Durkheim, Lasch, Goffman, Riesman, Baudrillard and Giddens, *The New Narcissus in the Age of Reality Television* constitutes an insightful analysis of the modern ideology of greatness, perfection or 'being the best', that permeates society – an ideology that overwhelms and ultimately drives the individual to dissemble and project an artificial self. A compelling argument for the importance of understanding the persistence of a powerful and dangerous trait in modern society, this book will appeal to scholars of sociology, social theory and cultural and media studies with interests in reality television, celebrity culture and modern narcissism.

Megan Collins is Assistant Professor of Sociology at Prairie View A&M University, USA.

Classical and Contemporary Social Theory

Series Editor:
Stjepan G. Mestrovic, Texas A&M University, USA

Classical and Contemporary Social Theory publishes rigorous scholarly work that re-discovers the relevance of social theory for contemporary times, demonstrating the enduring importance of theory for modern social issues. The series covers social theory in a broad sense, inviting contributions on both 'classical' and modern theory, thus encompassing sociology, without being confined to a single discipline. As such, work from across the social sciences is welcome, provided that volumes address the social context of particular issues, subjects, or figures and offer new understandings of social reality and the contribution of a theorist or school to our understanding of it.

The series considers significant new appraisals of established thinkers or schools, comparative works or contributions that discuss a particular social issue or phenomenon in relation to the work of specific theorists or theoretical approaches. Contributions are welcome that assess broad strands of thought within certain schools or across the work of a number of thinkers, but always with an eye toward contributing to contemporary understandings of social issues and contexts.

For a full list of titles in this series, please visit: https://www.routledge.com/sociology/series/ASHSER1383

We Count, We Matter
Voice, Choice and the Death of Distance
Christopher Steed

Depressive Love
A Social Pathology
Emma Engdahl

The New Narcissus in the Age of Reality Television
Megan Collins

Existence, Meaning, Excellence
Aristotelian Reflections on the Meaning of Life
Andreas Bielskis

The New Narcissus in the Age of Reality Television

Megan Collins

Routledge
Taylor & Francis Group
LONDON AND NEW YORK

First published 2018 by Routledge

2 Park Square, Milton Park, Abingdon, Oxfordshire OX14 4RN
52 Vanderbilt Avenue, New York, NY 10017

Routledge is an imprint of the Taylor & Francis Group, an informa business

First issued in paperback 2019

British Library Cataloguing in Publication Data
A catalogue record for this book is available from the British Library

Library of Congress Cataloging in Publication Data
Names: Collins, Megan, author.
Title: The new narcissus in the age of reality television / Megan Collins.
Description: 1 Edition. | New York : Routledge, 2017. | Series: Classical and contemporary social theory | Includes bibliographical references and index.
Identifiers: LCCN 2017026399 | ISBN 9781138206977 (hbk) | ISBN 9781315463490 (ebk)
Subjects: LCSH: Narcissism. | Self. | Consumption (Economics) | Reality television programs--Social aspects. | Lifestyles.
Classification: LCC BF575.N35 C65 2017 | DDC 155.2/32--dc23
LC record available at https://lccn.loc.gov/2017026399

ISBN: 978-1-138-20697-7 (hbk)
ISBN: 978-0-367-33295-2 (pbk)

Typeset in Times New Roman
by Taylor & Francis Books

Contents

Figures

Series editor's preface

In this discerning study, Professor Megan Collins makes a significant scholarly contribution to both the theoretical understanding of the concept of narcissism, and reality television. Her conjunction of these two phenomena is significant because the prevailing views of both are pitifully shallow. The existing literature regards narcissism as a private problem afflicting a small percentage of individuals. Collins goes beyond the dutiful citations of Freud in discussions of narcissism, which fail to account for the social and cultural dynamics of narcissism. Even psychiatrist Christopher Lasch's often-cited *Culture of Narcissism*, while using the word 'culture', fails to go beyond the atomistic model of such culture as a collection of individual narcissists. As for the vast literature on reality television and media in general, Collins is not content with the prevailing assumptions that reality television is merely a cultural expression of authenticity, interest in ordinary people, connectedness, and other truisms. She demonstrates convincingly that the reality shows she chooses for analysis are replete with classic symptoms of narcissism: hoarding, perfectionism, selfishness, deceit, fake emotions, manipulation, and chronic boredom.

To achieve this link between narcissism and reality television, Collins moves beyond Freud to include Emile Durkheim on the classical end of social theory, and beyond Lasch to include David Riesman, Todd Gitlin, Sam Vaknin and Jean Baudrillard on the more contemporary end of social theory. She is correct to say that that Durkheim's concept of anomie includes the 'infinity of desires' that is so similar to the insatiability of narcissists. But sociologists have neglected Durkheim's characterization of the 'bottomless abyss' of desires as a symptom of anomie in favor of the meaningless and incorrect understanding of anomie as 'normlessness'. Durkheim never used the word 'normlessness' or any concept similar to it. And his overall point is that the desire for infinity becomes the norm in anomic societies, and is caused by society, not by individuals. Modern economies depend upon the assumption that there is no end or satiation point for the consumption of goods, fame, experiences, or achievement. In contemporary parlance, narcissism becomes the new normal in dysfunctional, anomic societies. Similarly, Veblen's well-known concepts of *conspicuous* consumption, leisure, and waste – as well as the *vicarious* nature of each of these three phenomena – resonate with classical understandings of the narcissist as always performing before an audience and craving the attention of others. The accent is on the words conspicuous and vicarious: contemporary types feel compelled to and are obsessed with posting what they consume on electronic media, and just as obsessed with counting the number of 'likes' that they receive (or fail to receive) from the vicarious watchers of their consumption. For example, it is common practice for people to post images of what they eat on electronic media, and just as common for others to 'follow' them online and thereby consume their experiences vicariously. Durkheim and Veblen ought to be included alongside Freud in discussions of the theories of narcissism.

Collins revives the once famous theories of David Riesman and Jean Baudrillard (who were both heavily influenced by Veblen), and more importantly, connects them to the concept of narcissism. Thus, she demonstrates convincingly that Riesman's concept of the 'other-directed' *social* type adds a cultural dimension to the individualistic understanding of the narcissist as craving the admiration and attention of others. It is anomic, other-directed society that socializes recent generations to judge every experience that they consume in their lives with a 'like' versus 'not like' on social media: persons, images, ideas, news stories, etc. Riesman was prophetic in his claim that increasingly, we are all judged by the jury of our peers – Collins updates him by pointing out all the judging that goes on in the media, and especially reality television. As for Baudrillard, Collins rightly ignores the label of post-modernist attached to him – a label that he often denied – and focuses on the content of his claims that resonate with symptoms of narcissism. For example, Baudrillard claimed that when we 'connect' to so-called others via the Internet and media, we are really plugged into our own brains. The so-called 'connectedness' of the media age is actually a narcissistic loop of self-reference. As illustration, one may easily witness contemporary persons 'plugged' into their electronic contraptions of various sorts at coffee shops, bus stops, classrooms, or any public places. They are oblivious to the actual others in their surroundings and 'connected' to images on screens, encapsulated in their own solipsistic worlds. Again, discussions of cultures of narcissism need to move beyond Lasch and include Riesman and Baudrillard.

Armed with these deeper as well as broader theories of narcissism, Collins has selected and analyzed six reality television shows. I shall not try to condense the rich understandings she offers in a few sentences. The significant point is that the narcissistic trends she uncovers – largely unrecognized because narcissism has become the new normal and because the existing theory is limited – are evident in other television programs as well as films. Watchers consume depictions of narcissistic symptoms on a regular basis, and are socialized in narcissism. The very addictions to and obsessions with television bespeak narcissistic conditions of boredom and infinite craving for novelty. The opposites of narcissism, what Veblen called the instincts of parenting, workmanship and curiosity, and what Durkheim called social solidarity and cooperation, fade in imagery and reality with each successive generation. Collins offers a deep and compelling discussion of this dark state of affairs.

1 Introducing the new narcissus

A tale that seems to be as old as humanity itself, one with a moral warning for all: the tale of Narcissus. Early versions by Conon and Ovid speak of a beautiful young man who was very much aware of his exceptional appearance. As a result of his egoism, Narcissus left behind a trail of broken hearts. At some point, via a jilted lover, he is cursed to love only himself for all eternity. Narcissus, upon seeing his reflection in a pond or riverbank is so enamored with his reflection, with himself, that he cannot part from his gaze. Suicide by obsessing over one's self. Obsessed with the reflection seen looking back at us.

> ... god-like
> ... ...
> He had a cruel heart, and hated all of them,
> Till he conceived a love for his own form:
> He wailed, seeing his face, delightful as a dream,
> Within a spring; he wept for his beauty.
> Then the boy shed his blood and gave it to the earth
> ... to bear.
>
> ('New light on the Narcissus myth' n.d.)

The above quoted passage is believed to now be the oldest version of Narcissus' tale, dating back to the middle of the first century BC. The translation is by W. B. Henry, who believes the author to be the poet Pathenius. Pathenius would later become the tutor of the renowned poet Virgil (Keys 2004).

Narcissus was 'god-like'. Today, many people idolize individuals who achieve greatness: celebrities, movie stars, the wealthy, and the brilliant. Individuals, that to many appear as god-like. Reality television has provided individuals the opportunity to access the lives of celebrities and others. Pathenius' story of Narcissus, believed to be the oldest version on record, describes Narcissus as having 'a love for his own form'. Today over 2,000 years later, what would someone writing a moral story about our present humanity say?

This book will attempt to piece together different stories. Stories that paint a picture of a broader message about our social world and the messages individuals internalize. Reality television may answer deeper, more existential questions about how we define our sense of self and how we as individuals relate to the rest of society. There are many avenues of our social world that are drastically changing on a daily basis. The growth of social media and reality television alters the way we look at others and ourselves. Youth are found posing in front of bathroom mirrors, fixated upon their reflections, sharing these images with those around them seeking out attention and admiration. A new cultural narcissism is present in social media and reality television. This encouragement to be narcissistic is a growing concern for our youth and for the future of humanity. Few are discussing this matter and reality television is just one part of society that reflects the social changes that are encouraging narcissistic behavior. What may be most haunting in the discussion to follow, are that these reality television shows portray an alarming and consistent message about our social world. We are living in a society obsessed with greatness, of being the best and most admired. You may be asking yourself at this point, what is so concerning about an ideology of greatness and being the best? With a little patience, and more importantly your curiosity, I will attempt to unpack the deep consequences of the messages found within reality television, messages that reflect an alarming consequence of socialization: the new narcissus.

Media immersion and the self

How is it possible that our society is becoming narcissistic? Where did this begin and how did it develop? Television and the other media are fairly recent developments in our world. Prior to television the newspaper and then the radio seeped into our lives to inform our thoughts and ideas. The extent to which all of media affects the individual has been debated for decades. In the most basic understanding, all agree that media does effect the individual in some way, shape and form.

Individuals have long been concerned with their sense of self and defining who they are as a person. What is different about our sense of self today and how we are developing our identity is that the process is now a mediated experience. Television, radio, print, and film are engulfing our lives and we are submerged in this mediated world from the moment we are born. Today, births are recorded, photographed, posted on Facebook and tweeted. The growth of a child is tracked and photographed then posted for all the parent's Facebook friends to follow. Does the child have a choice about their life being put on display? Reality television shifted from the periphery to primetime slots in the late 1990s. Social media followed closely behind, emerging in the 1990s and really blasting onto the scene in the early 2000s.

It is important to pause and reflect on the idea that the self is an ongoing, socially constructed process. As Peter Callero states:

> [T]he social construction of selfhood is also about the meanings and understandings associated with the public self, the self that is visible and

> known to others and encompassed by what we come to accept within the cultural category of personhood.
>
> (Callero 2003: 121)

Family, friends, religion and the media influence our identity and personality. Media is a reflection of our local communities and cultures providing insight into the unknown and unfamiliar. As reality television becomes an increasingly central aspect of our culture today it is important to understand the common themes and messages found within these programs and how those messages impact the formation of one's identity.

Todd Gitlin's (2001) work *Media Unlimited: How the Torrent of Images and Sounds Overwhelms Our Lives*, delivers insight into how the growth of media saturation in the United States is affecting the individual. 'The United States is the world capital of tinsel and celebrity, the homeland for the manufacture of images and soundtracks in unprecedented numbers and at unprecedented velocity' (9). Gitlin, who was a student of David Riesman, argues that we are now living our lives in the presence of the media. This research supports Gitlin's argument that an individual's constant connection and immersion in media (radio, television, film and Internet) is beginning to alter the formation and maintenance of the self. 'Media are occasions for experiences – experiences that are themselves the main products, the main transactions, the main "effects" of media. This is the big story; the rest is details' (2001: 10). Constant contact with the media provides the individual with opportunities to feel or experience feeling. Think about the last time you were moved by a sad movie or when you laughed until you cried at your favorite comedy. The media provides opportunities to *feel*. Gitlin argues that the increasing saturation of media in our lives leads to confusion as to what constitutes *authentic*, meaningful feeling.

> We are on our way here into a society of nonstop popular culture that induces limited-liability feelings on demand – feelings that do not bind and sensations that feel like, and pass for, feelings. A society consecrated to self-interest ends up placing a premium on finding life interesting.
>
> (41)

A society focused on finding life interesting doesn't sound so bad; after all, a life of boredom lacks appeal too. This research hopes to point to how the increase of reality television may very well be portraying the negative effects of media saturation. Where does an individual find authentic, meaningful feeling: in their interactions with others or through the consumption of reality television? The answer is likely a bit of both. The more important question is: what do individuals consuming the messages of reality television internalize?

Life has become discontinuous and full of anxiety for the individual. Social institutions are disembedded, otherwise understood as the 'lifting out of social situations from local contexts and their rearticulation across indefinite tracks of time-space' (Giddens 1991: 18). For Anthony Giddens, media serves as an example of such an institution that causes time and space to be separated from one another, placing the viewer in a position where they are physically separated from what they are watching. Media is a 'mediated experience' according to Giddens, reliant on language to link time and space and to link viewers to the lives of those they are watching. Giddens is extremely concerned with the increase of mediated experience in modern times and how it affects the self. Media does not necessarily display or mirror reality but in a sense helps to form it. There has also been a vast increase in the number of options available to the viewer and Giddens explains that it becomes 'a question of selecting between possible worlds' (Giddens 1991: 29). With modernity comes increased specialization and disembedded social institutions separating time and space leading to an increased focus on individuality and concern with defining one's sense of self.

Existential questions such as *who am I* and *who shall I become*, aid the individual in making the self a reflexive project. One becomes focused on constructing one's own biography and defining who one is as a person. As a result, Giddens argues that the self becomes fragile, brittle, fractured and fragmented, anxious about the world and themselves. The 'child learns about its body primarily in terms of its practical engagements with the object-world and with other people' (Giddens 1991: 56). The important relation of the body and self is important for understanding how one may go about constructing one's identity.

Giddens draws upon the work of Kierkegaard and Foucault arguing that the self is essentially separated from the body, causing it to act as if under remote control – an ironic description of this relationship considering we are looking at the effects of television on defining one's sense of self. Questions of what to do, how to act and who to be, cause the individual to be completely wrapped up in shaping their own individuality. Emile Durkheim articulates that '[r]eflection [...] has about it something personal and egoistic; for it is only possible as a person becomes detached from the outside world, and retreats from it into himself' (1951: 279). An individual can reflect upon his or her actions and decisions in a healthy way. However, '[t]he moment the individual becomes so enamored of himself, inevitably he increasingly detaches himself from everything external and emphasizes the isolation in which he lives, to the point of worship' (1951: 279). Angela McRobbie also discusses our current situation in what she refers to as 'reflexive modernization' where there is an 'unhealthy degree of belief in the self' (2001: 3). The self becomes a project to work on: being defined and then redefined as a result of social change.

Similarly, Erving Goffman discusses changes in the self in our modern world. Goffman argues that individuals are constantly performing depending upon the current situation they are involved in. For example, in a work environment we might perform differently than when on a first date with someone. Individuals 'present a front for an organization as well as for themselves' (Goffman 1959: 77). Presenting a front for an organization would look like behaving in a professional manner at a business lunch or putting on a face/personality that reflects that particular organization. Goffman indicates that this process of putting on a front is not only for the organization but also for the individuals themselves. What does it mean to present a front for your self? In today's world we can present ourselves as we like via social media avenues such as Facebook.[1] I want people to see me as *this type of person* who likes certain types of people, food, activities, movies, products, etc. Does presenting ourselves in a certain way alter who we are as individuals? If on a daily basis we present ourselves one way when deep down inside we are a different person, at one point do we lose sight of our true selves?

Children are growing up in a mediated world. The influences from peers and the media help shape the child and help to define one's sense of self.

> Under these newer patterns the peer group becomes much more important to the child, while the parents make him feel guilty not so much about violation of inner standards as about failure to be popular or otherwise to manage his relations with these other children.
>
> (Riesman et al. 1950: 37)

If children are expected to 'fit in' with their peers and be popular they will begin to look to others to aid in defining their sense of self. What am I supposed to like? How am I supposed to act? Cues are taken from one's peers as to how to appropriately behave. Riesman refers to this shift of the individual as the other-directed person.

> The other-directed person must be able to receive signals from far and near; the sources are many, the changes rapid. What can be internalized, then, is not a code of behavior but the elaborate equipment needed to attend to such messages and occasionally to participate in their circulation. As against guilt-shame controls, though of course these survive, one prime psychological lever of the other-directed person is a diffuse anxiety.
>
> (Riesman et al. 1950: 334)

Durkheim argues that we need social interaction in order to understand our place in the world. To learn what the rules and expectations are and to help us feel connected to our community and society. What is different about our current culture is that the media is heavily influencing our sense of solidarity. Individuals are becoming anxious, like Riesman describes above, by constantly looking to others (and the media) for guidance. This results in a feeling of pressure for the modern individual, a pressure to stay up to date with trends and expectations. Constant. Endless. 'While all people want and need to be liked by some of the people some of the time, it is only the modern other-directed types who make this their chief source of direction and chief area of sensitivity' (Riesman et al. 1950: 38). Riesman rightly points to this change in an individual's way of thinking. People today are more concerned about the perceptions of others, a concern that for many has morphed into an obsession.

Stjepan Mestrovic argues that as a result of these changes we are now living in a post-emotional society. A place where our emotions and feelings are artificially produced, packaged and sold by advertisers, corporations and governments. 'A new hybrid of intellectualized, mechanical, mass-produced emotions has appeared on the world scene' (1997: 26). Mestrovic argues that Americans' emotional lives are being manipulated on a highly organized scale to the point where freedom and choice is seen as a staple of our lives when in fact we are free to choose very little.

> The contemporary consumer is not just a mass society automation, as Adorno claimed, but an agent convinced that he or she possesses some degree of freedom to choose group identities, and this belief makes the agent a target of manipulation by corporations who pitch advertisements in relation to specific subgroup versions of emotional reality.
>
> (Mestrovic 1997: 81)

An emotional reality. Has our constant connection with emotions that are artificially constructed by advertisers and marketing experts created a desire for real, authentic feeling? Has the individual lost sight of real, authentic feeling vs. artificial and false feelings? The growth of technology and increased media saturation can arguably affect one's ability to understand authentic feeling. Where human interaction and community involvement once provided meaningfulness to an individual's life we now see an increased television consumption coupled with the growth of reality television. Emotional reality and understanding the depth of authenticity within reality television will be a recurring theme within this research.

In *The Perfect Crime*, Jean Baudrillard delves deep into the world that is obsessed with appearances:

> Doomed to our own image, our own identity, our own 'look', we become our own object of care, desire and suffering, we have grown indifferent to everything else. And secretly desperate at that indifference, and envious of every form of passion, originality and destiny.
>
> (1996: 131)

Individuals care about other's perceptions of themselves, resulting in our obsession with our own image. How we appear to others has become the focus for many, resulting in a craving for that which is truly original, passionate and real. Today, we can fake a certain persona in the hopes of being attractive to others. Attractive, not only in the romantic sense, but in the sense that you are a likeable, amiable person that others want to be around and even … be. We are now 'unhappy consciousnesses extracting from this necrological mirror an identity which is itself wretched' (1996: 137). Baudrillard argues we are extracting an identity from a dead mirror, an identity that should be sought by many. What does the identity look like in this necrological mirror? Reality television may provide an insight into this ideal persona, one that is desired by many and achieved by few. 'Projecting ourselves into a fictive, random world for which there is no other motive than this violent abreaction to ourselves. Building ourselves a perfect virtual world so as to be able to opt out of a real one' (1996: 37). Why would we choose to opt out of our real world? What is driving us to escape into reality television?

The process of adaptation in modernity

Modernity is no doubt absorbed by consumption and consumerism. 'Modernity confronts the individual with a complex diversity of choices and, because it is non-foundational, at the same time offers little help as to which options should be selected' (Giddens 1991: 80). As individuals we are bombarded with endless options and possibilities yet we have no choice but to choose. Our lifestyle choices not only define how to act but who to be and this is at the very core of self-identity. Baudrillard states 'consumption from this Durkheimian perspective is seen not as enjoyment or pleasure, but rather as something which is institutionalized, forced upon us, a duty [...] we must be trained, we must learn to consume' (1998: 4). Learning to consume from a young age will be explored in Chapter 2 on the reality television show *Toddlers and Tiaras*. Others have discussed the importance of material objects and consumption patterns in defining one's identity (Rose 1992; Rose 2002; Pecora 2002; Philips 2005; Bullen 2009; Tudor 2009). Anxiety becomes a characteristic of individuals as they are overwhelmed by the plurality of choices, yet Giddens argues that daily rituals and routines help one cope. Durkheim and Baudrillard expand upon this idea of being overwhelmed and full of anxiety as a result of consumerism. Baudrillard states that there is a 'catastrophic anxiety which is the deep effect of the market economy and generalized competition' (1998: 67). Constantly striving to have the best and newest material possession is repeatedly the focus of many. Durkheim originally made an important observation about consumerism and the pursuit of material wealth:

> All man's pleasure in acting, moving and exerting himself implies the sense that his efforts are not in vain and by walking he has advanced. However, one does not advance when one walks toward no goal, or – which is the same thing – when his goal is infinity. Since the distance between us and it is always the same, whatever road we take, we might as well have made the motions without progress from the spot. Even our glances behind and our feeling of pride at the distance covered can cause only deceptive satisfaction, since the remaining distance is not proportionally reduced. To pursue a goal which is by definition unattainable is to condemn oneself to a state of perpetual unhappiness.
>
> (Durkheim 1951: 248)

In a sense, the accumulation of material possessions is limitless. Therefore, when we aspire to obtain objects that satisfy us how is it that we are truly satisfied when there is no limit to the amount of possessions that we can acquire? As Durkheim goes on to explain, 'inextinguishable thirst is constantly renewed torture' (1951: 247). One may be satisfied with one's new shoes, bag, car, house, experience, but as soon as that object/possession is obtained do we not begin to dream of the next car, house, etcetera, that we can someday acquire? This analysis will address how this false belief in limitless aspirations is doing more harm than good for our own health as well as the health of our relationships with others.

Fatalism, or a resigned acceptance to the events in our lives, is a characteristic of modernity discussed by Durkheim. Is it any wonder that a feeling of powerlessness overwhelms individuals as a result of the multitude of choices and decisions we are faced with? What happens when our goals or objectives are not met? When we cease to feel satisfaction from material possessions that promise eternal happiness? Unrealized expectations or goals set by an individual can have extremely detrimental effects on one's self-esteem. The individual may withdraw as a result of shame or become completely narcissistic in order to shroud their shortcomings. Baudrillard explains that 'the true message the media of TV and radio deliver, the one which is decoded and "consumed" deep down and unconsciously is not the manifest content of sounds and images, but the constraining pattern' (1998: 122). This constraining pattern is that of the consumer society, to believe, trust and ultimately accept the structure. Baudrillard goes on to state that 'the closer one gets to true documentary [...] the greater does the real absence from the world grow' (1998: 122). What a powerful message to consider. With technological advances and the rise of reality television, more time is spent away from human contact yet we feel connected by this very technology that separates us. Reality television is just a new form of vicariously experiencing the lives of others. Or is it a form of voyeurism? When people engage with the media they are not only learning about the lives of others, they are also internalizing messages about their own self. The question remains as to how meaningful and truly valuable this interaction is.

Media can also be a method of therapy for individuals. Giddens believes that therapy today has replaced the morality religion once supplied. While there are many that still practice their faiths, others are turning to therapy to help cope with the ills of our society. The media takes therapy one step further by encouraging the viewer to participate in self-therapy as a result of what they watch, thereby further separating them from meaningful human interaction. The therapeutic culture of the self is discussed by Nikolas Rose in his article 'Governing the Enterprising Self,' where viewers' dependence on TV 'experts' also serves as a mechanism through which the viewer can help *themselves.* Rose calls it democratizing therapy, a self-therapy via what one consumes on television. Figure your problems out by consuming the messages of TV experts.

Deborah Philips (2005) examines the relationship of expert knowledge in television programs like TLC's *What Not to Wear*. The 'experts' chastise the individual chronicled during the 30-minute segment about their choices in fashion and 'school' them about what is appropriate attire. Philips rightly points out that shows such as this applaud narcissistic tendencies when stars emerge from these reality TV programs. Philips refers to these programs as 'aspirational television' which 'employ taste experts who market particular forms of style and confirm that investment in *their* cultural capital will result in profit' (226–227). Reliance on experts and the role of therapy in the formation of the new narcissus will be discussed in Chapter 3, which chronicles A&E's program *Hoarders*.

Other studies focus on the consumption of taste, experts, and the role media plays in relation to identity and consumerism (Hirsch 2000; Andrejevic 2002; Ong 2009; Pecora 2002; Philips 2005; Bullen 2009). Since consumption is so intimately related to many television shows, and media in general, we begin to see stark contrasts between who is 'in' and who is not. Unless you are buying the right products you may be labeled as 'other' and excluded from the 'in' group. Taken one step further, there is advocation that it is not simply a matter of 'us' vs. 'them' but me/I vs. everyone else. 'It is a network of anxious relations [...] it is no longer a question of "asserting oneself", of "proving oneself", but of relating to and gaining the approval of others, soliciting their judgment and their positive affinity' (Baudrillard 1998: 171). What is it about myself that makes me a unique individual? How will I be best received? These questions plague the minds of many individuals in our society whether they consciously recognize them or not.

Vincent Pecora clearly articulates how our society has increasingly become one focused on surveillance, resulting in an 'orgy of capitalist self-promotion' which leads to narcissistic tendencies in individuals (2002: 354). In a capitalist society what one consumes defines one's uniqueness. Therefore, for some, what we consume on television may help define our own unique individual nature. This relationship between consumerism, television and the individual can be problematic when we refer to Durkheim's concept of anomie. 'The state of derangement, or anomy is thus further heightened by passions being less disciplined, precisely when they need more disciplining' (Durkheim 1951: 253).[2] Consumerism allows for the possibility of accumulating an infinite amount of goods and possessions. When a person is hungry, they usually stop eating when their body tells them 'Hey, I'm full.' Yes, overeating and ignoring that natural trigger is commonplace in our society. However, this same idea, of a satiation point is present in all living creatures. Animals know when they have had enough food. With consumerism there is no end point: 'a rule the lack of rule from which they suffer' (Durkheim 1951: 257). When there is no end in sight, individuals may become overwhelmed and may be confused as to how to appropriately function. Goals, dreams, desires and pursuits are infinite. There is nothing to place a limit on the amount of material possessions that have become so important to many. The forthcoming exploration of reality television will explore the disastrous effects anomie can have on the individual when they are no longer capable of checking themselves.

The surveillance of others and growth of narcissism

Another important observation is that of the growth in surveillance and the effects it has on the individual. 'The expansion of surveillance capabilities is the main medium of the control of social activity by social means' (Giddens 1991: 149). Mark Andrejevic and Vincent Pecora also examine the growth of surveillance and how fictional worlds are becoming indistinguishable from real ones. Surveillance is seen as good and required for verification/acceptance in society, public and private spheres are blurred and there has been a growth in the lack of concern for others. The more one uses technology the more one may become separated from meaningful interactions with other individuals. Instead, there is a surface level relationship, intent on seeking out acceptance and admiration simultaneously. 'Narcissism is intrinsic to the culture of surveillance shaping reality TV' (Pecora 2002: 355). People have developed an interest and desire to expose themselves and jump at the chance to participate in reality television programs. Look at me, here I am, don't you think I'm great?!? I need to know that you think I'm great! Mark Andrejevic believes this phenomenon is both 'a fascination with voyeurism on the one hand and fame on the other – pathologies of a society in which the public sphere has been eclipsed by the private one' (2002: 253). How often does one find oneself bombarded with personalized advertisements as one surfs the web? It was eerie at first seeing advertisements that directly related to my own interests and pursuits. Andrejevic states that 'consumer control boils down to the ability to have preferences monitored in detail' (2002: 256). Our preferences are not only being monitored by advertisers but by our friends in real life and in online communities. Do we accept this surveillance or feel powerless in its wake?

Sigmund Freud's *On Narcissism* articulates that most individuals are born without an ego, yet children develop a love and need for admiration of their 'self'. Most individuals then mature and are taught (through their parents) the importance of interacting with their social environment and retaining a healthy level of care for the self. When individuals instead place an extreme focus on receiving attention and admiration for their 'self' this is when unhealthy narcissism emerges. In a sense, individuals in our culture may be attempting to cope with the consumer structure of society. Many are maintaining an extreme focus on the self and regressing to childhood, where we develop an unhealthy reliance on others in order to feel needed and loved.

Sam Vaknin's work *Malignant Self-Love: Narcissism Revisited* provides the reader with a very clear understanding of narcissism and its devastating effects. Vaknin, who claims to be a narcissist, defines narcissism by nine (extremely important) criteria adapted and altered from the definition provided in the *DSM-IV.*

1 Exaggerates accomplishments, talents, skills, contacts and personality traits to the point of lying, feels grandiose and self-important.
2 Obsessed with fantasies of unlimited success.
3 Firmly convinced that s/he is unique and, being special, can only be understood by, should only be treated by, or associate with, other special or unique, or high status people (or institutions).
4 Requires excessive admiration, adoration, adulation, attention and affirmation (Narcissistic Supply).
5 Feels entitled, has unreasonable expectations for special and favorable priority treatment.
6 Uses others to achieve his or her own ends.
7 Devoid of empathy, is unable or unwilling to identify with, acknowledge, or accept the feelings, needs, preferences, priorities, and choices of others.
8 Constantly envious of others and seeks to hurt or destroy the objects of his or her frustration.
9 Behaves arrogantly and haughtily, feels superior, omnipotent, omniscient, invincible, immune, above the law and omnipresent. Rages when frustrated, contradicted or confronted by people s/he considers inferior to him or her and unworthy.

(2001: 32)

The *DSM-V* has since been released and still retains eight criteria for Narcissistic Personality Disorder (NPD) that can be diagnosed if a patient exhibits five or more traits. There was also much debate about whether or not all of the ten Personality Disorders (PDs) would remain in the *DSM-V* as a result of the difficulty in diagnosing and treating people who suffer from these disorders. Interesting to note that work began on the *DSM-V* in 2007 with an expected release and publication in 2013 (which did indeed occur). However, during this time the Personality and Personality Disorder (PPD) work group collaborated on what was to be included, changed, and deleted in this updated version of the *DSM*. On February 10, 2010 the PPD work group posted the official proposal for the *DSM-V*, which did not include NPD nor four other PDs (see Campbell et al. 2010: 640). Half of the personality disorders were simply excluded from the draft of the forthcoming *DSM-V*. This caused quite a bit of uproar within academia and psychiatry. Ultimately, NPD would remain as one of the ten original personality disorders, but I do not believe this would have occurred had it not been for the efforts of several psychiatrists and academics who spoke out in opposition to the work group.

These traits of narcissism will be repeatedly observed in all the reality television episodes discussed in the following chapters. Some might argue that anyone who agrees to be on reality television show is a bit of a narcissist. However, the behaviors of the people present in these episodes are not entirely unusual and out-of-the-ordinary for many people that one might encounter on a daily basis. Vaknin goes on to observe that

> [N]arcissism is a defense mechanism intended to deflect hurt and trauma from the victim's 'true self' into a 'false self' which is construed by the narcissist to be omnipotent, invulnerable and omniscient. The Narcissist uses the false self to regulate his or her liable sense of self-worth by extracting from his environment Narcissistic Supply [admiration, adoration, adulation, attention and affirmation].
>
> (Vaknin 2001: 33)

The new narcissus is the false self. Some research examines narcissism from an individual perspective; arguing that this disorder emerges within the individual. The fields of psychiatry and psychology often take an individual approach, attempting to 'cure' the individual of their personality disorder. My research instead argues that the new narcissus is a symptom of a societal disorder. I intend to argue that our society, with a focus on consumerism and being the best, encourages the development of the false self in order to succeed. For if one does not have extraordinary or unique traits, but one can fake it, then success is still possible.

Americans are now living in a society surrounded by media, searching for meaning and validation through the cues of others. In the late 1970s Christopher Lasch wrote that America was becoming a narcissistic society. Individuals were developing an obsession with celebrity while a simultaneous spread of bureaucracies began to increasingly stifle the individual. There is an immense pressure to be more like stars and celebrities. One is constantly bombarded by this pressure, through tabloid magazines, entertainment news reports, and now through reality television (that often chronicles celebrities). If an individual lacks faith in their inner self, becoming narcissistic can provide an outlet through which to gain that attention, admiration and adulation that celebrities are afforded.

> The narcissist has many traits that make for success in bureaucratic institutions, which put a premium on the manipulation of interpersonal relations, discourage the formation of deep personal attachments, and at the same time provide the narcissist with the approval he needs in order to validate his self-esteem.
>
> (Lasch 1978: 44)

This is where a growing narcissistic society becomes problematic. If individuals today are exhibiting narcissistic traits, or are constantly shown narcissistic individuals on television then this must have an impact on culture and how individuals construct their sense of self. If you are unable to achieve greatness due to the strangling effects of bureaucracies and consumerism then maybe if you begin to be narcissistic you will achieve that success. Bureaucracies allow individuals to easily manipulate their relationships with others for their own personal gain. Currently, 'impressions overshadow achievements', and the narcissist is purely interested in how they come across to others (Lasch 1978:

60). By manipulating the impressions of others around them, the narcissist can gain a sense of satisfaction that they would otherwise not receive. Christopher Lasch focuses most of his discussion on the impact bureaucracies have in the formation of narcissism. While this is important to consider, this research also argues that narcissism can be encouraged through the home, family and media. A society of manipulative, inauthentic individuals, only concerned with their own personal gain, will have disastrous consequences for society. Understanding how our society is becoming narcissistic, what causes it and through what avenues, aids in understanding the formation of the new narcissus today.

This story explores six different reality television shows in the hopes of showing a progression of narcissism and the development of the false self through several different stages in an individual's life. In Chapter 2, The Learning Channel's (TLC) program *Toddlers and Tiaras* serves as an example of how the new narcissus can be encouraged and developed at a very early age. In Chapter 4 the exploration of Music Television's (MTV) program *Catfish* provides insight into adolescence/young adulthood age group in relation to narcissism and the false self. Chapter 5 chronicles TLC's *Sister Wives* that provides an in-depth look at the lives of a polygamous family. Chapter 3 on A&E's *Hoarders* and Chapter 6 on VH1's *Celebrity Rehab with Dr. Drew* will serve as two examples of the ills of narcissism, consumerism and our obsession with celebrities. To explore whether or not the messages of the new narcissus are found internationally, Chapter 7 compares the *Real Housewives* franchise in the U.K., Australia and the U.S. The story will uncover deeper messages within seemingly different reality programs, shedding light on the devastating effects of the new narcissus. When one mentions any of these television programs or the phenomenon the programs are portraying, an immediate reaction may be one of repulsion and disgust at the participants' behaviors and lifestyle choices. However, when one takes a closer look, these programs all are portraying many important themes about our own society and the individuals within it. There are deep implications here, not only for our own society and its perceived ills but also for the audience that takes on the role of voyeur when watching reality TV.

Reality television is produced and in many ways constructed behind the scenes. Individuals (whom the audience never sees or hears) often conduct interviews with the cast members in the form of confessionals and voiceovers. Encouragement to behave or act a certain way may be coming from the production staff as well. The entire economic aspect behind reality television, from commercials and audience polling to focus groups before the show even airs, are all aspects that should be taken into consideration when attempting to discern the messages found within reality television programs. At the end of the day reality TV is a product to be sold to the audience. The audience is the commodity for each of these different television networks. In order to make a profit, the show must have a large audience in order to obtain advertising sponsors. What content gets the most attention, admiration, adulation and adoration (Narcissistic Supply) from the people watching television? The television networks need an audience that *pays attention* in order to survive. The question remains: are these messages of narcissism within the reality television programs, and within the economic aspect of the production of these programs, trickling down and encouraging narcissism within the modern individual?

This story aims to capture the essence of reality television and discover the understandings of meanings and actions for the individuals portrayed within the different programs studied. Reality television is a reflection of human behavior and merits further analysis in order to uncover the trends of narcissism, consumerism and falseness within our society. This analysis will focus on how this emergence of the false self is a symptom of society, not just an individual disorder. My purpose in this analysis is not to test a hypothesis or prove a theory. Rather, I intend to use detailed studies of reality television programs as illustrations of various theoretical perspectives on narcissism and modernity. Our culture is increasingly becoming dominated by reality television, an overshadowing mirror of our culture's ideologies, behaviors and identities. Will our culture become so fixated on our own realities, our own beauty, fame, and fortune to the point that we lose ourselves? Will we suffer the same demise as the old story of Narcissus committing suicide via our obsession with self? Some may believe that reality television is not a reflection of reality and that the audience is not observing aspects of our selves. The threat and fear that we *are*, however, looking at our selves within what is portrayed in reality television is worthy of further examination. Reality television is a part of our culture today and the messages found within it need to be deciphered in order to better understand the impact it has on individuals.

Notes

1 At the time of Goffman's writing (1951) media was in its infancy. Television would not enter the homes of individuals until the end of the 1950s. Goffman's concept of impression management is often utilized today in terms of the individual's interaction with media. However, Goffman's original conception of the term did not incorporate media.

2 The concept of anomie is commonly misinterpreted in many sociological texts and readings as being a state of normlessness. This definition is misleading, as Durkheim never uses the term. Instead, one can see here that he uses the term 'de-regulation' or 'without regulation'. The word comes from Greek ανομία, namely the prefix a- 'without', and nomos, 'law'.

2 Learning the importance of falseness

Toddlers and Tiaras

> I wear fake eyelashes but it's pretty cool and feels weird when you first put it on but after, it just feels like your regular eyes.
>
> (Sims 2009)

Seven-year-old Alicia's profound statement embodies the focus of this chapter: falseness may feel a little weird at first, but after a while, the falseness will begin to feel like your regular self. The new narcissus depends on a perfected presentation of falseness to others in order to secure attention and admiration. Media is a socializing agent for the modern individual and is a vessel through which messages about an individual's role in society are communicated to the viewer. Understanding the implication of those messages is of importance when discovering the process through which the new narcissus develops today. Modern individuals must prove that they are the best through competition, and one's personality and confidence will help in winning and coming out on top. Even more, there is the notion that artificially enhancing one's self can help one win too. Individuals receive the contradictory messages of being real and authentic yet by being false and insincere one can also achieve the same results.

Toddlers and Tiaras is a reality television program that chronicles the lives of young girls who compete in child beauty pageants. The Learning Channel (TLC) is owned by Discovery Communications, whose slogan is 'the number-one nonfiction media company'. The show *Toddlers and Tiaras* first aired on 27 January 2009 and continued for six consecutive seasons before a short-lived ending in October 2013. *Toddlers and Tiaras* would return for a new season in August 2016. This particular reality television program has been met with much controversy as to the behavior of the parents in placing their young impressionable children in such an environment as a beauty pageant. What may be disturbing for the reader is that the messages and lessons explored henceforth are intended for young children who are at a delicate, impressionable stage of development and socialization. The messages found within 'National Gold Coast', which is the fourth episode of the second season, will be the focus of this chapter.

In childhood, individuals are socialized to learn what is expected of them as an individual: one's goals, aspirations, correct behavior, language and values.

> [T]he California Gold Coast pageants is an originator of pageants. We have started over 35 years ago. When we did start we started with babies and children where a lot of the 'teen' and 'miss' pageants didn't offer that. California Gold Coast Pageants were featured in *Little Miss Sunshine* and it was quite excitement for the whole pageant world at that time. Many girls in our pageant have been picked up by an agent and have gone on into the movie business: Michelle Pfeiffer, Beverley Mitchell and Mariska Hargitay. You'll see nothing but glitz and glamour from Hollywood.
>
> (Sims 2009)

From the moment this episode begins, the audience is exposed to an emphasis on celebrities: implying the possibility that by competing in beauty pageants these young girls might one day be famous too. Hollywood is 'nothing but glitz and glamour' and that's the expectation for the young girls competing. Fame is often equated with success: the idea that an individual has excelled, in some aspect of life, to a point to which they deserve recognition throughout all of society. Young people often dream of being famous or having lots of money because our society has instilled in us this idea that success equals fame and fortune, arguably because of our increased interaction with media: the platform on which fame and success is built is made apparent for all to see. While the pageant director speaks, the viewer is shown images of young girls performing on stage at the pageant. The viewer is then introduced to the three girls and their families that are highlighted in this episode: Alicia, Rylan Lee and Emily.

'My name is Alicia, I'm seven years old and I love pageants' (Sims 2009). Alicia's mom is then introduced: 'I'm April and my seven year old daughter Alicia loves to have all eyes on her'. Mom then grabs a crown from a display case and places it on her head (see Figure 2.1).

'This is the crown I won when I was in a pageant with Alicia.' The camera zooms out to reveal Alicia standing next to Mom with a crown on her head as well, looking up at her mom. Both mother and daughter in their initial interaction with the camera choose to emphasize the symbol of their past victories: a crown. Instantly, audience members must understand that Alicia and her mom are winners. Even more than that, *Toddlers and Tiaras* is supposed to focus on young little girls who compete in beauty pageants. However, this initial interaction between mother and child indicates that much more is happening beneath the surface when little girls compete in beauty pageants. The idea that mothers want to live vicariously through their children is not an uncommon discussion when looking at child beauty pageants. Mommy never competed in a beauty pageant but now, due to the existence of a daughter, she can experience what it means to be in a pageant and even win. Alicia's mother even states that Alicia likes to have 'all eyes on her'. It is pressing to

Figure 2.1 Alicia's mom with her crown

know whether or not Alicia truly loves attention because the message she is receiving from her mother is clear: Alicia loves attention. The narcissist relies upon the attention from others in order to survive. The clear message to viewers early in the episode is that having attention from others is valued and important. April introduces herself in the same breath that she describes her daughter as loving attention. People are watching television and there is an urgent need to understand the messages that the audience is internalizing about our social world. All of the families portrayed in this reality television series are reliant upon thousands of dollars in order to compete in pageants. The children are constantly imitating their parents behaviors and reliant upon their 'coaching' in order to compete.

In an interview Alicia's mom states

> when we first entered Alicia in pageants it was because she got sick and was being diagnosed with a kidney disorder and she had stopped growing and all the little kids were starting to tease her so we thought that pageants would be a good way for her to start having more confidence.

Now Alicia and her mother are shown looking at all her crowns and trophies that take up a whole wall of her bedroom. 'You've won a lot … [mom looks at camera] hopefully we're going to add another one!' The message that confidence is of the utmost importance is present for many parents and all those involved in pageants. Parents and coaches constantly reiterate winning and being the best. *You must win another crown at this next pageant Alicia.* The message that there can be only one true winner in the pageant is also conveyed. Alicia then states 'I've won Grand Supreme and its one of the biggest crowns I've wished of in my dreams and I got it. I got my dream!' The dream is to win the highest title of the pageant: ultimate grand supreme. This is the only acceptable title to win. At this point in the episode confidence appears to be the best way to obtain a crown and a title.

'My name is Rylan Lee and I'm four years old and I wanna win a crown at Gold Coast Pageants' (Sims 2009). The pageant director informs us that Rylan Lee is a novice in the pageant world as she has only competed in six pageants. Rylan states in her interview: 'I have twenty crowns and I love 'em.' Rylan speaks robotically as though she has practiced introducing herself to the camera and ultimately the audience. When the viewer is introduced to Rylan's mother she explains: 'We actually saw a couple of pageant shows on TV and Rylan said "Mom, I want to do that."' Images found on the television screen, in addition to the interaction one has with others, can be used to socialize individuals to know their place in the world. Rylan learned about beauty pageants through watching television and then desired to be in one herself. Consumer society is based upon the belief that material possessions result in happiness for the individual. Acquiring trophies and crowns proves to the individual their success in competing with others, and as being the ultimate winner amongst a group of rivals. Competition is a necessary component of a consumer-based society. Therefore, individuals are often labeled and come to know their sense of self in terms of winning and losing.

Rylan and Mom show the cameras all of Rylan's trophies and Mom helps Rylan count the number of sashes she has. Rylan states 'We don't say I'm the best. We only say "I can try it, if we don't win that's ok." If we do win, we're excited.' The viewer cannot help but wonder if Rylan is speaking or if her mom is speaking through her. Rylan knows that she is supposed to be okay with not winning but ultimately, in order to be excited, she has to win. 'The actions of the body become more and more dead, unreal, false, [and] mechanical' for the modern individual (Giddens 1991: 61). Already, a four-year-old child is displaying elements of a detached body and self. Rylan knows she is supposed to think and feel one way about pageants but often how she is *supposed* to think and feel contradict with her true feelings. Even Rylan's attempt at repeating the advice of her mother seems mechanical, almost robotic in nature. It is important to note that throughout any episode of *Toddlers and Tiaras*, the little girls that compete in these pageants receive the same contradictory message: that it is 'ok' not to win, but ultimately, winning is the only *acceptable* outcome. Nothing else will suffice or make them happy. The advice of Rylan's mom is not uncommon for parents; however, the message is clear: not winning is just 'ok' while winning equals success. Already, these young girls are learning what it means to be an individual in a consumer-based society dependent upon competition: being the final victor is most important.

'My name is Emily Salazar, I like to walk the stage' (Sims 2009). Emily then informs the viewer that she is a daddy's girl. We are introduced to

Emily's father: 'my name is Alex, I'm a pageant dad and I'm proud of it'. Emily's mom discusses how Emily is a daddy's girl and how Alex loves to be involved in the pageants and was very excited when he won an award for his involvement in the pageants.

Alex exclaims 'Emily has about 165 trophies.' Alex has a crown on his head as Emily and her parents show all her crowns and awards to the viewer (see Figure 2.2). Emily exclaims, 'Mine looks cute!' to which Alex responds 'But I got a better smile.' Emily's dad then asks Emily what her favorite award has been and Emily responds by rubbing her fingers together and says 'Money.' Alex and Emily's mom laugh. Already, the viewer cannot escape the exposure to consumerism, competition and the importance of coming out on top with the ultimate prize being money. Even Emily's father is competing with her and reminding her that having the *best smile* is important. One's smile is an aspect of one's self that can be subject to competition with others. At this early point in the program (less than 5 minutes in) the viewers are asked to note that success is equated with winning the pageant and obtaining the ultimate prize of money. The pageant is glitz and glamour just like Hollywood and if you are successful in the pageant you might became famous like people in Hollywood too. The lessons of capitalism often loom beneath the surface, occasionally rearing their head as an reminder that possessions, money, and self-customization should always be kept in focus.

The viewer is then exposed to the three girls' practices and how they prepare for the pageants. Alicia's mom explains: 'to prepare Alicia practices and even when there's not a pageant we practice' (Sims 2009). All of her brothers

Figure 2.2 'So how do we look?'

and her dad act as judges while she is practicing 'so to reminder her of looking at all the judges'. Alicia must learn to acknowledge the judges and smile at them. Alicia's older brother states 'give 'em the same smile when you want Dad to buy you something', and everyone laughs. Four-year-old Emily has dolls set up as her judges. Both Mom and Dad work with Emily, referring to their positions as 'coaches'. Mom and Dad inform the audience via voiceover that Emily usually begins practicing three weeks before a pageant with an increase in coaching the closer they get to the pageant. For Rylan, her mom explains, 'we just play pageant for about 15… 15–20 minutes'. After a short stint at practice, Rylan's mom asks calmly from the couch if Rylan would like to try her beauty walk. Rylan declares 'No!' Rylan's mom asks nicely again and Rylan begins throwing a tantrum and pulling up the rug on the floor completely wrapping herself up in the rug. Dad steps in and tries to persuade Rylan to work a little bit longer on her routines and Rylan continues to roll around on the floor, hiding by the couch. Mom explains to the camera that she is tired. Rylan mumbles something under her breath and Mom says 'We don't say stuff like that.' Rylan says 'You're a fool!' Then, Rylan's mom says 'Nope, let's go to bed,' and then smiles at the camera as she escorts Rylan out of the room. Rylan yells 'No!'

With the first commercial break the viewer is provided an opportunity to reflect upon the newly presented individuals and their lives. Judgments can be made or very well may have already been.

> The mass media routinely present modes of life to which, it is implied, everyone should aspire; the lifestyles of the affluent are, in one form or another, made open to view and portrayed as worthy of emulation […] stories are developed in such a way as to create narrative coherence with which the reader or viewer can identify.
>
> (Giddens 1991: 199)

The viewer in the first ten minutes of programming has been exposed to three young girls and their families, why they have chosen to participate in pageants, and how they prepare and practice for pageants. Anthony Giddens argues that regardless of the reasons why individuals watch television there is still an interaction that takes place between what is witnessed on the screen and the individual (or audience). The viewer has been allotted the opportunity to assess the children as individuals and what types of personalities they have developed as well as insight into the types of parents each girl has. Many may choose to watch such a program purely to critique these families and the decisions they make. Others may identify with the families or individuals because the viewer is a part of a similar family or aspires to be like them. And yet others may simply be intrigued by the behavior of the girls and their families, or disgusted. The motive for watching will not be a central area of concern in this book because regardless of motive, the messages transmitted to the viewer are consistent and important to understand. Individuals in a society will conform to the expectations, values, wishes and beliefs of others in order to feel connected and integrated even if that means the expectations witnessed and internalized from the media. This reality television program exposes when and how the message that *falseness is acceptable* is not only communicated to viewers in the audience but to these young girls who compete in beauty pageants as well.

A common reaction to this television program is that these mothers are vicariously living through their daughters. Sam Vaknin discusses the female narcissist and her behaviors: '[T]he smothered and spoiled child is dehumanized and instrumentalized. [Her] parents love [her] not for what [s]he really is but for what they wish and imagine [her] to be: the fulfillment of their dreams and frustrated wishes' (Vaknin 2001: 198). Vaknin is stating that vicariously living through your child can be traumatic for that child. A child often develops their own desires and wishes, and if these do not coincide with parental desires and wishes, conflict can result. Even more, the trauma experienced by the child of being unable to live up to the expectations of their parent(s) can cause the child to develop a mentality that states over and over again in their head: 'never good enough'. Also, Vaknin expresses that spoiling a child is a form of trauma. If a child constantly receives everything they want, then they learn that the world is always able to fulfill their desires, wishes and wants. However, many individuals today know that this is not the case and that they cannot always have their desires fulfilled. If these young children are internalizing the idea that they will always get whatever they want, then, Vaknin argues, this is a form of trauma and abuse, because this message does not coincide with reality. Vaknin goes on to articulate that childhood trauma can often lead that child to grow up to become a narcissist. 'Narcissists tend to breed narcissists' (Vaknin 2001: 208). Children, such as those witnessed in this reality television program, learn to value attention and admiration from others as the ultimate source of satisfaction. 'Alicia loves to have all eyes on her.' The family is an influential agent in socializing an individual. Interactions with parents and siblings help to incorporate that child into their social world so that they come to understand their place in it. If Mom and Dad rely on attention from others in order to achieve satisfaction this has a higher likelihood of being internalized by the child as a necessary condition for survival. Similarly, participation in beauty pageants communicates that attention from judges will lead to winning. In time, narcissistic supply can become a coping strategy and means through which the individual attempts to fill the void deep inside them. Parents can even socialize children to see themselves as an object. If the parents treat their child as something that is created, often through artificiality, then the child is internalizing the message that they are an object to be worked on and created. Both Alicia's mom and Emily's dad also presented the viewer with their own crowns that they had won at pageants. It is very possible that these parents are indeed narcissistic and possibly dreamed of being a beauty queen or having a relationship with one. Now, they are able to fulfill that dream by using their daughter as a mechanism by which to do so.

Confidence and competition

Following the commercial break Alicia's mom explains to the camera that 'pageants have taught Alicia how to get what she wants and just be able to go after whatever it is and have the confidence to do it' (Sims 2009). Alicia's mom has already instilled in her child the importance of getting whatever it is that Alicia wants and in order to do so she must have confidence, otherwise she will be unsuccessful in her endeavors. These are pretty powerful messages that Alicia is being exposed to at the age of seven. Giddens clearly describes this as 'confidence in the integrity and value of the narrative of self-identity' (1991: 66). In a sense, Alicia's mom is teaching Alicia that if she is comfortable with her 'self' she will be able to get whatever it is she wants. But what happens when she is confident in her 'self' and she is unable to get what she wants, such as winning the pageant crown? Furthermore, we must examine the self that Alicia is being encouraged to construct. All individuals, through the process of socialization, come to form an understanding of their 'self'. However, Alicia is learning that an artificially constructed self is important and that working to create that false self will result in the obtainment of a pageant crown, happiness and money.

The viewer then witnesses the Salazar family spend 5 hours at the salon for Emily. She has a manicure, pedicure, facial, massage and her hair done while her parents stand idly by, watching, at her side, asking on several occasions if Emily 'feels like a princess'. Emily's dad states 'I honestly feel that it's going to help her. It does like pamper her, it makes her feel like a princess so it gives her that self-confidence, so' (Sims 2009). Both Alicia's parents and Emily's feel that by pampering their children and placing them in pageants, the child will gain self-confidence. Emily's dad, Alex, explains: 'I say she's loved and *I express my love by buying her things* and she's our only child so I guess you could say she's spoiled because she's daddy's little girl.' Identity and one's uniqueness can be determined by what they buy. The American myth (dream) has long informed its citizens that money will buy you happiness. Alex's father feels that by buying things for his daughter he is expressing his love for her. Sam Vaknin states:

> [O]verweening, smothering, spoiling, overvaluing, and idolizing the child are all forms of parental abuse. There is nothing more narcissistically-gratifying than the admiration and adulation (Narcissistic Supply) garnered by precocious child-prodigies. Narcissists who are the sad outcomes of excessive pampering and sheltering become addicted to it.
>
> (Vaknin 2001: 142)

Vaknin is indicating that the likelihood these young girls will grow up to be narcissistic is very strong. A young viewer may also begin to think about their parents as expressing love for them through what they buy. If money is equated with happiness in so many avenues of our daily lives it is not unusual to see money, and buying things, as a means through which love can be communicated and happiness and satisfaction obtained for both parties. Vaknin warns that children may become addicted to this 'pampering' and come to expect it. The young girls witnessed in this program are learning that salon trips, getting what 'one' wants and confidence are most important for the individual. If an individual is able to successfully portray confidence to others, then more pampering (salon trips, material possessions and attention) is sure to follow suit. The message to the viewer is that parents can express their love by buying consumer goods for their children. Likewise, child viewers might internalize the message that when parents buy them things that means they love them. The individuals witnessed in this program have adapted to the structure of a consumer society. Material goods can be an expression of your love for family members.

Meanwhile, while Emily is busy being pampered at the salon we witness Rylan Lee and her parents go to a fitting for pageant wear. 'When someone is looking for a pageant dress we meet with the parents and the child so I can see what her personality, hair coloring, eyes and personality is. That does have a play in it.' The dressmaker emphasizes personality as being important and being a part of the package to win the ultimate prize. Apparently, the little girl's personality also helps determine the type of dress she should wear too. Dad (in an interview) exclaims '[f]inancially, I'd prefer not to know the cost of the dresses' (Sims 2009). The dressmaker informs the audience in an interview that dresses start at $650 and go up from there depending on the type of dress. Mom wants to have two dresses made. The dress-maker as she is measuring Rylan says 'Oh! Perfect girl. Keep that! Perfect shape!' (see Figure 2.3). Sure, this may seem like a nice compliment to some but to a young, impressionable four-year-old girl the dressmaker's words may have a deeper impact. The dressmaker has essentially just informed Rylan that she has a 'perfect' body and that she should keep it. What happens if Rylan doesn't keep this 'perfection?' Giddens explains that 'shame depends on feelings of personal insufficiency, and these can compromise a basic element of an individual's psychological make-up from an early age' (1991: 65). The viewer has now witnessed an encouragement to maintain some standard of 'perfection'.

If an individual is unable to *naturally* present an acceptable body image they can then alter themselves to fit that standard. Even more so, in order to maintain 'perfection' one must understand that keeping a child-like body is essential. Giddens warns that if a child comes to understand messages such as those witnessed within *Toddlers and Tiaras*, then not only will the child's psychological make-up be compromised, but now these little girls will grapple with feelings of shame constantly. It is physically impossible to keep the perfect shape of a child's body, but despite this, that message is often reinforced by parents, coaches, pageant directors and judges. Even if pageant children come to understand that a child-like body is unobtainable, the drive to maintain 'perfection' still exists. Durkheim warns that constantly striving towards an unobtainable goal results in a state of anomie for the individual, characterized

Figure 2.3 'Perfect shape!'

by intense feelings of anxiety, exhaustion and never obtaining satisfaction no matter how much one tries. The dresses that these little girls wear in beauty pageants are extravagant not only in their appearance but in their price. The modern individual is constantly faced with this exorbitance and pushed to obtain what is necessary to succeed, even if it lies outside their financial means. In this particular example one must spend lots of money in order to win the pageant, as money can buy not only lavish dresses but also the confidence needed to succeed.

Alicia also goes to a spa to have a manicure and pedicure, but not to the extent of Emily's salon experience. Mom explains that 'glitz to me is the *presentation of yourself* and your nails are done and your hair, your eyelashes, makeup. You're a whole package from head to toe' (Sims 2009). Essentially, Alicia is commodified into a package that is sold to the judges and the best and most appealing product will win. The glitz package is entirely artificial: fake hair, fake eyelashes, spray tans, fake nails, fake teeth, and lavish dresses never worn outside the pageant realm. 'The child is totally objectified' (Vaknin 2001: 187). This dichotomy of presenting your self, but first, you must modify it and add lots of artificiality to it, is repeatedly witnessed in this program. The children learn to see themselves as an object to be worked and artificially constructed. You're not good enough as you are, you need to be altered, added to, covered up and enhanced. Alicia goes on to tell the viewer: 'I can't get color on my nails because the judges don't want color.' Alicia is being molded into the most sellable package, the most appealing candidate for the judges regardless of how Alicia wants to really appear. Giddens declares that 'self-actualisation is packaged and distributed according to market criteria' (1991: 198). One constructs their sense of self by consumption and this is reflected in the way Alicia's mom discusses Alicia having her appearance altered in order to be 'glitz' for the pageant. Being 'glitz' is essentially expressed in the sense that the contestant who has the most of it will win. The lesson young Alicia and even viewers may be learning is that a false, artificial self is the most beneficial. Individuals are adapting to a consumer environment packed full of illusions. The modern individual is encouraged to be illusory, artificial. For beauty pageants, the artifice is crucial.

> The absence of things from themselves, the fact that they do not take place though they appear to do so, the fact that everything withdraws behind its own appearance and is, therefore, never identical with itself, is the material illusion of the world.
>
> (Baudrillard 1996: 2)

Jean Baudrillard's work on the disappearance of reality is made apparent in this episode of *Toddlers and Tiaras*: the idea that personality wins but this is just the appearance of reality; the actual reality is the presentation of falseness, an illusion. Consumer capitalism creates a society dominated by appearances, which in turn leads the individual to search for the 'unblemished, socially valued self' (Giddens 1991: 172). Beneath the encouragement to be authentic lies the reality: focus on constructing the self that will be most valued by others. One must always be ready to be judged on their appearance, confidence and personality. Alicia seems disappointed that she can't get color on her nails because the *judges* don't want color. It appears that the judges want a natural look but through *artificial* nails that appear as though they're natural. These young girls are already being molded to fit the standards of a capitalist society that encourage the creation of a self that will receive the most attention and admiration (narcissistic supply).

Rylan is then taken to her private dance lesson and her mom explains that 'it really helps with her pretty feet and standing for the pageants' (Sims 2009). Dad explains to the camera during the dance lesson that 'I think she chooses me over Mom to play games with and stuff so it's fun.' Dad makes a reference to how he is more involved than Mom in the playing aspect of their relationship with their daughter. Rylan's mom explains, 'My relationship with Rylan is great but she's daddy's little girl. They are inseparable and like two little kids.' There appears to be a slight tension between Rylan's parents. They may just be stating their observations about their relationships with Rylan Lee, yet this may also be a reflection of competition between the parents for Rylan's affection and attention. Competition is an essential element of a capitalist society so would it be surprising to see it's grasp in the relationships between parents and children? Even more, narcissistic supply is required in abundance by the narcissist. Often, narcissistic parents will have children in order to secure a consistent amount of their drug: narcissistic supply. Children are ideal sources of attention, admiration, adoration and adulation, that which is needed in order for the narcissist to survive. Rylan Lee is an only child and she is the most desirable source of narcissistic supply.

Glitz and the artifice

On the day of the pageant the director informs the viewing audience 'pageants are a big business. You need a package in order to be in the pageant. The dress, the hair, the makeup, the spray tanning, it all helps to win the pageant' (Sims 2009). This aspect of the program is what may be most unsettling to the viewer. The notion that the best artificially constructed appearance of little girls is the most important aspect in being able to *win*. Unfortunately, we are a part of a society obsessed with appearances. How we present ourselves to others, who we are, how we behave, what we buy… these features are all concerned with appearance. Giddens uses the metaphor of camouflage to relate how individuals will adapt and change their 'self' in order to better fit into certain environments: '[the] individual has as many selves as there are divergent contexts of interaction' (1991: 190). Since Giddens' initial insight, individuals have adapted to different social interactions in an even more extreme sense. They do not alter their selves in different ways for different situations. The individual is now creating an artifice to be used in all social interactions. Some of the girls wear fake teeth referred to as 'flippers'. In this particular episode none of the girls chose to wear them. Young pageant girls are encouraged by parents, coaches and pageant directors to wear fake teeth, hair extensions/wigs, fake fingernails and even spray tans to make their skin darker. Already we witness the young girls in this program encouraged to present an artificial self but also the viewer may internalize the message that the little girl with the most thought-out, carefully constructed artificial presentation of self, wins. Emily's dad states, 'we had just started getting her professionally groomed. I had said from the get-go when she was younger that I would never put makeup on her but I said we'd never do it and we did start putting her makeup on.' There may be resistance to the presentation of artifice at first but after a while parents realize that to win, their child's beauty must be 'enhanced' with makeup. As Emily is shown having her hair done she says to her mom 'This is not a wig. This is my real hair.' It is interesting to see little Emily, at 4 years old, having to learn that sometimes she wears fake hair and sometimes she can just have her real hair. Rylan's mom says

> I try to intertwine a glitz but more of a natural glitz approach. We use no hairpieces. We use no flippers. We use no heavy makeup. We use no eyelashes. We do get her hair done. I do have someone do her makeup, very light. Her natural look makes her glitz.

Interesting to note that Rylan's natural look is glitz yet it still needs to be altered for the pageant.

The first category of the competition is beauty wear. There are twenty-two girls in Rylan's division, including Emily Salazar. Right before Rylan goes on stage her mom asks her 'how do you feel?' (Sims 2009). Rylan says 'I think I'm gonna win.' To which Mom replies 'Good job.' Emily's mom explains in an interview: 'we weren't expecting this many people, but it's good. It's good competition. We like to see how she does with a big crowd.' Again, the audience bears witness to the theme that competition and winning are most important. Healthy competition can encourage individuals to try harder and make improvements. However, when the façade of the competition is that the little girl with the best personality wins but in reality the one with the best artificially constructed appearance wins, the results can be detrimental. Rylan's mom states 'I think Rylan will definitely stand out. She's not full glitz so I definitely think she'll stand out with her blue dress on and her personality.' Rylan is not *fully* artificial yet her appearance (her dress) still helps her win. During Rylan's beauty walk on stage the viewer is left with the impression that Rylan is able to display her personality to the judges through looking pretty and smiling at them. The focus is on presentation therefore an individual may put even more focus and emphasis on creating an even better false self. Emily's dad is shown in an interview talking while Emily completes her beauty walk: 'Beauty for me is inner. I'm not a superficial person, you know? If Emily feels confident she is confident and it does show.' The artifice, the illusion, is that confidence and personality win the pageant, when in reality, the best artificially constructed contestant wins above all. In case the viewer missed the message about personality and confidence the first two times via Rylan and Emily's parents, Alicia's mom exclaims, 'I think Alicia is going to stand out in her competition for a couple of reasons, number one her dress is really not like the typical pageant dress and I think that her personality is really what makes her stand out.' Again, Alicia's dress will help her win and her personality that is shown by walking to different spots on the stage and smiling. In Figure 2.4, Alicia is seen standing all the way on the right looking at two of the other young contestants. Her look is one of concern and analysis. Alicia's dad then states 'a glitz pageant to me is one where they don't pretend, the makeup and the fake hair and the teeth. I guess the flapper? I think that's what they're called. I like it when the little girls show the fact that they're missing teeth cause they're growing up.' This is a disheartening, conflicting message of presenting authenticity when in reality the presentation is of falseness. Alicia's appearance is not natural nor that of a little girl.

She does indeed have makeup on and darkened skin from a spray tan and her dress does not look that different from other contestants. Alicia then states, 'I love how I go up there and show them who I am.' By walking in a beautiful glitz dress with her hair done, her makeup done, with a spray tan and artificial nails and artificial eyelashes Alicia can show the audience, judges and viewers of the television program *who she is*.

Following another commercial break, the scene opens with a little girl fully dressed in pageant wear sitting with her feet in the hotel sink full of soapy

Figure 2.4 Alicia's glitz look

bubbles smiling at the camera with two ladies working on her hair and dress. It is apparent from the in-depth look into these three girls' lives and others at the pageant that these little girls are indeed treated like princesses. Drawing upon the works of Erik Erikson, Giddens writes that '[b]asic trust is established in a child as part of the experiencing of a world that has coherence, continuity and dependability' (Giddens 1991: 66). Little girls are dependent on their parents and other consistent and significant individuals within their lives to show them how to behave and act within our society. They are dependent upon what these individuals are teaching them. Erikson warns that if basic trust is not established at a young age, or if children learn the opposite of trust – mistrust – then that individual will never have a solid footing for the future. Mistrust will persevere and individuals will constantly lack trust in other individuals and even the world as a whole. The individual will then be forced to come to rely on themselves only, be suspicious of others, and see the presentation of falseness as the only way to protect one's self from others. The question remains as to what will happen to these little girls' sense of trust when they are no longer treated as royalty and if they are unable to achieve their goals that their parents lead them to believe are obtainable so long as they are confident and *themselves.* Being treated like a princess will not last. Even more, placement of trust and faith in parents, pageant coaches, pageant directors and judges that are most interested in maintaining a façade not authenticity, ultimately results in failure, shame, anxiety and the possibility of narcissism for these young girls. Giddens warns: 'shame is directly related to narcissism' (1991: 68). When a little girl loses the pageant after being repeatedly told that confidence and personality win, then the little girl repeatedly learns that her confidence and personality were not good enough. A child is not able to distinguish between the conflicting messages of authenticity and falseness. Emily pointed out to her parents that her hair was real and not a wig, exemplifying the difficulty in distinguishing artifice from reality. Adults and viewers have a higher chance of understanding that what really wins the pageant is the girl with the best package; however, the children are not given that same message. Instead, confidence and having a great personality are what the girls are encouraged to focus on. The more these children lose, the more shame and inadequacy they will feel in relation to their shortcomings in confidence and personality. These young girls are taught to create an artifice because that is what wins yet they are told that practice and your personality is what will ultimately win the competition. If a little girl creates an artifice and practices yet still does not win, what will result? Giddens argues that shame is the result and can lead to even more narcissism. The narcissist focuses on the self and, most importantly, the creation of a false self. The creation of a false self is an attempt to shield the individual from feelings of inadequacy and shame. Alicia felt that when she was on stage she was showing the judges who she really was. She felt as though she was showing the judges her personality. Competition encourages individualism, but at what point does individualism become a 'preoccupation with the self' (Giddens 1991: 170)? At such a young age, it may be difficult for these young girls to recognize the impact their constructed 'package' might have in regards to how they come to define their sense of self. The pageant director/judge voice then announces 'for [the] swimsuit [competition] they should be upbeat, fun, spunky, showing lots of sparkling personality too'. Rylan is standing at the stairs that lead onto the stage. Rylan is stepping from left to right in nervous anticipation and/or excitement that she is about to go on stage. Rylan's dad exclaims 'I love watching her up on stage. I'm just really excited and cheer her on as much as I can, you know? Let her know there is one person out there that cares she's up there.' This seems a bit contradictory to what they are participating in: a competition where there is ultimately only one winner and 149 losers. It appears as if the dad is even aware of this painful reality that ultimately there is only one winner, and all audience members at the pageants are only concerned with one person doing well: their own child.

Rylan exits the stage after her swimwear routine, Rylan's mom tells her 'you did so good' twice in a row and Rylan acts as though she is trying to get away from her mom (Sims 2009). Mom asks for a high five and Rylan is already walking away from her as Mom says: 'There's daddy.' Rylan walks over to Dad who tells her good job and she gives Dad a high five, four times. The viewer is again exposed to the tension between the parents and their possible struggle for Rylan's attention. 'All individuals actively, although by no means always in a conscious way, selectively incorporate many elements of mediated experience into their day-to-day conduct' (Giddens 1991: 188). Rylan apparently became involved in pageants when she saw them on television and said 'Mom, I want to do that.' Might other young viewers at home also develop an interest in competing in beauty pageants? According to Giddens, in today's society individuals incorporate their experiences with the media into their daily lives. Vaknin warned that narcissistic parents tend to create narcissistic offspring. Repeated exposure to a consistent idea increases the chances a young, undeveloped mind will come to accept that idea as normal. Even if the mediated experience is subconscious, many messages remain consistent: artificially constructed selves are key to 'winning' in pageants and even in life, and money is a necessary component and the more money one has, the higher the chances one will win.

Emily is next. While Emily is on stage the camera cuts to Rylan who is watching Emily with a very intense, disapproving and worried look. The camera goes back to Emily as she exits the stage and the audience begins clapping. The camera once again goes to Rylan but from a wider angle so that the audience can see her standing next to her kneeling father with her mother a good 10 feet back behind them. Rylan is clapping for Emily. Another important socializing message for the individual is that one must constantly compare one's self to others. David Riesman's concept of the other-directed individual is apparent through Rylan's intense attention to Emily.

> Social mobility under these conditions continues to exist. But it depends less on what one is and what one does than on what others think of one – and how competent one is in manipulating others and being oneself manipulated [...] mobility drives are still imbedded in their character. But the product now in demand is neither a staple nor a machine; it is a personality.
>
> (Riesman et al. 1950: 46)

Rylan has been consistently told that her personality and confidence will win the pageant. Now she must pay careful attention to her competition, Emily, in order to compare Emily's confidence and personality to her own. This is a new condition of the modern age, to be painfully aware of others as a source of approval and disapproval for one's behavior. Riesman's other-directed individual finds it difficult to excel since one is constantly comparing themselves to others. Anxiety and feelings of insufficiency abound for the other-directed individual because they often feel that there is always going to be another peer that is better. Again the message that one is *never good enough* is repeated for these little girls. One judge explains:

> I think every judge is different but what I have come to learn in the last few years of judging is the more simple the better. They're all very glitzy. They're all made up. They all have hairpieces on, they all have their little teeth in, but if you get that child that's that natural beauty without all the artifice that child is going to get my highest vote.
>
> (Sims 2009)

This is surprising considering the judge is supposed to be judging the little girls based on exactly what she is not looking for: 'the artifice'. Personality is constantly brought to the viewer's attention as being essential for each contestant. 'For fourteen years I've been doing pageants and I have been the judge and it's just that factor. When they get on stage are they emanating that kind of confidence, radiance, personality and that's what I'm looking for.' Another judge states, 'I look for a complete package, glitzy, the hair, the dress, the makeup'. And yet another judge states 'there are so many beautiful girls, it's very hard, so I think it's coming down to personality'. All of the judges, in one way or another have this focus on personality, yet the contestants never participate in an interview. Instead, they simply parade around on stage in their artificially made up appearance. The pageant director exclaims: 'For swimsuit they should be upbeat, fun, spunky, showing lots of sparkling personality too.' How much personality can one really show while posing, blowing kisses and waving? This is a clear example of the endorsement of a false self. Yes, the parents play a role in 'the package' that their child is placed in; however, the rules of the game are that they need to be in a package behind this façade of personality. Riesman warned that personality, for the other-directed individual, is now of prime focus. One's personality is how an individual will achieve social mobility, yet it is soon apparent that the artificially constructed appearance is what is most sought after, not one's personality. All of these little girls' appearances are completely fake, yet no one chooses to recognize this fact, and instead personality is thought of by many as the deciding factor, not the fakeness. This dichotomy of personality and falsity is confusing not only for the viewer but for the little girls as well. It is left up to them to determine what to make of these competing messages. Comparing one's self to others is a repeated process for children who compete in beauty pageants. Having the best personality is what will win the pageant and 'because such a premium is put on sincerity, a premium is put on faking it' (Riesman et al. 1950: 223). In effect, the child who can perform the *best* personality, regardless of its authenticity, will win the pageant. Even taking Riesman's ideas a step further, the 'glitz' package can be considered an attempt to present the best personality considering the judges consistently point to all of the false constructions (fake hair, teeth, nails, eyelashes, etc.) as being the most important components of the competition. The intention may be to focus on the little girls' personalities yet this cannot be determined by walking around on stage. The true criterion for judging one's personality is the artifice and one's artifice is always up for scrutiny and comparison to others in the competition.

The moment all the parents and little girls have been waiting for: the crowning ceremony. As a judge declares, 'This is an amazing pageant. It's almost like a state final. There's so many beautiful girls, it's very hard, so I think it's coming down to personality.' The *Tiny Miss* category, which is the 4–5 year-old age group, includes Rylan and Emily. Rylan wins Most Photogenic Award and Character Centerfold Award. Emily Salazar wins Miss Personality

Award but she is not back from her room yet to claim her medal. Rylan wins the Sweetheart Queen Award and the Beautiful Face Award. Rylan then wins 3rd runner-up for her division. While on stage Rylan immediately looks down at her trophy and touches the top of it with her finger. She then immediately looks to her left and right at the other trophies placed on stage for the 2nd and 1st runner-up and Gold Coast Queen Overall Division Winner. Rylan is no longer smiling but standing posed with her arms in a low V position. Emily Salazar ends up winning the Gold Coast Queen for this division. Rylan is visibly dissatisfied with all of the awards just received. Instantly, Rylan begins to compare her trophy to the other, better trophies on stage. Even though Rylan won many top awards for her division the satisfaction is clearly missing. Emily has now made it to the stage and is clearly out of breath as she is handed all her trophies and medals for the awards she won. Rylan leans forward to look at Emily receiving all the awards she missed at the beginning of the ceremony. It is clear that Rylan is very upset that she has lost and immediately begins to compare her shortcomings to the 'comings' of others. Giddens articulates the devastating effects that Rylan is experiencing as shame. Again, 'shame occurs when a goal is not reached and indicates a short-coming' (Giddens 1991: 68). It is extremely difficult for any of the girls competing at the pageant to feel satisfaction when ultimately there is only one winner. Even the girls that win the title for their division struggle to find happiness because they know it is not the best prize at the pageant. Then in the dressing room we see Rylan trying to come to terms with how she feels about not winning the highest award for her division:

> Rylan: Mommy, daddy?
> Rylan's dad: Yeah.
> Rylan: Why was Emily better than me?
> Rylan's dad: Well, she just had a better day.
> Rylan: Why?
> [Dad shrugs and turns up his hands.]
> Rylan: But I wanted it.
> Rylan's dad: I know, well, it's like we said, sometimes we win 'em and sometimes we don't, so you just got to practice a little bit harder.
> (Sims 2009)

Dad holds up his hand for a high five and Rylan pushes into his hand with one finger putting all of her weight behind that little finger as she looks away from her dad and down at the floor. Rylan's dad exclaims 'Hey! That's not the attitude!' Well, what attitude should little Rylan have? The lesson that these little girls learn is that even if one works hard and has all the attributes required to fulfill a role, this does not necessarily result in the achievement and fulfillment of that goal. Confrontation with the truth is painful not only for the young girls but for the parents as well. When Rylan's dad was confronted with the question of 'Why was Emily better than me?' he was unable to respond. Would it have been possible for Rylan's dad to have stated that 'Emily has more confidence and a better personality? The structure of the consumer society is infiltrating the minds of individuals to the point that people are adapting to false promises and unrealized goals. Even when an artifice is created, this does not guarantee success, however, the message that it can help you achieve success is persistent. The unrealistic goal for pageant contestants being able to win via an appealing personality is grooming these children for catastrophic failure and ultimately devastating trauma; a trauma that could lead these children to turn to narcissism as a coping mechanism.

In the end both Alicia and Emily are eligible to win the High Point Supreme title, the highest award in the pageant, but neither one does. The pageant director exclaims, 'lots of happy winners and some not so happy winners, but overall it's been a great day'. Alicia's mom tries to comfort Alicia immediately after she has learned she did not win High Point Supreme: 'We're proud of you, ok? You can't win everything, can you?' (Sims 2009). Alicia nods her head yes. Alicia's mom smiles as though she is amused by her daughter's response and says 'No, no you can't, because somebody else has to win too.' Alicia shakes her head no. Mom, still amused, says 'Yes.' This may be amusing for the mom to witness her daughter attempting to come to terms with why she can't always win. As she exclaimed at the beginning of the show however, she allows her daughter to participate in pageants because she hopes that if Alicia is comfortable with her 'self' she will be able to get whatever it is she wants. Unfortunately, Alicia had to learn the hard lesson that this formula does not work. Hard work and confidence do not always equal success and the result of coming to terms with this disturbing reality can be very unnerving. Durkheim discusses an individual who is presented with unlimited aspirations: 'he aspires to everything and is satisfied with nothing' (Durkheim 1951: 271). Even though Alicia won for her division she was not satisfied because she did not win the overall prize. In Alicia's interview she exclaims, 'The saddest moment of the day today is when I didn't win the 500 dollars' (being the prize for the overall winner of the competition). Is it surprising that these young girls are not satisfied with winning the highest prize in their division? Taking an even broader perspective, beyond the experiences witnessed within this reality television program, individuals in a consumer society often achieve momentary satisfactions. Saving up to buy a dream car, pair of shoes or other material good will only result in temporary satisfaction. As soon as one has obtained the object or experience, the newness and excitement that once existed slowly fades from view. The individual is then left to plan, save and ultimately obtain the next momentary satisfaction, all the while feeling confused and agitated that happiness is not consistent and reliable. Part of being a narcissist is seeing the world as black and white, and not as a balance of both. There is no room for middle ground in a narcissistic set-up. Similarly, there is only one acceptable award at the pageant: the highest title. The momentary satisfaction the division title holds is quickly forgotten when the highest title at the pageant comes to the forefront. Consumerism promises the individual satisfaction, similar to what these young girls are experiencing, however, the satisfaction is only momentary. Individuals are doomed to a state of deceptive satisfaction. Alicia's dad exclaims, 'For a seven year old it's a little tough, you know? When they get the rug pulled out from underneath you, so a little tough for her.' How is one supposed to be confident in a self that is constructed and not the deep down true self? Might all individuals, even adults, struggle with this reality that momentary satisfactions plague our life, and artifice and falseness can achieve the same results as authenticity and truth?

Some might view the experiences of these three little girls as educational and good character-building activities. However, I would argue that instead it is fostering an environment that encourages the development of the new narcissus. An environment where the individual is determined to define themselves as unique and special by what they consume and how they present themselves and appear to others. 'The obstacle, for example, against which the victim of insatiable desires dashes may cause him to fall back upon himself and seek an outlet for his disappointed passions in an inner life' (Durkheim 1951: 288). Never satisfied, even amidst the countless awards and prizes received at the pageant. The young girls and even the parents struggle with this reality and at times are confused and upset by the experience of shame, confusion and anxiety. Similarly, Vaknin warns that '[o]ne of the abused and traumatized child's coping strategies is to withdraw inwards, to seek gratification from a secure, reliable and permanently available source: from one's self' (2001: 150). Reliance on self-promotion and constantly comparing one's self to others and feeling as if one is in a constant state of competition does not produce healthy individuals. If basic trust is damaged and not established for the individual at a young age, that child will learn to withdraw inwards and rely only on themselves. All other individuals are to be treated with suspicion and mistrust. Protection will become a prime focus for the individual and one can ensure that protection through the construction of an artifice. The artificially constructed self can deflect trauma, injury and pain by the presentation of falseness instead of one's authentic self. The authentic self has already been damaged, often beyond repair; the artificially constructed false self is a defense mechanism, the last resort for the individual to protect themselves from the pain inflicted by the outside world. 'If we put forward this anarchic competition as an ideal we should adhere to – one that should even be put into practice more radically than it is today – then we should be confusing sickness with a condition of good health' (Durkheim 1957: 11). Individuals in a consumer society must first adapt to the structure and in turn create an artificial self. The structure of society cannot guarantee stability and happiness even though the presentation of the world to the individual promises such things. Instead, the individual experiences temporary, deceptive satisfaction, that only results in constantly renewed torture for the individual. Rely only on yourself, for you cannot rely on the social structure; construct yourself in such a way as to receive the most attention and admiration, for this can guarantee success. That is the promise that individuals have faith in; however, this is not the message we should be spreading. Instead, trust is made vulnerable and one may become anxious in order to avoid the shame that is associated with not being able to fulfill one's aspirations and desires in life. As young Alicia states: 'I wear fake eyelashes but it's pretty cool and feels weird when you first put it on but after, it just feels like your regular eyes.' The new narcissus begins to whisper softly in the ears of young modern individuals today, like the young girls witnessed in *Toddlers and Tiaras.* The new narcissus promises to help in coping with the hurt and trauma of not living up to ideals that individuals are being taught to aspire to at such a young age. At first, the falseness one must project as the new narcissus may seem wrong, like a lie, but after awhile, the falseness just begins to feel like one's regular, honest, authentic self.

3 Consequence of believing the lie

Hoarders

> Compulsive Hoarding is a mental disorder marked by an obsessive need to acquire and keep things, even if the items are worthless, hazardous, or unsanitary.
>
> (Sharenow and Berg 2010)

Hoarders is a reality television show chronicling the lives of individuals who suffer from hoarding. This particular program first aired on the Arts and Entertainment (A&E) channel on 17 August 2009 and was the most watched season premiere in A&E's history with 2.5 million viewers. This chapter will explore the messages found within the sixth episode of the second season that aired on 14 January 2010. After a 60-second introduction showing upcoming moments of the episode the above quote appears in white against a black screen. Then a second text appears: 'More than 3 million peoples are compulsive hoarders. These are two of their stories.' Even if a viewer has never seen the program they have now been told what 'Compulsive Hoarding' is: 'an obsessive need to acquire and keep things, even if the items are worthless'. How do individuals today determine value and worth? The previous chapter that explored *Toddlers and Tiaras* uncovered a focus on material possessions as a source of prestige, power, notoriety and ultimately, self-worth. In this chapter, we will witness the disastrous outcomes of encouraging too much self- interest, the disregard of others, and the false belief that objects provide more meaning and value than humans.

> My name is Deborah, I'm 49 years old and I work as a sales consultant in a ladies boutique. My mom tended to do all of the cleaning and I was really not forced to do that much so … don't have a lot of discipline in that area.
>
> (Sharenow and Berg 2010)

As Deborah speaks the viewer is shown different shots of Deborah's home and the amount of objects and clutter that seem to cover every possible surface. In the same breath that Deborah is introducing herself she is providing the viewer with an excuse for her behavior. 'The narcissist is a partial adult. He seeks to avoid adulthood' (Vaknin 2001: 141). A narcissistic individual makes excuses for their behavior and refuses to accept the responsibilities of adulthood. Deborah also exposes instantly that she was not disciplined when she was younger. Sam Vaknin warned that children who are spoiled from a young age become addicted to that pampering and come to expect it for the rest of their lives. The viewer then meets Ron, Deborah's husband. 'My name is Ron, I'm 50 years old and I'm Deborah's husband' (Sharenow and Berg 2010). A voiceover of Deborah then begins as an old photo of Ron appears before the viewer. 'He was a flight attendant for 23 years and we met when I was living in New York and I was his waitress.' By this time what appears to be an old modeling photo of Deborah has appeared on the screen (see Figure 3.1).

As the camera zooms in on the photo of Deborah a voiceover of Ron states 'I met her and I was just floored. She was just the most beautiful thing I'd ever seen.' Sam Vaknin explains: '[narcissists] may have once been rich, famous, powerful, brilliant, or sexually irresistible, but they no longer are' (Vaknin 2001: 49). Why the old photos of Deborah and Ron are shown to the viewer is not exactly clear except for the possibility that Deborah and her husband Ron feel that they were once beautiful, attractive individuals and either they or the producers want the world to know it.

In the first two minutes of the episode there is a message being communicated to the audience about one's past. Our socialization process is never ending and our past experiences (and traumas) impact our present. A photo of Ron and Deborah on their wedding day has appeared as a voiceover of Deborah begins to discuss how her hoarding started. 'When I had kids, I was

Figure 3.1 Deborah

just so immersed in having my child and I just wanted to be with him every single second, but then I let everything else go' (Sharenow and Berg 2010). Deborah feels that her immersion in her children caused her to avoid cleaning and maintaining her home environment. Hoarding does not occur overnight. It is an ongoing process of accumulating things. What the opening quote fails to address in the definition of hoarding is that items to hoarders are indeed valuable. The items they possess are so valuable that they cannot bring themselves to rid these objects from their life. This chapter will uncover how the new narcissus is a consequence of modern individuals attempting to adapt to the social structure of their world.

Anxious individual

As Deborah continues to discuss her hoarding she concludes by stating 'something's missing, something's wrong' (Sharenow and Berg 2010). Indeed, for many individuals today something is very wrong. The wise words of Durkheim come to mind once again.

> To act morally is to do one's duty, and all duty is of a finite nature. It is limited by other duties. We cannot give ourselves over to other people, absolutely and utterly, without an abandonment of ourselves. Nor can we develop too much our personality without falling into a state of egoism.
>
> (Durkheim 1997: 184)

For Deborah and other individuals who suffer from hoarding what is missing is a lack of focus on the importance of interpersonal relationships with others. One's duty becomes the need to pursue wealth and to prove one's success through the accumulation of material objects. The new narcissus loses sight of their original true self because the falseness that surrounds them (possessions) promises satisfaction. The new narcissus is always in pursuit of more: more attention, more admiration and even more *things.* Hoarders believe that all the possessions they keep hold value and that by acquiring more and more things they are surrounding themselves with more value. By default the hoarder may then come to believe that they are making themselves more valuable by surrounding themselves with more objects. The new narcissus encourages the individual to focus on accumulating more and individuals who suffer from hoarding make this their prime focus, even in the face of damaging the relationships with those closest to them.

The viewer learns that Deborah and Ron have two sons: Lewis, age 14 and Sam, age 11. More text appears on the screen: 'Deborah's hoarding led to a very serious encounter with Child Protective Services'. Deborah states, 'since that day, I see a police car – I get panicky, if someone comes to the door – I get panicky'. As a result of Deborah's encounter with protective services, due to her hoarding problem, she is suffering from constant anxiety that someday her two children will be taken away from her again. 'The worst thing that could ever happen to me in my life would be to lose my children because they are everything to me. Everything. So why do I do this?' (Sharenow and Berg 2010). Deborah has suffered from the threat of having her children forcefully taken from her by CPS as a result of her behavior. But even in the face of this threat Deborah cannot stop her obsessive need to acquire and keep things.

> Ron: I've had enough. I've had enough of everything. I drank a half gallon of straight vodka and that would have done it but Deborah said that she had a weird feeling at work that day and she came home real early.
>
> Deborah: I just all of the sudden got this strange feeling that I had to go home. I came in the back door and I found him laying on the kitchen floor with a note. I couldn't even totally concentrate on saving my husband because all I could see: the ambulance and the police coming in and seeing the house, and I thought I'm about to lose my husband and my children.
>
> (Sharenow and Berg 2010)

The dialogue here is astounding. First, Ron states 'I've' had enough, not past tense, but present. He'd had enough of the hoarding and it appears that he has still had enough. Then, the fact the Deborah was more concerned with herself and what would happen to her as a result of her husband possibly committing suicide in their home, than the fact that her husband was lying there dying and in need of medical attention, is astonishing. 'Narcissists, however, remain dependent on others for their self-esteem and self-confidence [as opposed to] one's sense of inner worth' (Vaknin 2001: 142). Deborah was more concerned with the fact that she might lose her source of narcissistic supply (attention, admiration, adoration and adulation) than the actual loss of her husband. The relationship between hoarding and a narcissistic personality disorder is not unreasonable; in fact, many individuals suffer from multiple forms of disorders in conjunction with one another.

Hoarding as a mental illness was first published in the fifth edition of the *Diagnostic Statistical Manual* (*DSM*) of the American Psychiatric Association and defined as 'persistent difficulty discarding or parting with possessions, regardless of their actual value' (2013: 247). There is a deeply felt anxiety in Deborah that may stem from her adaptation to the structure of society and its promises. She has created an environment full of objects that she believes hold the utmost value. Some may argue that this anxiety stems from her hoarding problem; instead, we should understand that this constant state of nervousness does not result from an individual abnormality or mental illness but is indicative of her adaptation to consumerism. Ron and Deborah have adapted to the structure of consumerism in a drastic way. They have successfully accumulated a massive amount of material possessions in the pursuit of satisfaction. These are the priorities that have been encouraged from a young age for the individual today. Ron and Deborah followed this message and now have what is known as a compulsive hoarding disorder. Deborah has an obsessive need to keep and acquire material possessions, often over-valuing their perceived importance. Might we, as a society, over-value our perception of the importance of material possessions? Is it not our life experiences with others that hold the most value? Experiencing life and not *new* things. The objects we acquire are mere tools to be utilized in our experiences. Instead of a tool, these things have morphed into an obsession and are sought after more so than the life experiences themselves. Deborah has placed an extreme amount of value in the things that she possesses even to the point of damaging her relationships with others. She has adapted in an extreme way to the structure of a consumer society: accumulate material possessions and you will achieve satisfaction.

Jim: confusing value with sickness

Jim, the second hoarder to be featured during this episode, is a 66-year-old resident of Indiana and a beekeeper. 'I don't see myself as piling up stuff, here, there, and everywhere, but, uh, the evidence is all around me, isn't it?' (Sharenow and Berg 2010). Heather, Jim's daughter, will not allow her infant daughter to visit her grandfather at home. More text appears on the screen: 'Jim is an atypical hoarder. He doesn't actively acquire things by shopping. He passively acquires things from his many activities and friends.' His daughter Heather states: 'I'm sure he can *tell a story* about every single thing in there or have a reason for him keeping it. I think that's the problem, everyone justifies why they have stuff.' Jim's daughter is right about the problem and this problem is not just for individuals who hoard. How often do people 'justify why they have stuff?' This understanding of utility and value has become twisted and something of malice. When did we start valuing objects more than our relationships with others? When did things begin to take precedence above all else in our lives?

Jim then discusses a shoehorn that he got from his father's dresser: 'it's a trivial little item, but it has a lot of connections for me'. Again, we are presented with evidence that what we consume defines who we are as individuals (see Figure 3.2). This is indicative of a symptom of consumer society: possessions hold just as much value as people, and at times even more value.

> Jim: I have at times been unable to pay bills when they needed to be paid. I had a justified fear of not having money and I responded to that by hanging on to what I had. I just sort of feel like I'm, I'm vulnerable. If I just tight walk through this convoluted space and if the piles in the office don't fall over and kill me then maybe everything will be alright.
>
> (Sharenow and Berg 2010)

Jim is adapting to the fear and anxiety that comes with living in consumerism. Individuals are promised satisfaction and happiness by accumulating material

Figure 3.2 Jim in his home

possessions. Our failure to feel happy and satisfied is never addressed or this failure to 'succeed' is blamed on some other aspect of an individual's life. Jim, in order to combat his anxiety about money, cannot let go of any of his material possessions. Jim's profound confession of vulnerability and vision of dying is heart wrenching. As stated earlier, Durkheim's concept of anomie applies to this runaway character of our capitalist society: '[i]nextinguishable thirst is constantly renewed torture' (1951: 247). For Jim and Deborah, they are tortured by their obsession with accumulating material possessions. They have both fulfilled their duty as consumer to buy and consume the objects of their desire. Instead of experiencing the promised satisfaction that comes from buying what we want, Deborah and Jim and many other individuals today, instead experience anxiety, frustration, stress and fear. We learn that Jim travels for much of his work and this aids in his dilemma. 'One of the ironies of my life is I can escape. I get in my truck and off I go. I close the door and this house kind of disappears' (Sharenow and Berg 2010). Jim's home, what serves as the source of security and comfort for most individuals today, instead serves as a place of torture, a repeated reminder of Jim's failure to feel satisfaction from the accumulation of material goods.

Jim, by appearing on this reality show, is confronted with the reality that he has created a false environment for himself. He has transformed his place of refuge into something that reflects the dark message of our world: his entire existence rests on an illusion and he in turn has created an illusory self. Jim has created an artifice to help him cope with the drudgeries of consumerism. Hoarders focus on collecting things in a way that is still fulfilling the obligations placed upon the individual within today's world: the obligation to consume. Likewise, the new narcissus focuses on obtaining more attention and admiration from others. Through manipulation and deceit, the new narcissus uses other people to achieve whatever goal they have in mind and the new narcissus is unable and unwilling to identify with the wants and needs of others.

Both Deborah and Jim struggle to confront the artifice they have surrounded their lives with; this artifice that promised happiness, satisfaction and success that never came. 'The narcissistic personality has only a shadowy understanding of the needs of others, and feelings of grandiosity jostle with sentiments of emptiness and inauthenticity' (Giddens 1991: 172). Shame and narcissism are closely intertwined. Shame results when one's expectations about how one is *supposed* to behave or how things are supposed to turn out in one's life are not met. Deborah has feelings of shame and of being a prisoner as a result of her disorder. 'I'm tired of being ashamed. I'm tired of being a prisoner to my home. It affects everything in my life.' Deborah sees her home as a prison and Jim feels as though he's escaping every time he leaves his home. How often do other individuals in our society, who aren't suffering from a hoarding disorder, feel as though they are a prisoner of their possessions? To feel the weight of debt can feel very much as though one is shackled to some illusory individual that never materializes but ever more demands pieces of your soul as you struggle 8–5 to make enough money to pay off enough of next month's bill so that the interest rate doesn't explode. Our world shackles us to our possessions. Many are able to loosen the chains a bit and experience more fulfilling aspects of life, but how many are caught in the thick of the chains, struggling with an addiction to shoes, purses, cars, drugs, alcohol, sex, shopping, food … the list seems to be endless. The dark message is to always strive for *me*, to be more and to do more. What happens when an individual focuses too much on themselves and only begins to care about how *they* are affected?

Throughout the episode and interviews with Deborah she appears totally ignorant of the needs of her husband and children. Deborah refuses to acknowledge the needs of the rest of her family and has been completely selfish in her endeavors to accumulate all of these possessions. Vaknin explains how narcissism and hoarding may be closely related:

> When a person persists in a dysfunctional, maladaptive or plain useless behavior despite grave repercussions to himself and others, we say that his acts are compulsive. The narcissist is compulsive in his pursuit of Narcissistic Supply. This linkage between narcissism and obsessive-compulsive disorders sheds light on the mechanisms of the narcissistic psyche.
>
> (Vaknin 2001: 196)

Compulsive hoarding, as a new mental disorder, may have emerged as a result of an internalized message to always consume. Individuals today are urged to compulsively indulge in the consumption of goods and services with an added inextinguishable thirst for the attention and adoration from others. This artificial self needs reassurance and attention in order to continue functioning and to continue consuming. This artificial, false self is a façade for the emptiness that is inside the individual. This emptiness has built up from the inability to feel long-term, meaningful satisfaction from society and from one's possessions. Jim states that he can escape the home he has created for himself, while others in our society may turn to drugs or alcohol to help escape from the amoral character of our capitalist society that encourages this infinite pursuit of material goods. Suzanne, a clinical psychologist, comes to Deborah's home to meet her and her family.

> Suzanne: So how do you feel about me coming in?
> Deborah: I am very embarrassed and nervous.
> Suzanne: Well, I'm not here to judge. I'm here just to look and to help so let's take a look.
>
> (Sharenow and Berg 2010)

Again, the audience is exposed to the anxiety, fear and shame that Deborah is experiencing in this moment. As Deborah continues to show the psychologist her home she says 'this looks exactly like how the inside of my head and stomach feel'. Husband Ron says 'sometimes she just feels so tired all the time that she just wants to lay [sic] in bed and watch TV'. It appears that Deborah does not want to face her dilemma and at times withdraws completely from the world she has created around her in order to avoid dealing with her behaviors. Giddens says regarding this retreat into media representations: 'confrontation with the real phenomena themselves is psychologically problematic' (1991: 27). Both Deborah and Jim struggle to face the reality of their lives, their behavior and the falseness that surrounds them. Deborah's constant state of anxiety must be exhausting: to constantly feel unsettled and nervous about the state of one's home environment.

> A thirst arises for novelties, unfamiliar pleasures, nameless sensations, all of which lose their savor once known. Henceforth one has no strength to endure the least reverse. The whole fever subsides and the sterility of all the tumult is apparent, and it is seen that all these new sensations in their infinite quantity cannot form a solid foundation of happiness to support one during days of trial [...] Weariness alone [...] is enough to bring disillusionment, for he cannot in the end escape the futility of an endless pursuit.
>
> (Durkheim 1951: 256)

Hoarders, like the new narcissus, have too much focus on the self and selfish pursuits. By obsessively acquiring things, Deborah and Jim are surrounding themselves with an artificial promise of happiness. A state of anomie causes the individual to feverishly pursue an amoral goal of accumulating wealth and possessions. Deborah goes on to say 'I do not blame my problem on him [Ron] but just like my hoarding effects his depression. I think the alcoholism and the suicide attempt, um, it affected my problem. Vicious cycle!' (Sharenow and Berg 2010). Again we witness Deborah avoiding accountability for her situation. In the same breath that she says that she's not blaming her husband she claims that his behaviors cause her hoarding. One's possessions are not 'a solid foundation of happiness' nor can they 'support one during days of trial' (Durkheim 1951: 256). Hoarders and the new narcissus alike are suffering from the same societal disorder of failing to regulate individual passions. Instead the encouragement to pursue our seemingly infinite desires bombards us at every moment and some begin to pursue these passions even at the expense of others.

Isolation and avoidance

Deborah and Suzanne have gone upstairs and into one of the boys' bedrooms.

> Deborah: This is the children's room and there is a bunk bed hiding under there.
> Sam (voiceover): The last time that I slept in my bedroom I was probably about 5 years old.
> Lewis (in interview): I always sleep on the couch in the living room because our room is like the laundry room.
> Sam: I have to sleep in my mom's bed.
> [...]
> Suzanne: There seems to be a lack of intimacy in the lives of the mother and father.
> Deborah: Right now I isolate myself. We don't have conversations anymore. I'm just, I'm too, weighed down by all of this.
>
> (Sharenow and Berg 2010)

Deborah's two sons cannot sleep in their own room because of the amount of stuff piled up on the bed and the floor. Ron sleeps in his own room, the oldest boy sleeps on the couch and the youngest boy sleeps with his mother. 'The narcissist does his damnedest to avoid intimacy' (Vaknin 2001: 203). Deborah puts all her focus on the things that she owns and as a result of this accumulation of items she closes herself off from the rest of her family, refusing to recognize their needs and interests. Deborah does not have people over to her home only because she is fearful of having her children taken away but also because she has chosen to isolate herself not only from other people but from her family as well. '[T]he humans of the age of affluence are surrounded not so much by other human beings, as they were in all previous ages, but by objects' (Baudrillard 1998: 25). Deborah somehow feels that the things she has acquired are meaningful and significant more so than interactions with other individuals. She may not be consciously aware of this decision she has made but it is clear that she has placed the possessions in her life as her number one priority. Similarly, Jim articulates this same isolation: 'I'm not telling people about this. I have a lot of embarrassment. I have a lot of fear. It's terrible' (Sharenow and Berg 2010). As Deborah and Jim acquire more and more material possessions they begin to become isolated from those closest to them. This in turn leads to anxiety, fear and embarrassment when around others because they may feel out of touch with how to interact in normal social situations.

The act of hoarding is the consequence of selfishness, narcissism and the use of others for your own personal benefit. The false self, created as an adaptation to the modern consumer world, tricks one's true self into believing that the obsessive pursuit of possessions or attention from others is a worthy endeavor because it results in the most success and happiness. 'The consumer object isolates' and for those like Jim this isolation is coupled with fear and embarrassment (Baudrillard 1998: 85). Be unique. Be special. Be different. These are the messages internalized through many avenues today (work, school, family, media, sports, religion). Consuming, even though it may make you appear unique, is in reality making you the same as everyone else. The episode informs us that Jim's daughter, Heather, will not allow his granddaughter into visit his home because it is unsanitary and because there is a missing, loaded gun somewhere in the house. Jim states 'I respond to it [the stuff in his house] by leaving, by ignoring it'. Even faced with losing contact with his daughter and granddaughter, Jim still continues to hoard.

The audience is then introduced to the expert who is going to help Jim overcome his disorder: 'My name is Geralin Thomas and I'm a certified personal organizer, specializing in chronic disorganization.' Geralin proceeds to examine Jim's home and asks him why he chooses to leave things as he finds them when she opens up a kitchen cabinet to discover cobwebs and mice droppings. Jim has a cat and he explains that he thought it would help him deter the mice.

> Geralin: Do you ever think that you make excuses for your behaviors?
> [Jim laughs in agreement with Geralin]
> Geralin: The average person when they open this up would think 'Oh, I've got a wreck in here I'm gonna take ten minutes and clean it.' What is your thought? Close it and keep moving?
> Jim: I don't have time to deal with this now. […] I do a thing with my mind which is I intend to do it, therefore I have done it.
>
> (Sharenow and Berg 2010)

Jim, like Deborah, is unwilling to face his behaviors and choices because he is afraid of what he might discover, so he continues to acquire things compulsively (see Figure 3.3). He simply closes the cabinet and walks away. *I don't want to face these feelings right now so I'm just going to avoid this situation and leave.* Jim must continue to avoid the artificial self he has created. The new narcissus behaves arrogantly and feels that they are superior, therefore, intention or the feeling of effort is equated with real, actual effort.

Four '1–800–Got Junk?' trucks pull up in front of Deborah's home as Deborah reveals 'my mind and my emotions feel as cluttered and as nasty as the house' (Sharenow and Berg 2010). The audience is then introduced to

Figure 3.3 Jim and avoidance

Dorothy: 'I'm a professional organizing expert specializing in hoarding.' The crew, Dorothy and the family begin working their way through the clutter, boxing things up and throwing items away. Words flash up on the screen: 'Not long into the cleaning process, Deborah hits an emotional roadblock.' A small dish, which had belonged to Deborah's recently deceased mother, is broken. Deborah explains how the loss of her mother has affected her: 'It's sort of stopped me from what I need to do in everyday life.' As Deborah begins to cry while holding the dish (see Figure 3.4) the organizer asks what Deborah would like to do with the item and Deborah replies 'I feel like I'm

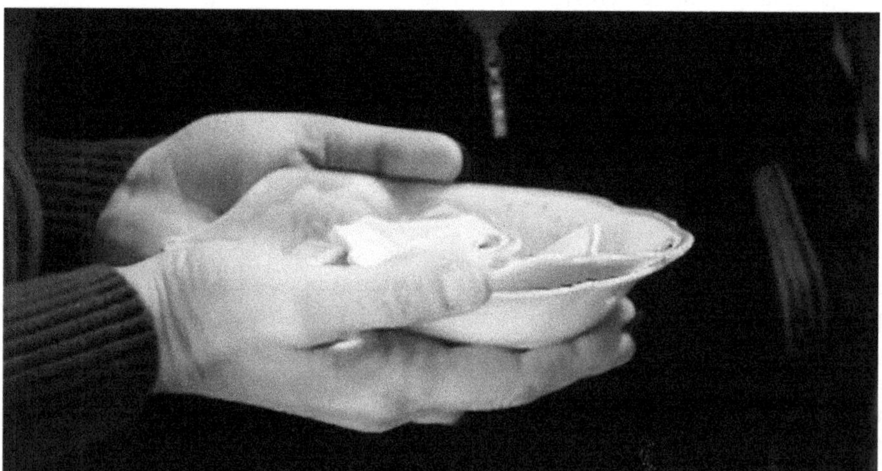

Figure 3.4 Deborah and the teacup

throwing my mom away.' This teacup not only symbolizes Deborah's mother but Deborah feels as though if she threw away the teacup it would be comparable to throwing her mom away. Deborah's warped understanding of value is not unusual. How often does our need to keep up with the latest and greatest thing or gadget interfere with our everyday life? Previous research has explained how individuals may define their lives and identities in terms of the things they consume. 'They give material form to a particular narrative of self-identity' (Giddens 1991: 81). For Deborah, and others, the things you consume help define your personality, who you are as an individual. Deborah has given significance to all the material possessions in her life, even to the point of viewing objects as representations of people. Individuals like Deborah and Jim are adapting to the relentless message that consumer goods are of the utmost importance as they provide the individual with seeming uniqueness and exceptionality. Consume more and maybe one will receive more attention and admiration. Objects for Deborah have even begun to replace her relationships with other people. Accumulating more and more goods is the focus and intent for her daily life to the point of valuing the maintenance of these objects more than other people.

Jim experiences similar feelings concerning the objects he hoards but attributes the objects to memories rather than people in particular. The organizer exclaims 'he is so worried about forgetting things that he hangs on to things because he doesn't want to forget about them' (Sharenow and Berg 2010). Jim begins to become resistant to the clean up and removal process of his belongings. 'My life is in memories of things and things are memory triggers for me and it's a very powerful thing.' The items that Jim has collected over the years are like gold to him and that's why he cannot bring himself to let things go. 'Wealth, on the other hand, by the power it bestows, deceives us into believing that we depend on ourselves only' (Durkheim 1951: 254). Jim has withdrawn into his house and his possessions, attributing significant meaning to each and every thing. What matters are the memories that belong to Jim and the memories become real by embodying all of his possessions. 'My life is in memories.' One's life should be thought of in terms of the memories and experiences one has had; however, Jim has adapted to our modern world and its dark promise. Instead of seeing his life through his memories he sees his life in terms of the things he owns. The things themselves have come to replace experiences, memories and his relationships with others. The organizer interjects, 'If we were to let things go, do you think you could still remember them without the things?' To which Jim replies, 'My memory is terrible.' Giddens observes that a '[l]ack of coherence in ideals, or the difficulty of finding worthwhile ideals to pursue, may be as important in relation to shame anxiety as circumstances in which goals are too demanding to be attained' (1991: 69). Jim and Deborah have pursued the ideal of obtaining as many material possessions as possible; the pursuit of this goal is exhausting and causes shame, fear, anxiety and frustration for them. Durkheim also warned that having goals that are too demanding can cause fatalism, or a resigned acceptance to the events in our lives. Jim truly believes that if he rids himself of the multitude of things in his possession that he will no longer be able to remember his life. We then witness Jim describe in detail the importance of bricks he has been saving as they were bricks from his high school that was torn down. He describes the details of the building and his experiences at school and the organizer exclaims that it appears Jim has a great memory to which Jim responds with laughter. Jim appears unable to believe or come to terms with the fact that he does indeed have a good memory and that he has been convincing himself otherwise.

Deborah is outside the home smoking a cigarette and Ron is with her drinking a soda. Both are watching while the cleaning crew pile up furniture in the front yard. The organizer is upset by the parents' lack of involvement in the clearing process, while their two boys are eagerly helping. Deborah comes in the house to see the cleared dining room and gets very excited. The organizer tells her that the boys did all of it without even being asked. The organizer informs her that it is Deborah and Ron's turn to do some work. 'See, all we had to do was ask. If someone doesn't take charge it doesn't happen, so the parents have to actually be the ones to take charge not the children' (Sharenow and Berg 2010). The new narcissus often behaves like a child, free from discipline, and will lash out when confronted with their behavior. Deborah has participated in avoidance for years now so it is no surprise she is still avoiding facing her over-accumulation of material goods even when presented with an opportunity to alter her behavior. Deborah has internalized the adaption to consumer society: objects are her life to the point of denying the real and avoiding the choice to change.

Sam, Deborah's youngest child, appears to have been most affected by his mother's behavior (see Figure 3.5). Several times throughout the episode he

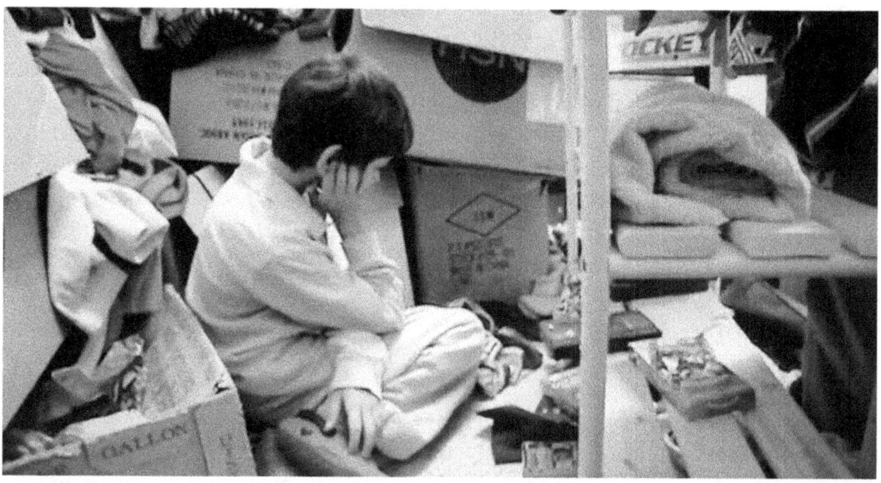

Figure 3.5 Sam's isolation

retreats to isolation and at other times is overly enthusiastic about the cleaning process. Sam, the unspoken victim of this environment, is also experiencing the consequences of restricted socialization. Through his parents' isolation, he has also become isolated because of their hoarding. He is unable to have friends over so his interaction with others is limited. The organizing expert Dorothy informs the audience: '[Deborah] thinks he's got some hoarding tendencies.' In addition to suffering from isolation, Sam is also learning to keep and acquire things just like his Mom. Deborah later tells Sam, at the encouragement of the psychologist and organizer, 'Sam, it is not your job to take care of your Mom and Dad. It is Mom and Dad's job to take care of you' (Sharenow and Berg 2010). The camera then reveals Deborah in an interview exclaiming 'my loved ones have had to adapt because of all of this'. We witnessed in the analysis of *Toddlers and Tiaras* that individuals may camouflage themselves and adapt to different environments, encouraging development of the false self. Sam, a human who is still learning about his place in the world, the expectations for what it means to be a member of our society, is internalizing very dark ideals. In an interview Sam explains: 'Sometimes I do feel that I have to grow up faster than other kids because I have to deal with things.' In her interview Deborah states 'I don't think the children even know what they've had to adapt to because it's all they've ever known.' However, Sam is clearly aware that something is very different within his home and within his family otherwise he would not react the way that he does. Near the end of the episode Suzanne is sitting outside with Sam on the curb. As the sorting continues, Sam becomes very upset when he realizes the crew will be leaving soon.

> Suzanne: Tell me again, because everybody's what?
> Sam (crying): Everybody's fun and nice.
> Suzanne: Everybody's fun and nice?
> Sam: And I'm gonna miss everybody.
> Suzanne (interview): Why would a child reach out to people that he just met for a few days here and be so sad because they are leaving?
> (Sharenow and Berg 2010)

Unfortunately, this is most likely the result of limited interaction with other people. Instead, Deborah, in her misguided socialization, has collected 'meaningful' things to fulfill her life and the life of her family all the while completely disregarding the needs of others. Suzanne accurately states that 'he's reaching for some kind of real connection'. This is a consequence of our society and represents this idea of the false self. We are encouraged in this society to have faith in material possessions. We are encouraged to believe that these material possessions are representative of power and success and therefore should have a significant weight and importance in our lives. *Hoarders* provides an extreme example of what can happen when we focus our lives on the things we possess and, worse yet, attribute to these possessions meaning, significance and our sheer existence as human beings. Our connection to ourselves and to others is lost. Will anyone be remembered for what they owned? The things they possessed? Or the wealth they had? People are remembered for their contribution to the betterment of humanity.

The audience is taken back to Indiana and Jim's process of clearing through his possessions. Jim explains why his office looks the way it does: 'apparently the piles of paper was like building a little fort. My feeling financially insecure led me to be insecure about a lot of things' (Sharenow and Berg 2010). Jim begins to recall his mother as a bookkeeper in 1958 making $5,000 a year, which wasn't enough to live on. His uncle would help them out because he also worked for the firm. Jim remembers, as a little boy, sneaking in and looking at the ledger at his mother's job, seeing her account and it piling up – '5, 10, 15, 20 …' – in reference to thousands of dollars. Jim breaks down: 'At the end of the year he [Uncle] would always find a way to declare a dividend to clear that account.' Jim is now crying. 'There is not enough memories.' The organizer asks 'Do you think you maybe hang on to all that stuff for that reason? Because there aren't enough memories?' To which Jim replies 'I don't know, maybe.' Giddens explains that 'human beings react against social circumstances which they find oppressive' (1991: 175). Individuals adapt by creating an environment surrounded by material possessions that can provide meaning. For Jim, they embodied memories and for Deborah, relationships with other people. This focus and obsession with consumer goods forces individuals to adapt in any way possible. Some, like Jim and Deborah, adapt in extreme ways. An artificial self is created as a coping mechanism or as a way to achieve success, and when confronted with the dichotomy of the artifice and the real, individuals will avoid facing the truth. They keep faith in the artifice, all the while avoiding what may be truly meaningful in life. Insecurity, anxiety, fear and shame all stem from this root problem of financial insecurity. Our social structure's primary goal is reflected back at us. The image that the new narcissus sees is a disturbing one and must be avoided at all costs. *Keep focusing on the artifice.* This limitless race towards an indefinite goal of material wealth can cause only momentary satisfaction and should anyone fail at this primary goal, then a relentless state of insecurity and anomie will result.

Jim thinks memory loss and financial insecurity are the source of his oppression so he keeps everything in order to maintain his belief that these things will eventually bring about security because he will be able to *remember.* Instead, the false self has convinced Jim to keep consuming and acquiring possessions. A feeling of powerlessness results when one is not satisfied and fails to experience the promise of our society and of the new narcissus. A loss of care and concern as a result of these feelings of powerlessness may encourage the individual to focus on the self and self-promotion, or in Jim and Deborah's case the hoarding of material possessions. The episode ends with the audience being exposed to Jim's granddaughter coming over to his house for the first time and being asked to babysit. Deborah is going to continue attending therapy in order to work through her anxiety issues but there is still a large amount of clutter in the house. Her boys now have their own rooms and have had friends over for the first time.

As a society, we must begin to understand that hoarding is not just a mental disorder suffered by individuals, but is instead indicative of the consequences of our social structure. Our society is suffering from an anomic state of existence ruled by the relentless pursuit of material wealth to the point of extreme narcissism and disregard of others. As Geralin says to Jim: 'Your whole life can't be a keepsake box.' The new narcissus is enamored with their reflection (the selfish pursuit of material wealth) and struggles to pull their gaze away from this pursuit. Even when everyone around them is pleading for them to stop, the reflection continues its false promise of more satisfaction. The new narcissus needs only to continue working on the artifice, the reflection, and their ultimate self.

4 The ease of falseness

Sister Wives

The Learning Channel (TLC) aired a new program, *Sister Wives*, on 26 September 2010. The show provides an insider's look into the lives of a polygamous family in Utah. This particular program was also met with much controversy, as polygamy is illegal in the United States. However, the family wanted to open their lives to viewers in the hopes of exemplifying the *positive* aspects of polygamy. The Brown family was not so much concerned about the possibility of a criminal investigation as exposing their 'wonderful' lives. This chapter will examine how the false self can creep into an individual's life with such ease that this individual may be completely unaware of the lies they tell themselves and others. The audience meets Kody Brown, the father of the family, at the very beginning of the first episode as he is driving a luxury convertible and talking to the camera.

> My name is Kody Brown and you've gotta meet my family. I'm a polygamist but we're not the polygamists you think you know. I like marriage, uh, and I'm a repeat offender, so … I have adopted the faith that embraces that lifestyle, uh, in fact, it recommends it. And uh, I like to reward good behavior so if you're good with one marriage they figure you'll be good with two. I hope they think I'll be good with four. [smiles big] Let's go ahead and go home and you can meet my family. They're special and you'll like them and um, I'm excited about introducing you to them.
>
> (Gibbons et al. 2010)

In the first few moments, the audience learns that Kody is an advertising executive and he currently has three wives and twelve children. Almost instantly, the audience is exposed to many important aspects of Kody that relate to the idea of the false self. 'A person's identity is not found in behavior, nor – important though this is – in the reactions of others, but in the capacity *to keep a particular narrative going*' (Giddens 1991: 54). Giddens is incorrect in assuming the reactions of others do not matter for one's identity today, however, he rightly points out the importance of narrative in communicating one's identity. Modern individuals today are expected to have a particular narrative or story about their life. This episode was full of long narratives, via confessionals, interviews and voiceovers, providing insight into the identities of each of the wives and the father. However, as we have seen, and will continue to see when examining this episode, identity is influenced by others' reactions. 'While all people want and need to be liked by some of the people some of the time, it is only the modern other-directed types who make this their chief source of direction and chief area of sensitivity' (Riesman et al. 1950: 38). Kody goes on to explain: 'Twenty years ago I married Mary and then seventeen years ago I married Janelle and then sixteen years ago I married Christine. I just fell in love and then I fell in love again and then I fell in love again.' Kody did not have any influence in his life that would stop him from marrying as many women as he wanted. In fact, Kody's moral foundation supports the belief of plural marriage and the taking of multiple wives.

Even though polygamy is illegal in the US, prosecution is usually only the result of child abuse or child trafficking. 'If there is nothing to control them they will not be able to control themselves' (Durkheim 1957: 11). Kody converted to his religion at the age of 20 and this faith encourages the 'multiplication of love' by accumulating multiple wives and children. There is another family featured on reality television: *19 Kids and Counting*, which features the Duggar family from Arkansas. The Duggars adhere to an extreme form of Protestant Christianity known as the Quiverfull movement. A passage from Psalm 127:3–4 states

> Sons are a heritage from the LORD, children a reward from him.
> Like arrows in the hands of a warrior are sons born in one's youth.
> Blessed is the man whose quiver is full of them. They will not be put to shame when they contend with their enemies in the gate.
> (New International Version)

Hence, another fundamentalist religious group encourages the accumulation of as many children as the Lord rewards you with. Some non-fundamentalist faiths still encourage refraining from birth control to allow married women to have as many children as the Lord intends. However, our social system rests on the notion that all individuals must pursue a goal that is free from limitations, without rest or relief, always to advance and have more wives, more children, more money. You may laugh but what is our purpose? What is our goal? Is it not the betterment of humanity and ourselves? Then, ought we not pause and reflect for a moment on the often-conflicting messages received today? Too much focus on accumulating wealth and success can then cause a misunderstanding about how to regulate other aspects of one's life. Advancing ourselves becomes confused with obtaining more money. Money that is used to then distract us and fulfill us via the accumulation of possession, wives or even children. Our obsession with pursuing more wealth and by default possessions and experiences results in individuals beginning to equate partners, children, pets, friends and people as possessions to acquire too.

The Brown family is shown gathered in a kitchen at home with several of the family members. Three of the older girls are standing by Janelle, the second wife.

> Aspyn (one of the daughters): We're sisters.
> Kody (from across the kitchen): Sisters from the same mister. She's a sister from the same mister and he's a brother from another mother.
> [laughter]
> Aspyn: Polyg talk.
> [laughter]
> Kody: She's got a mouthful; she said it's polyg talk.
> Janelle: It's polyg talk or polyg food and that's how most of us are known: polygs. Polygamists. I dunno, my name is Janelle.
> Logan (oldest son): Somebody referred to us as polyg-lets.
>
> (Gibbons et al. 2010)

Janelle's very profound statement of 'my name is Janelle' says a lot about identity and the view of the self. It appears as though it is difficult to maintain one's own identity in such a family when there are multiple wives and twelve children. While Giddens argues what is important is to keep a narrative going, Baudrillard states '[p]eople, then, are incapable of understanding themselves, of knowing what they are and what they want' (Baudrillard 1970: 169). Janelle may be saying 'hey, I'm an individual too,' not just one piece of the larger Brown family puzzle. Janelle does seem to be a bit lost amongst all the children. Janelle's 'my name is Janelle' comes quickly after she has said 'that's how most of us are known: polygs'. It's almost as if she is crying out to be heard and understood and received by the audience as an individual, not just a 'polyg'.

Meri, the first wife, has one child with Kody. She explains that they have three separate bedrooms and three separate sexual relationships.

> [We] don't go weird [...] when he is ornery with another one he gets weird with me and I don't want that, you know, so it's very important for him to have a good relationship and the sexual nature of it is definitely part of that good relationship and when he is off with somebody else I just don't think about that part of it you know why would I want to do that to myself ...
>
> (Gibbons et al. 2010).

Here we see Meri refusing to think about the sexual relationship of her sister wives with her husband. Why would she not want to acknowledge this? Meri appears uneasy about the understanding that her husband is sleeping with other women and appears as though it is still difficult for her to accept. Meri, at one time, may have been aware of her true self, but the false self overshadows the true self. The more the false self takes over, the less likely one is able to recognize the lies one tells to oneself. The false self says to the individual, ‘sharing your husband is fine’ and the true self says ‘something doesn’t seem right’. Is Meri allowed to have multiple husbands? Meri goes on to explain:

> I came from a culture and it’s not abnormal to get married when you are 19/20 years old. I was raised in a polygamous family. By the time I met Kody we were talking about marriage and stuff at that point he and I eventually knew that we would both take another wife or wives into the family [...] If you’re looking at this lifestyle just as you know, what can I do to help you or what can you do to help me, it works out totally well [...] It’s not something like I’m sitting there thinking: ok I’m, I’m ready to, take another wife, let’s go find somebody. It’s more of a situation of when uh, the, uh, uh, right person comes along.
>
> (Gibbons et al. 2010)

Throughout the episode Meri seems to justify the lifestyle that her family lives. The family wanted to participate in this reality television program to present the viewer with the positive aspects of a polygamous lifestyle. The family may be attempting to present their lifestyle in comparison to that of a traditional family of mainstream Mormonism found within the Church of Jesus Christ of Latter-Day Saints. Surprisingly there are many parallels between their family and non-polygamous families in our society. Giddens discusses how an individual determines the choices they will make in life: ‘the selection or creation of lifestyles is influenced by group pressures and the visibility of role models, as well as by socioeconomic circumstances’ (1991: 82). Meri grew up in a polygamous lifestyle and may have been accepting of her husband’s choice to marry other women because that is all she has ever known. A husband taking multiple wives had been normalized for Meri not only due to being raised in a polygamous family but also being surrounded by polygamy through her church and through close contacts. Even if a part of her did not want that sort of relationship, she had been influenced and encouraged to continue in it because that was how she was socialized religiously. There are many parallels between what Meri and the other wives may be experiencing in terms of cultural oppression and the socialization other individuals experience in terms of consumerism and narcissism. Consume material goods in the pursuit of being deemed unique, special and ultimately successful. Material goods are a measure of your success. Likewise, the accumulation of multiple wives or having multiple sexual relationships can also be a result of the limitless pursuit of wealth. Unregulated pursuits in one area of one’s life can lead to the acceptance of a pursuit of multiple sexual relationships and marriage partners. Why be satisfied with just one when you can have *many*?

During a group interview with all three sister wives and Kody, the third wife says:

> Christine: Yeah, you have to know, that Janelle and I might have never married Kody, we never would have married him on our own. It took Mary pulling some strings and Kody by himself would have never done it, he had to have Meri's back too.
> Kody: Meri bonded with Janelle and Christine before it was a serious thought in my mind. Meri's the bait.
> Janelle: No, she's in mergers and acquisitions, is what he says.
> [Laughter from everyone]
>
> (Gibbons et al. 2010)

Whether or not these statements are true, the viewer cannot help but wonder if there was some manipulation and convincing on Kody's part to get Meri to accept the addition of the new wives. Referring back to narcissistic traits laid out by Vaknin, the narcissist 'uses others to achieve his or her own ends' (Vaknin 2001: 32). The person in this family that is receiving the most benefit is Kody. He is the one that gets to sleep with three women while each wife is confined to being with her husband every third night and is only allotted one date a week. Janelle's comment about 'mergers and acquisitions' is funny to all of the parents but it is presenting the viewer with a very dark aspect of our society: how consumerism begins to seep into our very relationships with other people. The accumulation of multiple wives is very much a business transaction. There are finances to consider, living arrangements, and the adjustment of adding additional kids. Throughout the episode the wives will attempt to justify their lifestyle that they are convinced is a positive one.

The viewer is then exposed to Janelle, the second wife, who has six children with Kody. During her interview one is exposed to many interesting aspects of their family life.

> When I finally decided it really didn't seem so strange it was not … like this big … let me think about this, it wasn't a huge jump for me for some reason […] I've always been a career person, I've always worked. I would prefer to be working rather than be home with the kids […] Now that they're getting older and they text me and we communicate via the phone and stuff, that's nicer. I love it because I get my children and we do all the really fun things together but I get to be the mom but I don't have to do the cooking or the chauffeuring.

Janelle works ten to twelve hour days, and as she says she prefers it that way. Janelle's polygamous lifestyle allows her the freedom to work and not be at home with the kids. The advent of technology allows her the freedom to do what she wants to do without having to physically be in the presence of her children. Janelle can still 'be the mom' via a text message or phone call and not have the burden of being physically present all the time. The drudgeries of parenthood can be avoided so that Janelle can do whatever it is *she* likes to do.

> On my days home, all I do is drive the kids everywhere and I'm doing this and I'm doing that and I'm seeing to the homework and everything and you know what? I like working more, so let Christine do that. And Christine likes to do that! I can say 'I'm going to a movie, will you watch my kids?' And they have somebody to watch 'em. I don't have to do everything. I have time for the things I like to do too, not just household stuff.
>
> (Gibbons et al. 2010)

The dialogue here makes it seem as if Janelle's children are a burden to her and she would rather have Christine, the third wife, care for them. The new narcissus focuses on whatever they want even when it means overlooking the needs of others. She enjoys the fact that she gets to work and do what she enjoys the most, while someone else is raising her children. Janelle goes on to state 'Usually Christine will make dinner and I don't have to worry about that because I work with a bunch of women who are like "Ugh!" I've gotta go home and fix dinner!" And I'm like "Oh. Not me!"' Even on Janelle's days off she does not want to care for her children she would rather do things that interest her.

> If a sense of duty is to take strong root in us, the very circumstances of our life must serve to keep it always active [...] If we live amorally for a good part of the day, how can we keep the springs of morality from going slack in us? We are not naturally inclined to put ourselves out or to use self-restraint; if we are not encouraged at every step to exercise the restraint upon which all morals depend, how should we get the habit of it?
>
> (Durkheim 1957: 12)

Society, for the individual, serves the purpose of keeping individuals in check. Society helps to regulate our natural, animalistic impulses that can cause harm to others and ourselves. Today, the moral code of our society is *more*. There is never enough to be obtained and one's duty in life is the pursuit of more success, wealth, possessions and for some, even children and wives. Sprinkle a desire for a little narcissistic supply in with this steadfast duty to obtain more wealth and you have the ripe breeding ground for the development of the new narcissus. For Janelle, she focuses on her job and bringing in an income and fervently holds to this moral code that through the pursuit of *more*, happiness will surely follow for herself and for her family.

Freedom and choice

Freedom and autonomy are mentioned repeatedly, by the wives, as beneficial to maintaining a membership in a polygamous family. As Janelle states, 'this home is actually built by a polygamist and this is probably typical of what you'll find in most polygamist families: separate living spaces but interconnected and so the family functions as a whole but we all have our own autonomy' (Gibbons et al. 2010).

Figure 4.1 Brown family home

This is an interesting concept to think about. Freedom and autonomy are clearly valued in this family and they therefore have separate living spaces (see Figure 4.1). Meri informs the audience that her sister was the second wife in a polygamous relationship, and 11 months after she was diagnosed with cancer her sister passed away. Meri becomes emotional as she talks about how her sister's sister wives now take care of her sister's children.

> Janelle and Christine would be there to step up and raise my daughter just like … I want her to be raised, you know? With the freedom that she … deserves and the, you know, whatever she wants to do. So that's definitely a plus to this lifestyle.

Meri seems concerned about her daughter's freedom. The message to the audience is that the wives are free to pursue whatever it is that they want to do, a freedom that is unique to a polygamous lifestyle. However, the practice of polygamy in the US is notorious for marrying young girls off to older men. Might Meri's concern stem from a deep-seated fear she has felt as a result of her immersion in a polygamous family growing up? Meri goes on to explain:

> You know what? I hope our kids do what they want to do in their life, whether its live our lifestyle or have no religion at all, as long as they are strong and firm in what they want to do and what they want to believe and that they are not following somebody else.

How free are these sister wives? Did Meri feel that she was free to make her own choices and decisions regarding polygamy? Meri would most likely say absolutely. The polygamous lifestyle encourages wives to overcome their jealousy issues. Maybe Meri, and the other wives, feel they are free because they chose to marry Kody and weren't forced into a marriage. Baudrillard states that 'the consumer experiences his distinctive behaviors as freedom, as aspiration, as choice' (1970: 61). We have already seen through *Toddlers and Tiaras* and *Hoarders* that people become objectified in a consumer society, and a polygamous lifestyle follows the principle of accumulating more wives and children. If reality seems too difficult to accept and if the feelings stirred within you by living this lifestyle are too much to handle, then focus on yourself and create an artifice. 'Consumption [...] is the duty of the citizen' (Baudrillard 1998: 80). Durkheim warned us of an amoral aspect of our life becoming a duty and a worthy pursuit. If the moral duty of pursuing a limitless goal exists for us as individuals today then we are by definition in the pursuit of something amoral. Morality, by definition, is regulation. One must not be allowed to eat all the food or drink all the water or have all the women. Morality and regulation are key for a society and family to function. When the modern individual confuses amorality with being a worthy pursuit there will be 'no influence set above him to check his egotism' (Durkheim 1957: 12). As Janelle previously stated, by being in a polygamous family she has 'time for everything [*she*] likes to do'. During the parents' interview on the couch (see Figure 4.2) Meri exclaims:

> Meri: Having the lifestyle and only once every third night, frees up a lot of time for us ...
> Janelle (interjects): Oh, it's great!
> Meri: ... to go do what we need to do.
>
> (Gibbons et al. 2010)

Figure 4.2 Christine, Meri, Kody and Janelle in a group interview

By being a part of this polygamous family there is some level of encouragement to be narcissistic and focus on one's self. A marriage is no longer a partnership but a whole collaboration and team of wives under the leadership of their husband, Kody. Their religion encourages the wives to overcome jealousy, to stifle that emotion, and instead to focus on the freedom one is accorded. Since Kody is the ultimate narcissist in this situation, the wives are allowed the 'freedom' to pursue their own self- interest even to the point of developing an unhealthy level of narcissism. The new narcissus often emerges as a way for the culturally oppressed individual to cope with their life circumstances.

The Brown family, throughout this first episode, appears to be 'selling' their lifestyle to the audience. It is almost as if the Browns are saying 'Look, we know polygamy has got a bad rap and all: for the child brides, incest and pedophilia. But look, our reality show presents you with *our* lifestyle, that is also polygamous, but not as bad as you think it is!'

> It is a paradox of contemporary cultures that they simultaneously promote individualism as well as automatized reactions [...] advertisements sell feelings, moods, and emotions that are synthetically attached to a given product.
>
> (Mestrovic 1997: 81)

Expanding on Stjepan Mestrovic's postemotionalism, the new narcissus emerges as a result of too much focus on the self and the promotion of synthetic feelings and emotions. The modern individual cannot escape the constant bombardment of advertisements for products on the television screen, computer, even at the doctor's office or in school. Advertisements present the individual with products they should aspire to own because there is also a promise that by owning this product one will not only experience a feeling of satisfaction but also the opportunity to experience *a way of life*. Reality television is just another route through which modern individuals are routinely presented with different ways of life. Individuals on reality television must successfully sell their lifestyle to the audience in order to be well-liked so that the show has high enough ratings to garner more money from advertisers so that ultimately the show continues as a profitable enterprise for the production company and cable network alike. If the Browns successfully sell the audience their lifestyle then the Browns will benefit financially too. All three wives remind the audience that their lifestyle provides each of them freedom and autonomy and that their lifestyle really isn't that different from other families.

What does it mean to be free? Freedom and power are very closely intertwined. Many definitions of power exist and are usually understood in one of two ways: domination (power over others) or empowerment (helping others reach an intended goal). Power is the ability to bring about an intended outcome even in the face of opposition. Then is freedom not the ability to pursue a goal without opposition? Emile Durkheim articulates a very important aspect of freedom that seems to be missing from the minds of many modern individuals' understanding of freedom.

> [L]iberty is itself the product of a set of rules. I can be free only in so far as the other person is prevented from turning to his own benefit that superiority, whether physical, economic or any other kind, which he possesses, in order to fetter my liberty. Only a social rule can serve as a barrier against such abuses of power.
>
> (Durkheim 1997: xxxiii)

Over a hundred years since Durkheim's warning about the unchecked abuses of power within the economic realm, the modern individual is experiencing the devastating effects of immorality unchecked. The new narcissus is not only present on reality television shows but is springing up all around us. The new narcissus clings to the motto of unregulated pursuit of more: more attention, adoration, adulation and even emulation from others. These sister wives, through their socialization process, have internalized an understanding that polygamy is an acceptable form for a family, for as Kody states 'love should be multiplied, not divided'. The encouragement to pursue more wives and children is indicative of an infinite goal impacting all aspects of one's life. The maintenance of autonomy and freedom, as Durkheim warns, is only true freedom when it does not infringe upon the liberty of others. To subordinate others in the process of pursuing your freedom is characteristic of the new narcissus.

The final wife, Christine, is then introduced the viewer. Christine was also raised in a polygamous family, like Meri. Christine has five children and is currently pregnant with her sixth.

> I never wanted to just be married to a man, I always wanted sister-wives, uh, I just liked the idea of the companionship. I liked the idea of the freedom that it got me. There's too many things that I want to do and want to be, um, free for, and I just like the idea of having someone around. I just like the idea of sister-wives, a lot. Um, I, yeah, I honestly wanted sister wives more than a husband, for a good time of my life. I wanted the whole family, I didn't just want Kody. No, I wanted everything.
>
> (Gibbons et al. 2010)

Already, we see Christine justify her marriage, lifestyle and why she would enter into polygamy. However, there is more to her statements than just justifying polygamy. Christine states that she 'didn't just want Kody' she 'wanted *everything*'. In the previous chapters on reality television we saw the uncontrolled, runaway character of economic life as discussed by Durkheim and the dangers that can result. Durkheim says the individual apart of such a society 'aspires to everything and is satisfied with nothing' (1951: 271). The new narcissus emerges from our sense of duty to pursue wealth and the presumed freedom one feels in pursuing wealth and *choosing* material goods. Individuals are led to believe that this pursuit is not only a moral one but that the pursuit will bring about happiness, prestige and autonomy. Instead, individuals feel frustrated, unfulfilled, constantly advancing yet the satisfaction only seems to last but a short while before the hunger begins again. It's as though there is always a voice deep within us that repeats the same thing over and over again: *more*. The mindset of the new narcissus becomes even clearer to the viewer when Christine continues discussing how she came into the marriage (see Figure 4.3).

> And then a third wife comes along and they actually say if you are having problems, in, like, when you have two wives and you're having problems, marry a third, because it'll even it out. So I only ever wanted to be a third. I never wanted to be a first at all because I didn't want to be married to a guy by myself and then I didn't want to be a second, because I felt like they are a little wedge in the relationship and I didn't want to be the wedge. I only ever wanted to be third, because it sounded the *easiest* [big smile].
>
> (Gibbons et al. 2010)

Christine has already made it clear that she wanted everything and worse yet, what she wanted was the best position in the marriage according to her: that of the third wife. Regardless of whether or not the third wife actually is the best position, Christine has 'won' it! She won 3rd wife! 'Conspicuous existence is a form of conspicuous consumption, in which the consumed commodity is narcissistic supply' (Vaknin 2001: 66). The new narcissus is constantly seeking out the attention, admiration and adoration from others via the easiest route possible. Christine informs the audience that the first and

Figure 4.3 Christine smiling

second wife positions can be a bit too difficult because the first wife only has one source of narcissistic supply: her husband, and the second wife causes tension and conflict in the marriage. Kody then has a voiceover stating that Christine has a demanding job 'because she's actually mothering the twelve kids'. Christine is then shown interacting with several of the children, because, as Christine says with a smile, she is the 'domestic one' and designated caregiver of all the children. 'Savanah is technically Janelle's, but we've raised all the kids all together and so if someone tries to tell me that Savanah's not my child, I adamantly disagree (smiles)' (Gibbons et al. 2010). Christine often ends her comments with what appears to be a forced, fake smile. Vaknin explains that '[a] child, after all, is the ultimate source of Narcissistic Supply' (Vaknin 2001: 208). Christine probably loves the fact that she is in charge of all the children because they provide the most attention, adoration, and admiration (Narcissistic Supply).

This idea of forced emotions and fakeness is seen in an interaction between Meri and Christine during the parents' interview on the couch. Meri says, 'They say you have to work on being nurturing. You [Christine], even if it hasn't come by naturally, you do a really good job at it' (shrugs shoulders). To which Christine responds 'thanks!' while shrugging her shoulders (Gibbons et al. 2010). There is something very interesting about their body language when this compliment is given and received. It is as if they have never given or received compliments before and it is so strange and foreign to them that their body language clearly articulates the uncomfortable nature of the situation and possible falseness of the compliment. 'Mechanization has extended its imperialistic realm from technology and industry to colonize the last bastion of nature: emotions (Mestrovic 1997: 146). Christine and Meri seem machine-like in their interaction with one another. Postemotionalism, as defined by Mestrovic, 'is a system designed to avoid emotional disorder; to prevent loose ends in emotional exchanges; [...] to order the emotions so that the social world hums as smoothly as a well-maintained machine' (1997: 150). Similarly, an extreme focus on the self and the pursuit of narcissistic supply, to the point of damaging others, causes the new narcissus to avoid any emotional encounter that may be too much to handle. In the forthcoming chapters, the reader will witness the new narcissus' attempts to avoid emotional situations and more important, avoid confronting the artificiality they have constructed in their presentation of self to others. For Christine and the other wives, what may start as a forced, fake smile, can eventually become the norm for one's behavior, immersing the individual so that all social interactions contain this presentation of falseness.

Meri and Christine both grew up in polygamous families, and family is arguably the most powerful socializing agent for the individual. One's first interactions with the social world occur within the family and home. Meri and Christine learned that having one father and multiple mothers was a normal family environment. All of the sister wives and Kody are shown in a group interview.

Christine: We always home-schooled our kids and until about five years ago, we put our kids all in this one school that's a school for *our* people.

Kody: The private school's a home school coalition. It's a church school, a polygamous school.

Christine: Everybody that goes to this school believes in plural marriage. They all have *tons* of moms. All of them!

Not only are the Brown children learning the expectation of plural marriage from their experiences in their family but also through their school environment. One's family, school, religion and friends all support the principle of plural marriage. Just as the wives were socialized to understand the expectation to have multiple wives in a marriage, the children in this family are also learning this important expectation. Other latent functions are occurring for these young children as well. The understanding that only boys will be allowed to take multiple wives sends the message to both young men and women that it is acceptable for men to have many wives and women must learn to overcome jealousy and other emotions in order to share their partner with sister wives. Men must be free to pursue their thirst for novelty with the addition of more wives, and women must learn to accept their subordinate position as one of many wives competing for attention and satisfaction.

Maintain the artifice and suppress real emotions

'Her name is Robyn and she's 30. She's got three children and she grew up in the lifestyle.' Kody is nervous and excited to tell his twelve children that he is courting a woman who has the potential to become their fourth mom.

Janelle: We were beginning to feel like there was someone else. I was starting to feel like there was someone. Like I would comment to Christine, 'gosh we sure need another one, it's getting kinda boring, you know?

Christine: Yeah, Meri would make comments like that too and I'd be like 'you guys are insane'. It's fine how it is. I don't want to rock the boat.

Janelle: Yeah, but I sort of felt like there was somebody else coming. We had sort of started to talk to the kids about the possibility of another mother coming into the family so I don't think it was a foreign concept to them. They have peers who, several of them, who have just had new moms come into the family.

(Gibbons et al. 2010)

Janelle indicates that life was starting to feel a bit boring. How on earth could it possibly be getting boring when you have twelve children, three wives and a husband? As witnessed in the analysis of *Toddlers and Tiaras* and *Hoarders,* consumer society presents the individual with infinite possibilities that can be detrimental and unnerving. Potentially, there is no limit to the number of wives that Kody could obtain. This environment of several adults searching for attention and admiration encourages the desire to seek out more. The addition of a fourth wife (or more) and a need for even more children is one way to obtain more attention and admiration. 'Since man is, nonetheless, never satisfied, the same story begins over and over again, with the sterile self-evidence of old fables' (Baudrillard 1970: 69). This quote from Baudrillard clearly parallels that of Durkheim's concept of anomie. How are we to be satisfied when the possibilities are limitless? Sister wives and others living in polygamy think this lifestyle is a righteous one and that one's duty in life is to 'multiply love'. Multiplying love in the form of wives or children can help to create unity for the family when there is tension or division among the wives. The pursuit of *more* will surely bring about more happiness or more narcissistic supply or even the unfortunate distraction from one's true feelings and emotions. Even more, Janelle indicates that the children's friends have been getting new moms so maybe their family needs a new mom too! Outrageous as this may seem, imagine for a moment, the community the Brown family lives in. Their church and faith support plural marriage, their family is plural, the school their children go to is for polygamous children and therefore their friends are polygamous too. This community the Browns are immersed in normalizes the accumulation of wives and children.

Christine felt that it was 'insane' to speak of adding a fourth wife. Christine may feel that her title of third wife is in jeopardy with the potential addition of a *new* wife. If a new mom is added to the family, Christine will no longer have the ultimate title of *newest* wife. As Kody and the three wives sit down with their children to discuss the potential addition of a fourth wife, one of the children struggles to understand. Kody begins to try and explain and Christine interjects to try and make it clearer for the eight-year-old girl (see Figure 4.4).

> Christine: Sweetheart, there might be a girl that's going to be entering our family soon so you'll have another Mom and some other brothers and sisters but right now we're gonna keep it quiet. And when Robyn comes are we gonna go 'Robyn you're gonna be our new mommy!'?
>
> Little girl: No.
>
> Christine: No, because she's not in the circle right now so when she comes we just go 'Hi Robyn, how are you?'
>
> (Gibbons et al. 2010)

As Christine instructs the child to say the above statement several of them repeat the statement along with her as though they are practicing: 'Hi Robyn, how are you?' Christine is essentially teaching the children how to practice faking it (see Figure 4.4). Right after this statement is completed in unison Christine states in a very calming and soothing tone 'Very good.' *Good job children, learning to suppress your true feelings and emotions.* It appears as

Figure 4.4 Family discussion of adding fourth wife

though the parents are getting the children's help to *snag* a fourth wife. Robyn doesn't know that she is going to be the fourth wife yet, but she will soon. Kody then asks if anyone is concerned about this and then pointedly asks Aspyn, one of the older girls, who replies 'I think it'll be kind of weird at first but I think it'll be like, ok, after awhile.' Just as young Alicia stated in *Toddlers and Tiaras*, the fake eyelashes feel 'weird when you first put it on but after, it just feels like your regular eyes'. As another older girl in the family puts it, 'We'll get used to it.' Unfortunately, this is the lie promised by the new narcissus, to falsify one's true feelings and emotions and after awhile one will become *used* to the falseness to the point that it just feels normal, true and authentic.

Meri states 'I'm not gonna lie. There are jealously issues, you know? I mean there are, those are there, those are natural, and you know, hopefully that's something that I can overcome' (Gibbons et al. 2010). Meri is essentially stating that she hopes her false self can take over so that her natural self cannot be hurt and traumatized by Kody's decision to add another wife. Christine states 'I like three wives a lot and I'm kinda more hesitant adding another wife. I like it easy and so I kinda like just having three.' Christine appears to like just having three, because we have already witnessed the importance she feels her third wife position brings her. Sure, people are hesitant when change is introduced, however, Christine may feel threatened and ultimately there is now a fourth wife to take away some of the attention and admiration she receives from Kody and the children. Meri goes on to repeat 'I like my time with Kody and having sister wives makes it so that I do have less time with Kody. Jealousy is something that I want to overcome.' Unfortunately for Meri, she has been living with jealousy for twenty years now. She has likely created a false self as a coping mechanism in order to avoid the emotions that exist deep within her, emotions of jealousy and pain. It is with the possibility of even more time being taken away from her that these emotions emerge from deep down inside her where she has been placing them due to the falseness of the new narcissus always being at the forefront. Robyn, the potential fourth wife, is briefly shown at the end of the episode. A voiceover of Robyn says 'Kody's my soulmate. I love him,' as she is shown laughing with Kody as they leave to go on a date. The cameras then follow Kody and Robyn to a restaurant as a voiceover of Kody states 'because wives are comfortable with another wife in this lifestyle they're not comfortable with a girlfriend'. Even Kody's statement that he apparently understands his wife's feelings and emotions comes across as oblivious to the situation his family is living in. Robyn is significantly younger than all of his wives by at least ten years. As much as the wives speak of freedom and autonomy, Kody, is the only true free one in this equation, not the wives. Kody dating a potential fourth wife equates to cheating. A marriage and partnership, for many individuals today, rests on a basis of fidelity and faithfulness. Kody is instead free to do as he pleases and merely has to convince his wives that his decisions are the right ones (i.e. dating is not the same thing as cheating). Christine concludes the episode with an interview at a kitchen table.

> I don't want to be a boat rocker, and I don't want my boat rocked. So no, I'm a little hesitant to accept another wife, but if it happens, she just has to be absolutely amazing. [brief big smile – fake] Otherwise it might be a little difficult [raises one eyebrow].
>
> (Gibbons et al. 2010)

Christine may be hesitant to face the feelings and emotions stirred within her as the family considers adding a fourth wife. This addition could cause more pain, hurt and trauma for Christine and her sister wives. 'We are surrounded by waves of fake spontaneity, "personalized" language, orchestrated emotions and personal relations. "Keep Smiling"' (Baudrillard 1970: 161). Throughout the episode the viewer witnesses Christine's constant forced and fake smiles when discussing various aspects of their polygamous lifestyle. Referring back to Vaknin's characteristics of narcissists: they prefer to surround themselves with other special and unique individuals *only*. Christine will *only* be accepting of the fourth wife if she is 'absolutely amazing'. These wives may have very well entered into this polygamous marriage on their own accord. However, the way the wives have spoken about their marriage and relationship does not quite add up. '[N]arcissism becomes intensified as a reaction to the feelings of powerlessness thus engendered' (Giddens 1991: 173). It may be possible that over the years something inside each of these women has been broken to such a point that they have generated this façade of falsity in order to help them cope with their cultural situation. The façade, now in control, is constantly in search of more attention and admiration from others for this is the only way to survive. The children, Kody, and even the other wives can be a steady and consistent source of that supply. The new narcissus needs attention and validation from others in order to remind them that the artifice is indeed. A special and amazing individual. A fourth wife could jeopardize all that. Also, each wife is not alone in the repression of her feelings because there are two other wives that may be dealing with the same emotions. 'The narcissism of the individual in [a] consumer society is not an enjoyment of singularity; it is a refraction of collective features' (Baudrillard 1998: 95). The Brown family is surrounded by other polygamous families in their home, at church, at school and with their friends. The message is consistent from all avenues of one's life and from one's community: maintain the right image. Through the projection of falseness one is able to overcome true feelings of jealousy, pain and suffering. The children in this family are socialized to accept the roles of their mother(s) and father. Even more, the children internalize an understanding about their place in the world as men, women and ultimately as individuals. If the message is that one's true feelings must be repressed and instead replaced with the projection of artificiality, then the children are learning about the role the new narcissus may play in their lives as well.

The new narcissus is affecting more and more segments of the population. Reality television frequently portrays individuals who enjoy the pursuit of narcissistic supply and are themselves, narcissists. Is this the ideal individual we want to aspire to? One that shoves away their true feelings and emotions due to unhealthy goals and instead projects a falseness bent on obtaining that unhealthy illusion? Should we aspire to be someone who is free to pursue as many partners as possible even if that pursuit inflicts pain and suffering on those closest to us? This is the dark promise of the new narcissus: fame, satisfaction, attention and emulation from others but in the process artificiality, manipulation, deceit and pain. The new narcissus should not be the aspiration for modern individuals today.

5 Avoiding reality

Catfish: The TV Show

The way we communicate with one another has drastically shifted in the past thirty years. Cellular phones have only been widely accessible to many in the past fifteen or twenty years. Today, the cell phone seems to be an unavoidable tool for so many avenues of communication: social media (Twitter, Instagram, Snapchat, Facebook, etc.), emails, text messages, phone calls, Facetime and video calls, even gaming, weather, travel, banking, transit, television and movies, news, stocks, exercise/health monitoring, personal library, storage for any number of items like boarding passes, tickets, reservations, documents, presentations and reports. The modern phone really is the tool that can do it all. All of these so very crucial components of our daily lives would not be possible without the advent of the Internet.

The Internet provides individuals opportunities to form meaningful connections with other people, in a sense, providing a new social space for the creation and experience of community. Lest we forget, we are social individuals. Can an individual truly be social via an interaction with a computer, cell phone or television? Even if that device provides a visual view of the individuals one is communing with? 'The so-called community of Internet users is not a real community because one can enter and leave the interaction in cyberspace at will. One does not have such freedom in real communities' (Mestrovic 1997: 94). Even if an individual experiences connection, or social solidarity, and a sense of belonging to their online community, the interaction and experience of that particular form of community is very different from a face-to-face community. While in some instances, individuals can leave a community whenever they desire, more often than not, modern individuals are bound to their social groups with social expectations, and the fear of subsequent consequences prevents the abrupt exit from these groups. Individuals must follow the expectations of their given groups and if they choose not to then they may be forced to leave the group. All individuals need to belong and this need for belonging causes all individuals to adhere to the rules and expectations of society. The Internet allows for individuals to bypass those rules and expectations. One can enter into an online community and violate the norms and rules of behavior. Language and conduct that exist in normal face-to-face interaction can be altogether absent in online social interaction. One can say whatever one wants to anyone one wants online. There are no social cues against this behavior and far fewer repercussions. An individual can be abusive and manipulative in how they interact with others online. As I write this I am aware that others adamantly disagree about the level of community one can experience online. Clearly, communities, social solidarity and connection to others can occur via online interaction; however, the implications and consequences of the increasing presence of the Internet in our lives is worthy of examination. Now that individuals are spending a significant part of their day 'connected' via their cell phones, how is this impacting the way we view ourselves and others?

> The notion of an artificially authentic community seems to be an oxymoron at first glance, but appears to be the meaning of Disney culture, the McDonaldization of society, Internet 'communities', and other anomalies that postmodernists have already uncovered. It is no longer Adorno's culture industry, but a new authenticity industry that seems to characterize postemotional societies.
>
> (Mestrovic 1997: 74)

Stjepan Mestrovic's description of the experience of authenticity in a postemotional society sheds light on how our experiences online relate to the new narcissus. The Internet is now a primary source of interaction for many individuals today. It is possible that we are confusing authentic, meaningful relationships with other people as the types of relationships and experiences that occur on the Internet and through our phones and other devices. Relationships may *begin* online via a game, a blog, Facebook group, online dating website, photo sharing or online texts, emails and video calls but these relationships must then carry over into face-to-face interaction. If an individual confuses an online relationship or community as an end (meaningful, interpersonal relationship) rather than as a means to achieving that end, then that person is now vulnerable to the new narcissus' deception, betrayal and pain.

The reality television show *Catfish: The TV Show* first aired on 12 November 2012. It is about individuals who meet and fall in love online but have not met in person. A 'catfish' in this context refers to someone who has created a false or misleading profile on social media sites like Facebook or other Internet sites in order to make themselves more appealing. This particular episode, entitled 'Jen & Skylar', is the sixth episode of the second season and originally aired on 30 July 2013. Nev and Max (hosts of the program) receive emails from individuals who ask for their help in determining whether or not the people they are talking with online are who they really say they are, or if they are presenting a fake identity. The episode begins with Max and Nev reading an email from Jen, who is an 18-year-old high school senior in Iowa who has fallen for a 22-year-old college junior in San Francisco, California (see Figure 5.1). When Nev and Max read the email of Jen's story she explains:

Figure 5.1 Skylar

Nev (reading Jen's email out loud): I do have some concerns that he's hiding something from me even though I feel like I am completely open with him. I've been online since I was ten years old.
Max and Nev (in unison): Wow.
Nev (reading Jen's email out loud): In middle school I was bullied and found that people online did not judge me. Skylar is the one person that I would like to bring into my real world.

(Mussman 2013)

Jen is ready to take the romantic relationship she has developed with Skylar online into her real world. This is a profound idea, that the experiences we have online are in some way artificial or not quite the same as real world, face-to-face interactions. Jen's experiences in the real world were often negative so she found solace online.

Nev: So since middle school you've been actively socializing online?
Jen: Because people in real life don't like to talk to me. So I'm like I'm going to be who I am online. I'm not going to make a fake personality because I want people to like me for me.

(Mussman 2013)

Jen has adapted to the current structure of our society. She was bullied in school for being her true self and the Internet provided an opportunity for her to interact with other individuals who did not judge her or make her feel bad about her true self. Jen could no longer develop meaningful, close relationships with others in person; however, she could experience a similar relationship with others via the Internet. Now that she has developed a romantic relationship she needs Max and Nev's help in beginning an authentic, meaningful, face-to-face connection with someone she has only been able to superficially interact with up until this point. Jen's belief that online she can be real whereas in real life she would have to be fake is an indicative of the freedom that the Internet provides the modern individual: a freedom to pursue interaction with others, an interaction that is free from regulation and pre-prescribed codes of conduct that exist in the real world.

Anomie online

Online experiences can also be very isolating for the individual. Confusing relationships with others via our relationships that solely exist online cannot bring about a real, meaningful connection; online relationships that take the place of real life can be isolating. Can one truly experience another person's presence via online interaction? The experience of holding hands for the first time? Or of one's body language, or even of physical chemistry?

> [W]hat is most significant about mega-cities is that they are connected externally to global networks and to segments of their own countries, while internally disconnecting local populations that are either functionally unnecessary or socially disruptive [...] It is this distinctive feature of being globally connected and locally disconnected, physically and socially, that makes mega-cities a new urban form.
>
> (Castells 2010: 436)

The Internet connects us to others but also disconnects us from our local communities. Local businesses or small, 'Mom and Pop' shops are slowly being destroyed by the ease of Internet shopping. Jen chose to form relationships online because she was being bullied in real life. While social media and the Internet can provide opportunities for people like Jen to truly express who they are as a person, they can also provide opportunities for individuals who are projecting a false self to inflict harm on others through their selfish pursuits of attention and admiration. Some individuals may choose to be false in real life with their interactions with others as well as the interactions with others online. Many individuals like Jen want to develop meaningful relationships with others online.

'But something appears to be missing in these seemingly heartfelt disclosures of apparent authenticity. Part of what is missing is an authentic sense of community' (Mestrovic 1997: 97). Jen, and others who appear on this reality show, seem to experience what Mestrovic references in this statement about *heartfelt disclosures of apparent authenticity* – this illusion of authenticity. Jen, and others like her, believe that the individuals they are meeting and falling in love with online are indeed who they say they are. The individuals portrayed in this show often have been 'dating' or 'in a relationship' with this unknown online individual for many years before reaching out to Max and Nev for help. To maintain a relationship for years without ever meeting them in person or even having a video call seems to be a bit unrealistic because it is. A relationship with others solely via online interaction is not an authentic relationship.

Jen goes on to explain her feelings for Skylar and how they met through an online game site, and asks Max and Nev to help her meet him in person. According to Jen, she and Skylar talk on the phone and text each other almost every day but have never video chatted and he has only sent her two pictures of himself. He also claims to not have a Facebook profile. They decide to help Jen by finding out more about Skylar, and they conduct research on Skylar's phone number, his name, the photos he provided and whether or not he is enrolled at the university he claims to attend. The research does not produce many answers as to whether or not Skylar's identity is actually truthful, so Nev decides to call and talk with Skylar to see if he would be interested in meeting face-to-face.

> Nev: We're a little concerned that maybe you're not being totally honest with her. And we obviously did a little research just to see if we could find anything out about you and the only thing we did find was uh, that there isn't currently anybody named Skylar Hazen registered at San Francisco State University.
>
> Skylar: I mean, I do go to San Francisco State and everything. I just don't … if I want to meet her like I mean I feel like I could make it a point to meet her when I feel like. *This is like the worst time ever for this to happen.*
>
> Nev: I mean look, sometimes, you don't get to choose exactly when and how things happen.
>
> (Mussman 2013)

Already we see Skylar attempting to avoid the confrontation over whether or not he is being honest about his identity. Skylar also immediately points out that this is a terrible time for him to meet her and he wants to decide when and if they'll meet. This behavior is indicative of a narcissist who refuses to face his true identity and constantly focuses only on what is beneficial for himself. To refer to the fourth characteristic of narcissism expressed by Vaknin, the narcissist 'feels entitled, has unreasonable expectations for special and favorable priority treatment' (2001: 32). If Skylar does indeed have true feelings for Jen and has now been afforded the opportunity to meet her, then why avoid this? Skylar only seems concerned with his feelings and his schedule and is unable to take on the position and feelings of others. Mestrovic's discussion of the children's television show *Barney and Friends* provides insight into the development of the new narcissus today.

> In one episode, for example, they want to experience igloos but are thwarted by living in a warm climate. It is important to note that in this episode, as in all others, the group immediately supports the wishes of one of its members. No child ever objects to another child's fantasy. In

> any event, the frustration is not a problem: Barney instantly imagines them into an arctic setting in which they sing a happy song. There is absolutely no obstacle in life that cannot be overcome by wishing in *Barney and Friends*.
>
> (Mestrovic 1997: 54)

We are living in an age of entitlement where the norm communicated to members of our society (even young, developing children) is to always get what one *wishes* for. Throw in the illusory belief that everything is fine and nothing ever goes wrong and you have an environment ripe for the creation and encouragement of the new narcissus. If you are bullied in school and unable to make friends, go online and make friends where there are less rules and additional opportunities for manipulation and abuse. Adaptation to the structure, morals and values of our society commend the exceptional individual just as much as the artificial one who appears to be equally exceptional, when in reality the presumed exceptionality is but a farce. Skylar is exemplifying a modern individual who not only feels entitled but believes they are special and unique too. Remembering Durkheim, the norm for our society is to always strive for more and to never be satisfied with what one has. On top of this limitless pursuit of satisfaction the Internet is a place that is relatively free from regulation and restriction.

Skylar asks for time to think about whether or not they can come out to San Francisco to meet him. The next day Nev calls him back to find out what he has decided: 'Yeah. I mean, if she really wants to come. I think it would be best for her to come here.' Nev retorts by saying 'I need you to convince me a little bit more that like you are taking this as seriously as we are, and as seriously as she is' (Mussman 2013). Skylar seems extremely apprehensive about revealing his identity to the show and to Jen. Max, Nev and Jen fly to San Francisco to meet Skylar face-to-face. When they arrive at his address the man that appears is not the one from the photos.

> Nev: and uh, we brought her from Iowa, just like we said we would. What comes as a bit of a shock for Jen and also us is that you're not the guy that we saw in the pictures and your name is also not Skylar.
>
> Bryan: Yeah, I basically um, pretended to be Skylar. Because I never wanted it to reach that point where she would know who I am.
>
> (Mussman 2013)

Here is the dislocating, isolating and dangerous aspect of online interaction and confusion about interpersonal relationships that exist online. The new narcissus results from an adaptation to our social world, one that increasingly relies on the Internet for communication and the formation of relationships with others. The Internet also provides individuals with an opportunity to be whoever they want to be, free from restriction, judgment and control. Skylar pretended to be someone else online and exclaims that 'I never wanted it to reach that point where she would know who I am.' Skylar did not want Jen to know who he truly was. His authentic, true self was masked by Skylar's false one.

> Max: So let me just get this straight. Do you have true feelings for Jennifer?
> Bryan: I don't have any like emotional feelings towards her. I would never be able to have like a romantic relationship with her.
> Max: Then why the fuck are we here?
> Bryan: Well, she's actually not the only girl I spoke to. And I felt like out of all the girls this is like the perfect time, the perfect girl to finally come clean to and end, like Skylar.
>
> (Mussman 2013)

Skylar saw the Internet and online community as a way to develop relationship with women. In fact, Skylar could not only have one relationship with a woman online, he could have multiple ones. The Internet allows individuals the freedom to pursue unchecked desires. In the case of Skylar, he was able to pursue multiple women without the social ramifications that occur when an individual attempts to maintain multiple face-to-face romantic relationships. The new narcissus thrives on the opportunity to receive as much attention and admiration from others as possible. The Internet is a way to experience seemingly infinite relationships with others without the rules and regulations that exist, in regards to the treatment of others, in the real world.

> Nev: What are you ever hoping to gain from all these half true friendships that you have online? What's the point?
> Bryan: I wanted to like brush up my game it's just something I do.
>
> (Mussman 2013)

The new narcissus depends on others' adulation and adoration in order to function. The narcissist 'behaves arrogantly and haughtily, feels superior, omnipotent, omniscient, invincible, immune, above the law and omnipresent' (Vaknin 2001: 32). Developing pretend relationships was an opportunity for Skylar to not only receive narcissistic supply but it also served as a means of affirmation that Skylar is indeed an amazing person who is desired by many individuals of the opposite sex.

The new narcissus' 'gift'

Bryan (a.k.a. Skylar) had been lying about his true identity to Jen. He states that he 'never wanted it to reach that point where she would know who I am'. Bryan and Jen were texting, talking on the phone or communicating online almost every day, yet this level of intimacy was not sufficient for Bryan to reveal his true identity. On top of creating an artificial self that presented emotional, romantic feelings towards Jen, he has basically exclaimed that he used Jen for his own selfish pursuits of practicing his interaction with the opposite sex. Vaknin expressed that narcissists will use others for their own selfish pursuits and needs in order to obtain the drug that is so essential to their existence (narcissistic supply). Bryan (a.k.a. Skylar) had been lying about his identity to many women, not just Jen. An extreme focus on the self and encouragement to use others for your own personal gain, to feel better about yourself, can be witnessed here in Bryan's description of why he lied about his identity.

> Bryan: Because I feel like its good for her to finally know the truth and …
> Max: You could have told her that on the phone though, right?
> Bryan: Yeah, but in a way I wanted to end Skylar and I feel like by telling Jen who I am that ends Skylar.
> Max: Right but that's … all about you. That's you taking care of your business and not really caring how its effecting [sic] someone else. Its kind of selfish.
> [… Max then asks Bryan if he is sorry for what he's done]
> Bryan: I don't know if I'm sorry, but, its … it is what it is. I was giving her a gift of … being in that … that relationship.
> Max: You were giving her a gift?
> Bryan: Yeah, I mean, she was happy. I knew I was leading her on but I knew it would never be permanent.
>
> (Mussman 2013)

Bryan exclaims that it was 'good for her' to know the truth. The new narcissus is confident in all of their abilities and here Bryan essentially states that by humiliating Jen through publicly presenting his false self *she* is better. He goes on to exclaim that this whole fake relationship was a 'gift' for her (see Figure 5.2). 'The narcissist fervently believes in his own infallibility, brilliance, omnipotence, heroism, and perfection. He doesn't dare confront the truth and admit it even to himself' (Vaknin 2001: 22). Bryan seems to believe that his fabricated self, as well as the relationship he fabricated with Jen, was beneficial to both him and her because he gained attention and adoration from Jen and she received the satisfaction of someone providing her with a seemingly genuine, loving relationship. As a narcissist, Bryan received his narcissistic supply (attention, admiration, adoration) by his interaction with Jen and other women online. In turn, he believed they were also receiving a benefit of attention and adoration that comes from a genuine relationship. The new narcissus also believes that by being in relationships with other people, these people benefit from their interaction because the new narcissus is just such an amazing person. Why wouldn't people want to be around me? *It's a gift for you to be in my presence.* Even more, relationships with others bring happiness but the Internet, while connecting some, is also providing the platform for others to be false. Bryan's idea that his fake relationships with other women were 'gifts' and even more that they made these women happy is

Figure 5.2 The gift of Bryan

astounding. The women are only happy because they fervently believe in an illusion. As long as our belief in the illusion continues to exist so too will the illusion. In order for the illusion to continue, people need to believe that the illusion is real. How else will individuals continue to pursue the limitless race?

Bryan seems to be completely oblivious to the fact that a phoney relationship is not the same thing as a real one. He is avoiding the truth and the hurt he has caused. He also appears to be more interested in the public announcement of his lies than the hurt it is causing Jen. There is no such thing as bad publicity for the narcissist. Bryan has been able to appear on reality television: people will be talking about *his* outlandish behavior. Maybe he'll even experience a little bit of fame. Bryan, in his body language and dialogue, appears proud of his behavior and leads the viewer to believe he has actually done something meaningful and good. Being on the reality show is just another avenue through which Bryan can receive attention, even if it is negative. Jen has indeed brought Skylar (a.k.a. Bryan) into her real world. The new narcissus can be conceived in an online environment. Before fully immersing yourself in the illusion that you will present to others in the real world, you can practice your fabricated self online!

> Jen: Why did you even come down?
> Bryan: I wanted to come clean to you face-to-face.
> Jen: But did you want to come clean to me or did you just want to feel better about yourself?
>
> (Mussman 2013)

A need to come clean, face-to-face, yet it was ok to manipulate and deceive her behind closed doors. The new narcissus will take the easiest way out when it comes to getting exactly what they want (the attention, admiration and adoration of others). Lying and manipulating is much easier via the Internet and other forms of communication available to the modern individual. By coming clean in person, and on reality television, the new narcissus can be glorified or criticized for their formidable behavior. Good attention or bad attention, what matters is to receive attention. Bryan was able to maintain a steady and consistent source of narcissistic supply from the many women he was communicating with online. Reality television, like the Internet, is but a means through which to put your self on display.

> Bryan: I wanted to come clean to you because I felt like … I felt like you were special. You have a cool personality. You're different than any of those other girls.
> Nev: So you picked the coolest girl to reveal how much of an asshole you were?
> Bryan: It's more of a dick move to lie.
> Jen: But are you even admitting the fact that you're a dick, or are you just saying it because all these people are looking at you?
> Bryan: No, I feel like it's the best thing to come clean to you.
> Jen: I don't even know if I believe that.
>
> (Mussman 2013)

Jen struggles to believe what Bryan is saying because all the wonderful feelings and emotions that she has felt over the past two years for a man named Skylar have been destroyed in an instant by a man named Bryan who pretended to not only be Skylar but pretended about his feelings and emotions for her. A screenshot of a text message then appears on the screen: 'You mean the world to me.' Bryan (as Skylar) communicated to Jen that his feelings for here were genuine. 'Emotion has been mechanized' (Mestrovic 1997: xii). Social interaction today often has a tinge of mechanization and in some instances, individuals can seem so robotic in their responses (as we witnessed in *Sister Wives*) that the obviousness should cause discomfort in participants and viewers alike. A postemotional society has 'the tendency for emotionally charged collective representations to be abstracted from their cultural contexts and then manipulated artificially by self and others in new and artificially contrived contexts' (Mestrovic 1997: 1). The Internet allows the individual a platform on which they can present artificially created 'quasi-emotions' that can be a source of power for the new narcissus. 'Power is in being charming while inflicting pain and humiliation. Power is in tearing human emotions to pieces and putting them together again in new shapes without inducing the human agent to think about choosing' (Mestrovic 1997: xiv). Mestrovic draws on George Orwell's statement about power, in his famous novel *1984*, to aid in the understanding of postemotionalism. Bryan has gained power by advancing his game through manipulating and deceiving Jen and other women online. The new narcissus is often aware of the fact that their behavior is wrong but there is nothing to stop their pattern of abuse. Bryan even says he knows that it is 'more of a dick move to lie'. The new narcissus is fervently convinced that they are an amazing individual and even an awareness and understanding that lying and cheating is wrong does not stop them inflicting abuse on others. If anyone does stand up to them or call out their bad behavior, the new narcissus will simply disconnect from that source of narcissistic supply and move on to someone else.

> Jen: Did you consider the fact that I did like you?
> Bryan: No, I didn't. I wasn't as concerned about your feelings.
> Max: What you've done is cruel. Do you get that?
> Bryan (shakes head): No.
>
> (Mussman 2013)

The new narcissus finds power in their infliction of pain upon others since it reaffirms the false belief that their behavior is indicative of someone unique, special and worthy of more attention and emulation. 'There is almost nothing that the narcissist refrains from doing, almost no borders that he hesitates to cross to achieve renown. To him, there is no such thing as "bad publicity" – what matters is to be in the public eye' (Vaknin 2001: 127). Bryan did not care about Jen's feelings because the new narcissus not only fails to empathize with others but also fails to feel anything at all. Any sign of a negative emotion like shame, embarrassment or pain causes the new narcissus to shuffle that emotion away. Bryan continues to avoid confronting his behavior as a result of his artificially constructed self. He is receiving attention from Jen, Nev, Max, the film crew and over 2 million viewers: an ideal situation for the new narcissus. Remember, the new narcissus is 'devoid of empathy, is unable or unwilling to identify with, acknowledge, or accept the feelings, needs, preferences, priorities, and choices of others' (Vaknin 2001: 32). The new narcissus cannot identify with others because he can no longer identify with himself.

> What is unusual about the narcissist's sadistic behaviours – premeditated acts of tormenting others while enjoying their anguished reactions – is that they are goal orientated. [...] The narcissist [...] haunts and hunts his victims for a reason – he wants them to reflect his inner state.
>
> (Vaknin 2001: 52)

Vaknin explains that the narcissist projects this false self at the expense of others and he is hurting his victims for a reason. He wants them to feel the same pain and disgust that he feels deep down inside regarding his true self. Bryan cannot even fathom that what he's done is cruel because he has lost sight of what real feelings and emotions are. Bryan avoids the fact that he is indeed flawed by refusing to accept any negative aspects of his behavior towards others. The new narcissus feels entitled and special and therefore 'can only be understood by, should only be treated by, or associate with, other special or unique, or high status people' (Vaknin 2001: 32). The next day Max and Nev ask to meet with Bryan again to discuss what he's done and to ensure that he realizes his behavior is wrong. Nev clarifies that Bryan went online in order to improve upon his female communication skills, to which Bryan responds 'it wasn't like I sought out to go online, it happened online just naturally and I realized ok, maybe this is something I can do without getting too close to the person' (Mussman 2013). Bryan states that his intention wasn't to go online and inflict pain and harm on others but then the interaction with others online just happened 'naturally'. This is how easily the new narcissus can creep into an individual's life. The Internet was an easy route by which Bryan realized he could begin to develop relationships with women. Even more, individuals like Bryan can now interact online without getting too close. Close, meaningful, interpersonal relationships are what human beings need most and these are successfully achieved through the expression of authentic feelings and emotions that can be both good and bad. To try and eliminate all the bad or to avoid the bad and instead project artificial feelings and emotions is problematic. 'It is not cultural sterility but emotional sterility that plagues our present fin de siècle' (Mestrovic 1997: 26). The new narcissus encourages the individual to avoid all authentic feelings and emotions that endanger the deep down and fragile true self. To repeatedly project false emotions can result in an individual becoming numb to authentic ones.

As Bryan goes on to articulate, '[I was] hoping that they wouldn't get too close to me without realizing like, the repercussions it would have to the other person. I mean I'm certainly not cold-hearted, but I was kind of hurt in the past by like a girl and I felt kind of uncomfortable trusting, building a trust' (Mussman 2013). Max asks Bryan what happened in his past relationship that hurt him so much. 'Just someone kind of leading me on, pretending to like me. Not only leading me on like physically but like she knew that I was invested emotionally, then I realized she was doing this to other guys too' (Mussman 2013). Bryan has essentially inflicted the same trauma and pain he previously experienced onto Jen and others. This is one of the most devastating effects of the new narcissus. As Mestrovic states, 'the only value left is survival of the self' (1997: 38). Once a narcissist inflicts damage on others for their own selfish pursuits this can cause their victims to repeat that same behavior in their interactions with others. The damaged individual, isolated and lacking personal connection and acceptance, struggles to cope with their pain and trauma. The creation of a false self can shield them from experiencing that same pain again. For the new narcissus, creating such an artifice promises a life free from pain and suffering, but at the cost of one's soul; for one must create artificiality in one's interactions with others, thus creating a vicious cycle of artificiality and trauma.

Bryan continues to avoid the true nature of his actions when he states his intention was never to get too close to the women he met online and was hoping they wouldn't get too close to him either. This is the furthest from what actually transpired. Jen was emotionally invested and did get close to him and this in turn provided Bryan with a continual source of narcissistic supply. Bryan and Jen exchanged text messages and spoke on the phone frequently and spoke to each other as if they were in an emotional relationship. Bryan continued to say 'I'm not cold-hearted' and the intention was not there. yet it appears very clear from his previous statements that he felt he was giving Jen and other women the 'gift' of feeling as though they were in a real relationship.

> The narcissist simply discards people when he becomes convinced that they can no longer provide him with Narcissistic Supply. This evaluation, subjective and highly emotionally charged, does not have to be grounded in reality. Suddenly, because of boredom, disagreement, disillusion, a fight, an act, inaction, or a mood – the narcissist wildly swings from idealization to devaluation. He then disconnects immediately. He needs all the energy that he can muster to obtain new Sources of Narcissistic Supply and would rather not spend these scarce and expensive resources over what he regards as human refuse, the waste left by the process of extraction of Narcissistic Supply.
>
> (Vaknin 2001: 159)

The new narcissus often experiences waves of disconnection and isolation from others. When one's narcissistic supply is jeopardized the immediate reaction is to avoid and disengage, even if it means inflicting pain and trauma on those that are closest to them. A consumer-based society tells the individual that once something is broken there is no need to fix it – just buy a new, and better thing. Similarly, once an individual is 'broken' or no longer a source of attention and admiration, there is no need to repair the relationship – just disconnect, move on and find new sources of narcissistic supply.

Avoiding reality

Earlier in the chapter, we saw how Stjepan Mestrovic uncovered the darker messages about the frustrated desires and wishes of children, as portrayed in the children's television show *Barney and Friends.* '[T]he frustration is not a problem: Barney instantly imagines them into an arctic setting in which they sing a happy song. There is absolutely no obstacle in life that cannot be overcome by wishing' (1997: 54). The millennial generation, of which Jen and Skylar are apart, is often referred to as young, spoiled and entitled. If children's television programs send the message that you can get what you want simply by wishing for it, should there be surprise when people behave arrogantly and without regard for how their behavior affects others? Singing a 'happy song' by buying more possessions that promise happiness only pushes individuals to see others as a means through which they can obtain more attention and admiration. The new narcissus receives encouragement to manipulate, lie and cheat with impunity. 'Compassion would not be withheld from a suffering individual if he or she belonged to a wrong or unaccounted for group. Compassion should be the emotional glue that holds together all members of a society on the basis of a common humanity' (Mestrovic 1997: 97). If compassion is what holds community and society together and the new narcissus is encroaching more and more into the lives of members of our community, then there is a great cause for concern. The new narcissus is unable to feel compassion; like the robber barons and other tycoons of the 20th century and beyond, what matters most is the accumulation of more and more, free from any form of regulation. Some individuals who acquire massive amounts of wealth will later in life have a 'change of heart' and decide to give away much of their fortune to meaningful and worthwhile causes and charities. But why wait until the end of life? Might there be some sort of 'Aha!' moment for the modern individual who has so fervently adhered to the great motto of our society? The seemingly limitless pursuit of material wealth can never be quenched, and it may be that when someone nears the end of such a tiring and relentless race that they begin to realize that the race has been rigged the entire time. There is no winner and there never can be. No one can ever truly be satisfied under this amoral belief that pursuing a limitless goal brings satisfaction. The never-ending race is shifting the focuses and priorities of many individuals today.

The development of the new narcissus is a result of individuals struggling to adapt to this consumer society of false promises, and they are creating an artificial self in order to cope with the banality of life, or the traumas experienced from unlimited goals and pursuits. Individuals begin to believe in the artifice they have created just as they believe in the promises of a consumer society. When others warn of the danger of the false self or the problems with a consumer society and the current economic system, avoidance and denial of reality are a common reaction. Think of a small child who has been caught in a lie: this basic, human instinct still exists in many individuals, especially in those who have constructed an artificial self. The child, like the new narcissus, will deny their behavior and avoid facing up to their responsibility. Faking it while receiving the same benefits as someone who is authentic and genuine results in the repetition of that behavior. 'When one is no longer checked, one becomes unable to check one's self' (Durkheim 1951: 257).

Reality television portrays individuals who are not adhering to rules regarding honesty, courtesy and compassion towards other humans and who employ falseness and manipulation in order to achieve fame, success and attention from others. Normalizing behavior that goes against basic human decencies is extremely problematic. Turning a blind eye to the new narcissus and their infliction of pain and suffering on others or merely chalking it up to 'the way things are done' is not acceptable. Accepting that their behavior is indeed flawed would lead to the eradication of their carefully constructed self that they have erected in response to a consumer society and the exposure of their blemished true self. Pressure to maintain the 'right' image is felt by many segments of the population and to maintain this image you must believe in it wholeheartedly and deny any condemnations from others who may challenge your personal route to success and happiness.

In February 2013, Hollywood.com released a report claiming that *Catfish: The TV Show* is actually 'catfishing' America. The online source reports that online casting calls for people who want the show's help in meeting their online love interest, more often than not come from the person who is faking their identity and wants the show to profile them and their false identity. Five of six stars of the first season told Hollywood.com that it was actually the person who was faking their identity who contacted the show, not the person who was truthful with their identity. The possibility that this reality show (and others) is completely fabricated is not that shocking. The Hollywood.com article claims that the producers complete all the research before actually determining whether or not to profile the couple in an episode. If the show's premise is lying to the audience this would essentially be another reflection of the development of the new narcissus in our modern society. The show would be pretending to the audience that they have no idea whether or not the person's identity is false; Nev and Max appearing as though they are doing all the research to find out if this person really is who they say they are, when in reality they already know the truth. If this is indeed the case, then they are presenting false emotions and false sympathy for the individual who has to come to terms with this fact in front of an audience of millions. This individual has fallen victim to the new narcissus. The world may never know the truth behind reality television, for as we have witnessed thus far, the false self must prevent the exposure of the true self. The artificial self must be maintained. Reality television has developed as an adaptation to a consumer world that has an extreme focus on appearances and illusions in the hopes of garnishing the most attention and profit (or success). We are surrounded by illusions that claim to be real, just like reality television claims to document *real* life when in all actuality the entire show may well be a well-thought out and carefully constructed fabrication.

6 Experts of falseness

Celebrity Rehab with Dr. Drew

> Any discipline must [...] appear intolerable when one has grown over-accustomed to acting without any rules save those imposed by oneself.
>
> (Durkheim 1997: 185)

Celebrity Rehab with Dr. Drew was a reality television show that lasted for six seasons on the US channel VH1. Each season a new batch of celebrities checked in to the Pasadena Recovery Center in Pasadena, California in order to begin their recovery from some form of addiction. Dr. Drew Pinsky and his staff were on hand to oversee the patients' rehabilitation and to ensure their safety and well being throughout the process. Season three featured the following patients: Mindy McCready, Dennis Rodman, Mike Starr, Mackenzie Phillips, Lisa D'Amato, Heidi Fleiss, Joey Kovar, Kari Ann Peniche and Tom Sizemore.

Emile Durkheim warns us that when an individual becomes accustomed to a life without rules, the more intolerable all rules appear. Celebrities live lives free from the sanctions that so many others must conform to. Individuals today are now encouraged to see celebrities as the ultimate form of success, achieving the highest level of wealth, status and notoriety. In fact, this is one of the most alarming aspects of the new narcissus. Everyone, arguably, has some level of narcissism. Indeed, most individuals fit a sliding scale with some slightly more narcissistic than others and vice versa. Some amount of narcissism is healthy in order for the individual to survive. If people did not care about themselves and focus on themselves then they would be unable to function. This book attempts to uncover the darker, more extreme end of the scale: the unhealthy level of narcissism. The celebrities witnessed in this season of *Celebrity Rehab* are not only suffering from addiction but many may also be suffering from narcissistic personality disorder. In fact, Dr. Drew Pinsky, the host and primary physician for the celebrities, has also written extensively on celebrity narcissism in his book entitled *The Mirror Effect: How Celebrity Narcissism Is Seducing America*. Here Pinsky states that the narcissistic traits of: 'extreme self-importance, inflated sense of specialness, vanity, envy, entitlement' are found in all sorts of reality shows and that '[t]he people who succeed on these shows appear to have little use for education, hard work, or the discipline of climbing a career ladder. Instead, they pout, throw tantrums, stomp their feet, manipulate friends, family, and coworkers, and otherwise act out, all while wallowing in the lap of luxury' (Pinsky 2009: 65). Pinsky goes on to explain how reality television can be 'malicious', where 'unstable individuals' lives and interpersonal chaos are served up as entertainment' for viewers (2009: 65). What is surprising is that as a healthcare professional Dr. Pinsky fails to see that his show is doing the exact same thing as these other malicious reality shows.

> When *Celebrity Rehab* was created, I told VH1 producers that my goal was to do exactly the opposite of these shows: to *humanize* the celebrities we would feature, and to use the show to explain what was really behind the participants' outrageous and inconceivable behavior.
>
> (Pinsky 2009: 66)

Even though Dr. Drew had hopes of humanizing the celebrities featured on his show, ultimately, ratings are the bottom line and of the utmost importance for the producers and the cable channel executives. Humanizing the cash cow cannot be the goal or intention.

This show is a means by which celebrities who have fallen from the public's grace can have a chance at fame once again. Sam Vaknin makes the case that narcissists are addicted to being famous. By being on the show these celebrities will be talked about, possibly interviewed and even shamed for their addictions. However, as Vaknin points out, any attention, adoration, adulation and admiration (narcissistic supply) is what matters. 'There is no such thing as "bad publicity" – what is important is to be in the public eye' (Vaknin 2001: 124). By being on the show, these celebrities now have a means to obtain narcissistic supply – from other residents of the recovery center, from the staff who are treating them and most importantly from the viewers who are watching the show.

This is where the aspect of choice comes in. Does the audience have a choice in what shows it watches? Absolutely they do. But what is important is that people are choosing to watch, and that regardless of the reason why they are watching this or other reality television shows, the new narcissus is present throughout.

Whereas elite culture was once valued by many and accessible to only a few, more and more in the modern age individuals have vicarious access to the same experiences and lifestyles as celebrities. Furthermore, now the average individual can participate in some of the same experiences as celebrities. Social media now provide the modern individual an avenue through which they can post 'status updates' and pictures and slideshows and events that they are attending. These posts constantly receive feedback in the form of comments and 'likes'. Thus social media can serve as a platform for individuals to receive narcissistic supply (attention, admiration, adoration, and adulation).

Individuals can vicariously experience the extravagant lives of the rich and famous. Durkheim's observations about the ills of a consumer-based society are still applicable today.

Consumerism merely morphs and takes on a new shape in order to satisfy the market while we as individuals are left eternally dissatisfied with our latest and greatest gadget. One need only to turn on a major news station and examine the major headlines of the day. What are the top stories: war, technological innovation, crime, scientific breakthroughs, global warming or terrorism? Sure, those might be topics of conversation for the day, yet many news channels now choose to focus on celebrity status as major headlines. The ultimate form of success and achievement: to be well-liked and admired by others.

This chapter will attempt to show the reader the darker side of stardom and fame. Many individuals today may aspire to be wealthy. In fact, that is often a measure of one's success in American society. Many though, want to be famous and with that fame, wealth will surely follow. Celebrity status appears to be just as desirable as the achievement of wealth or success. An important question to ask is whether or not celebrity status should be the new aspiration for members of our society.

Consequences of idolization

> Shelly: Aren't you here because you have consequences of drinking?
> Rodman: No. I think I have consequences because I'm famous.
>
> (Pinsky 2010)

At the beginning of the very first episode of *Celebrity Rehab*'s third season, Dennis Rodman, one of the cast members/patients on the show, is introduced to the audience. Dennis is seen in an interview setting smoking a cigar, and he proceeds to introduce himself by saying that 'everyone on the planet knows who I am'. Rodman goes on to discuss his NBA championships and how he started his bad boy persona back in the day. Dennis is shown partying in nightclubs with intermittent shots of tabloids and newspaper headlines featuring Rodman's 'bad boy' persona, party lifestyle and arrest for domestic violence. A voiceover informs the audience that Rodman has been convicted and sentenced to three years' probation and court-appointed rehab. At the end of the introduction, Dennis Rodman is wearing sunglasses and smoking a cigar while exclaiming that rehab 'isn't going to do shit' for him. He then points at the camera and with an extremely haughty attitude exclaims, 'Try and help me Dr. Drew. Try!'

Right away the viewer has instant exposure to Rodman's aggression, alcoholism, arrogance and now what appears to be a challenge to his soon-to-be rehabilitation specialist. Narcissists do not believe that they need help and loathe the idea of it because in their eyes they are flawless even when they are in the midst of an addiction.

The *DSM-V* was released in 2013 and includes slightly updated characteristics of narcissistic personality disorder. 'Individuals with narcissistic personality disorder believe that they are superior, special, or unique and expect others to recognize them as such' (670). As noted in my introduction, after much debate, NPD and four other personality disorders remained in the final version of the *DSM* after an initial draft had excluded them. The fact that Rodman thinks everyone on the planet knows who he is adds insight to how he views himself: like a god. Can we though, as individuals living in the modern world, be surprised at this revelation? Do we not treat our professional athletes as though they were gods? To be treated like a god means these individuals are believed to be omnipotent, omnipresent and omniscient.

Professional athletes today are revered for their physical prowess and abilities, not only on the court but off the court as well. People today don't just want to be entertained by the game and its players. They want to be entertained by the players' lifestyles. These lifestyles are even admired and sought after as they are seen as the epitome of success. Professional athletes today make millions of dollars for playing a game. Yes, there are trainings and restrictions and diets and the scrutiny that these athletes undergo; however, many would probably argue this lifestyle and profession is an ideal life situation. Often the media and other individuals simply say 'he's full of himself' or 'arrogant'. However, there's much more to it than this. 'By the time they have been retired for two years, 78% of former NFL players have gone bankrupt or are under financial stress … within five years of retirement, an estimated 60% of former NBA players are broke' (Corben 2012). They are treated like gods and given the riches of kings, yet once the game ends so too does this dream. Professional athletes become accustomed to this 'baller' lifestyle, and once it ends and the paychecks stop coming they are at a loss for what to do. This is the anomic state Durkheim warned of for the modern individual: a seemingly infinite amount of wealth with unchecked behavior. Suddenly the spending behavior is normalized but the influx of cash no longer exists. Athletes hope for endorsement deals, broadcast positions or coaching jobs but those opportunities are limited.

To make matters even worse, competition is what many athletes become obsessed with: competition both on and off the field. As one professional athlete states, 'they like to gamble. It's just a part of our nature' (Corben 2012). Many professional athletes struggle with gambling addictions. While they are playing there is constant flow of cash to support their addiction. Players have spoken about the need to 'keep up with the Joneses', so to speak. Amongst the players themselves a competition develops to have the greatest car, the most beautiful women, the nicest house. Michael Jordan's father said 'Michael doesn't have a gambling problem he has a competitive problem.' When one former player, Charles Barkley, was asked how much money he'd lost gambling he replied 'probably 10 million'. John Daily, a professional golfer, claimed to have lost 50 million dollars gambling. This 'competitive problem' or gambling problem or addiction all stems from the current structure of our society and the norms for individual behavior. The economic realm of society rules all and there is little to no training or restraint when it comes to money. Saving is a learned skill that requires discipline, ironically, in an arena of life that lacks discipline and restraint. Yet we still blame and ostracize athletes for losing it all. Durkheim states that

> [p]overty protects against suicide because it is a restraint in itself. No matter how one acts, desires have to depend upon resources to some extent; actual possessions are partly the criterion of those aspired to. So the less one has the less he is tempted to extend the range of his needs indefinitely.
>
> (1951: 254)

Having less and a limited access to money helps to protect individuals, to some extent, from the dangers of a consumer-based society. Professional athletes, however, are vulnerable to the unchecked desires Durkheim warned about. Being treated as a superior human being for their exceptional athletic ability, and the immense fortune that goes with it, provides these individuals with an unchecked lifestyle. 'Wealth [...] by the power it bestows, deceives us into believing that we depend on ourselves only [...] The less limited one feels, the more intolerable all limitation appears.' Many professional athletes are lucky to last more than ten years in their sport. On average, many players see four or less years. These athletes, then, have a brief interlude of seemingly unlimited wealth, fame and the chance to play a game they are passionate about before it all comes to an end. What then are they to do? Dennis Rodman, the athlete chronicled in this season of *Celebrity Rehab*, begins to rely on alcohol to an unhealthy extent.

Narcissistic individuals feel as though they are gods and worthy of emulation, but also desperately need what Sam Vaknin has described as narcissistic supply: attention, adoration, adulation and admiration. The idea that we, as individuals today, idolize (admire, worship, emulate) celebrities and athletes is not new. However, I do not think people clearly recognize the consequences of this idolization for themselves and for celebrities. This particular reality show provides the viewer with a glimpse, a very small glimpse at that, into the struggles and consequences of idolizing mere humans. Addiction can happen to anyone. Dr. Pinsky makes this clear in the very beginning of the first episode. Some viewers may question why celebrities in particular struggle with addiction, when they have such fabulous lives. Addiction is not just a consequence for these celebrities. In fact, it is a reflection of a larger issue deeply rooted within our society today: an extreme focus on the self to the point of narcissism.

Another community service specialist informs the audience in an interview that while Dennis Rodman might have been a superstar in the outside world, in the Pasadena Recovery Center everyone is treated the same. It's interesting to hear this because there seems to be a disconnect from the staff at Pasadena Recovery Center. If Dennis was a regular person in the outside world he more than likely would not experience the same privileges that he is experiencing by being in a recovery facility instead of jail or prison. Dr. Pinsky even recognizes at the beginning of his own book how celebrities experience preferential treatment within the justice system in the United States, yet his role in perpetuating that preferential treatment goes unnoticed. In fact, Dr. Pinsky's work on how celebrity narcissism is seducing America fails to address how he profits and benefits from exploiting these addicts by chronicling their recovery in a reality television show.

'I hate people': a love for drugs and birds and the isolation of addiction

The new narcissus is a result of growing up in a world where we are encouraged to adapt to a lifestyle that demands our happiness through obtaining consumer goods. Mike Starr, who has the appearance of someone who is gravely ill, is introduced to the audience. 'It was really nice to have everybody love ya. Have all the people screamin' for ya. I was the best bass player entertainer there was' (Pinsky 2010). Starr goes on to talk about his time in the band Alice in Chains. He informs the audience that he never did drugs before he was kicked out of the band. Starr exemplifies a unique aspect of the modern narcissist: *all they have left is who they use to be.* In Chapter 3, the individuals chronicled in the reality television show *Hoarders* also struggle with who they used to be. 'They may have once been rich, famous, powerful, brilliant, or sexually irresistible, but they no longer are' (Vaknin 2001: 103). Many modern narcissists become focused on their previous, amazing lives. In the first few episodes of *Celebrity Rehab* Dr. Pinsky implies that Starr has one of the worst addiction habits of anyone staying in the Recovery Center since he has been struggling with addiction for decades now. In fact, throughout most of the show Mike Starr acts and behaves as though he is somewhat checked out. A viewer may wonder whether or not Starr's demeanor is the result of lacking any meaningful connection to others. Not only does he appear to be seriously ill, but he seems to be very lonely too. By being in the recovery center he is able to connect and engage with others in a way that does not involve drug use. Even though the new narcissus is obsessed with their self and who they used to be or who they are, the need for fulfillment from social solidarity and social belonging still exists. This is one of the most difficult struggles for the new narcissus: the need to belong and connect with others, yet seeing others simply as a means through which to obtain more attention and admiration.

As other cast members are introduced to the audience, this extreme focus on how great these celebrities used to be is apparent. Mackenzie Phillips introduces herself by stating 'I got fired from *One Day at a Time* for drug problems. I guess I sort of pioneered that teen star gone wrong on drugs' (Pinsky 2010). Phillips was definitely not the first teen star to struggle with drugs; however, it is interesting to note that she introduces herself this way. Another cast member, Heidi Fleiss, introduces herself to the audience. 'I'm

Heidi Fleiss and I was known as the Hollywood Madame. I was the greatest Madame that ever lived. I took the oldest profession on Earth and I did it better than anyone.' The new narcissus is convinced they are special and unique and will even get to the point of developing an illusion about their current or past social status.

Early in the season Dr. Pinsky is concerned about how all of the patients seem to be isolating themselves from each other. Dr. Pinsky discusses the importance of interpersonal communication in the recovery and rehabilitation process during a group session. Drew points out Heidi Fleiss' isolation from the other patients and she responds by laughing and stating she would 'horrify everyone in here'. Heidi briefly discusses her training to become a madame and Bob Forrester, a staff member, and Dr. Drew probe Heidi about her experiences.

> Bob: When they were training you how to be a madame and how to, how to manipulate and how to do those things. What were you thinking? You're a sharp girl. What were you thinking?
> Heidi: I was pretty interested. It was like so different so taboo.
> Dr. Pinsky: Let me ask a question, what is a prostitute?
> Heidi: Prostitution is, I think, the influence of money in your life.
> Dr. Pinsky: And what's money?
> Heidi: Money makes your whole world easier.
> [Pause]
> Some people say it makes it harder though.
>
> (Pinsky 2010)

'Money makes your whole world easier'. This is America's motto. The modern individual adapts to a world where unchecked and unregulated spending is the norm and expectation. Life does indeed seem easier when there is an unrestrained flow of apparently infinite cash. Heidi seems to quickly realize though, her mistake in saying 'easier' and follows up with 'Some people say it makes it harder though.' This is the social ill that Durkheim warned about, where a state of sickness appears as though it is a state of good health. Similarly, the phrase 'more money, more problems' also seems to circulate amongst the American people. It is as if individuals today know they are suffering from an unhealthy condition yet the causes of their disorder are so normalized within society that many are blinded from the true source of their frustrations and illness. The group session continues.

> Bob: Dennis you have people in your house you don't even know having parties every night. That seems like if it's not drug addiction and alcoholism could be dependency. That you wanna be liked and you want to take care of people and you wanna put on a show.
> Dennis: No dude, I don't want that.
>
> (Pinsky 2010)

Bob is calling Dennis Rodman out on his need to be liked by others. His 'dependency' on being liked by others is what Rodman is really addicted to. He needs the admiration of people in order to feel satisfied. The money is simply a means through which to obtain more narcissistic supply, that's why Rodman doesn't 'give a shit about the money'. Mackenzie Phillips proceeds to ask Rodman how many people party at his house every week, to which Dennis responds 'probably about two or three hundred'. Mackenzie then exclaims, 'That's really weird Dennis. I think that's really … that seems very strange to me.' It may seem weird or strange to Phillips and viewers that Rodman has parties with hundreds of people several times a week; however, this is an ideal situation for the new narcissus: hundreds of people, several times a week, to entertain you, admire you, tell you how great you are, is like a seemingly infinite source of narcissistic supply.

> Bob Forrester: You know what one of the things is? You're not upstairs alone by yourself, in a big house, there's 200 people downstairs […] might make some people who feel really alone feel like they're connected.
>
> Dennis: You think so?
>
> Drew: Let's put it this way. When I deal with people who are dying and they're trying to figure out the meaning of life. When they figure it out when they've come to terms with it they always will say it's the important people that give life it's meaning. The other relations, the people they love. That's why they live.
>
> (Pinsky 2010)

This is the very important message Dr. Drew is rightfully trying to convey to the patients: the importance of relationships with others. The new narcissus is the result of normalized behavior: seeking attention, admiration and fame, the worthy pursuits in today's world. The whole premise behind social media is the front that through engaging with social media sites like Facebook, Twitter, Instagram and the like, the modern individual is *connecting* to others. But can an individual be truly connected to someone without being in his or her presence? A deep, meaningful and lasting connection to others can be more than difficult to maintain via social media. Heidi Fleiss immediately responds to Dr. Drew's message of the importance of building meaningful relationships with other people:

> Heidi: I'm not at that stage yet [with a smile]. My life is centered around birds.
>
> Drew: And you don't have resentments about that?
>
> Heidi: Yes but I can't help it. Because I'll walk around angry or I'll be miserable everyday.
>
> Mackenzie: I get the feeling that, forgive me, but, that you are miserable everyday.

Heidi: I'm happy with my birds that's where I'm happiest.
Bob: Yeah this bird thing. What is that all about?
Heidi: I don't know. I can never part with the birds. Ever. [begins crying] I would hate myself.
Drew: Because …? I would hate myself …
Heidi: Because I love the birds.
Drew: Is that the only thing you love right now?
Heidi: Yeah.
Dr. Drew (voiceover): Heidi's love for her birds seems to be genuine but the fact that they are the only thing she loves is very unhealthy. The withdrawal from human contact is definitely something that will need to be addressed before recovery can be put in place.

(Pinsky 2010)

Everyone in the group session seems to be a bit confused by Heidi's obsession with birds. The viewer, as well as the other patients on the show, may question why the 30+ birds are the only thing she loves (see Figure 6.1). Heidi exclaims that the birds are what make her truly happy. Individuals today are misinformed as to the ways in which to engage and connect with others. Social media or having 30+ pets is not a way to develop meaningful connections. Encouraging narcissistic tendencies downplays the importance of meaningful, lasting connections with other humans. Later in the episode,

Figure 6.1 Heidi's birds

Dr. Drew, in a voiceover, states that he wants to have a one-on-one session with Heidi.

> Drew: Do you have any friends?
> Heidi: Not really. I mean I live with birds.
> Drew: I know.
> Heidi: Some days I spent 60 days with not talking to anybody and just playing with my birds.
> Drew: Are you fearful people won't like you or won't want to hang out with you?
> Heidi: I dunno. I have no idea what I think.
> Drew: Do you know … are you aware that people like you? Are you aware of that?
> Heidi: Sometimes.
> Drew: You like people but no friends.
> Heidi: Yeah,
> [smiles and then points both hands at Dr. Drew]
> because of drugs.
> Drew: Maybe.
> Heidi: Drugs make it so that I can't really socialize with somebody that um, that I would find um, mentally stimulating, that I would want to be with. How am I gonna go do something normal … stupid things you know?
> Dr Drew: Stupid things?
> Heidi: Yeah, you know, even getting high – stupid.
> Dr. Drew: But you're not stupid.
>
> (Pinsky 2010)

A focus on being the best: whether it is the best child actor, the best madame, the best bass player or the best model, what matters is to just be the Ultimate Grand Supreme in life. The difficulty lies in understanding the new narcissus. In order for innovation and creativity to occur there must be a degree of freedom all while encouraging individuals to be their best self. That message is valuable. What is concerning is when so many aspects of our daily lives project authenticity when the reality is actually fake. Today, falseness can lead to the same amount of success. If you can fake being the best at something and still receive all the same benefits of success and fame for doing so, then why not fake it? There is a blatant and repetitive message that ecourages lying, cheating, manipulating and using others with all the same rewards and very little risk involved if caught. Countless times throughout history, individuals have been exposed for illegal stock manipulation, insider trading, ponzi schemes, fraud, etc., and more often than not, these individuals are merely reprimanded and sentenced to very little jail time. Our society's understanding of deviance, or behavior that violates the norm, does not include being fake. White collar and elite crimes, when you really look at them, involve lying to people, presenting one's self and one's skills as one thing when the reality is not the same. As long as an appearance of wealth, which is often obtained through the illegal use of other people's money, is constantly maintained all will be well. The punishment for falseness, even though it can be the most costly to society, is minimal. Worse yet, many individuals that engage in these behaviors are never caught or if they are, can use their status, influence and wealth to buy their way out of trouble. Heidi Fleiss is choosing to isolate herself and live with her birds, the only things she loves, because of her addiction and isolation. The new narcissus' main concern is receiving the most attention and admiration from others.

Heidi's isolation and addiction intensified following her very public fall from grace, in the late 1990s, as a result of her conviction on three counts of pandering. She was known for her secrecy and refusal to name any of her high-end clientele who used her services. Back on 23 August 1993, *People* magazine ran a cover story on her entitled 'Heidi's High Life', which chronicled her rise to becoming the 'Hollywood Madame' and included a few quotes from her (see Figure 6.2). In the first paragraph she states '[t]hey're going to be writing books about me one day. I'm going to be a legend'; and later the article reads: 'Heidi, says a source, "liked to be out there, admired. She wants to be the rock star."' This bit of insight from 1993, when Fleiss was first criminally charged for her involvement in running a high-end prostitution ring, shows that she was concerned with not only being admired, but even in the face of criminal charges, was more excited about million dollar book deals and 'being a legend'. Fast-forward to 2016 and not much has changed in twenty-three years: the new narcissus is the result of this obsession with being famous and the best.

Now, Heidi lives alone with lots of birds. It is difficult for her to think about socializing, and she even mentions it would be hard to find someone worthy of her time, someone 'mentally stimulating'. The new narcissus will resort to isolation should there be a lull in access to worthy providers of narcissistic supply. Fleiss has a constant and consistent source of narcissistic supply: her birds. The birds need her for food, shelter and attention. In return, she has thirty or more birds that will admire her, love her, adore and attend to her. She even has photos of all her birds on the wall above her twin size bed at the recovery center, maybe to serve as a reminder of her reliable source of narcissistic supply (see Figure 6.1). The birds will not mistreat her or abuse or manipulate her; they are essentially a perfect source of attention. Her addiction to meth allows her to escape her reality and her birds may temporarily soothe any emptiness she may feel when sober.

More and more individuals today are beginning to see their relationships with animals as equal to relationships with people. Heidi may be replacing relationships with other people by acquiring lots and lots of birds. Individuals today may feel that it is easier to maintain a 'relationship' with a dog or other pet, than it is to maintain a relationship with a person. Animals are not only a great source of narcissistic supply but they can also be a great form of

Figure 6.2 Heidi and her cover story

therapy for any damage experienced in the past. Have people treated you badly? Animals can help with that!

Confusing sickness with a condition of good health

On Day 8, Tom Sizemore joins the other patients at the Pasadena Recovery Center and participates in a group session with the other patients. Tom Sizemore and Heidi Fleiss were once in a tumultuous relationship in the early 2000s that ended in Tom being convicted of domestic violence charges filed by Heidi and other women.

Bob: Are some people a lot sicker than other people in this room?
Mindy: I hope not anymore.
Mackenzie: Absolutely.
Bob: Some people in this room are way, way sick: both spiritually, psychologically and biologically, way sicker than other people in this room.
Drew: and in different ways.

(Pinsky 2010)

All of the celebrities who have entered recovery are suffering from some form of addiction. Some addictions may be more difficult to overcome than others. It is interesting that this is thought of as important to differentiate between the patients. Even in rehab, how addicted you are to something becomes a form of distinction. This is the state of our modern world: focus on being the best at everything, even your addiction. Bob then states 'and so what you've got to understand is that's why individually, everybody is kind of assessed, treated, treatment plan, right? Now Tom, Tom's a complicated case.' Bob seems to switch the focus on competing to be the most addicted to why it's important to understand the level of addiction in order to prepare a proper treatment plan. Heidi does not like that Bob thinks Tom is a 'complicated case', or worse yet, that Tom holds the title of 'sickest'.

Heidi: Oh, God. I'll walk out if I have to hear that. What's so complicated? He's a drug addict.
Bob: Here's the complication of it: in the face of all consequences that would wake up anyone in this room, including myself, he says 'fuck you' and smokes more drugs. That's complicated.
Heidi: It's flat out bullshit!
Bob: Heidi! You have a home.
[points at Heidi and then points at Tom]
He doesn't have a home.
Heidi: Yes he does.
Bob: No he does not.
Heidi (to Tom): You're homeless?
[Tom nods yes]
[…]
Bob: So there's different levels of addiction here, different continuums. Heidi, you got sober because they were threatening to put you in prison. [to Tom] He says 'fuck you'.

(Pinsky 2010)

Tom is a complicated case because nothing seems to stop him from using drugs. Addiction means to continue engaging in a behavior or substance even when one has experienced consequences because of that behavior or substance. Tom in the face of a huge magnitude of consequences still chooses to use drugs.

Heidi: You know what? I respect myself too much where I would never get to that point.
Drew: Did you think you'd get to this point?
Heidi: Where I play with birds? Never in a million years!
Drew: Ok, you wouldn't go where he's gone but you also wouldn't go where you ended up.
Heidi: I, I think I'm so lucky. I look at those birds and I think what did I do in my life to deserve these incredible creatures?
Drew: Yeah, that's right Heidi, you live with birds.
Heidi: *I'm alone, I live with birds.*
Drew: You need to be around people, that's how it works, that's how we're wired.
Heidi: I mean come on, my saying is 'I hate people' [shrugs].

This is the important issue here for all of the celebrities featured on *Celebrity Rehab*: not only their level of addiction, but the hatred of people. For a second time in a group session Heidi mentions the love she has for her birds. On this particular occasion she goes one step further and exclaims that she hates people.

Drew: Do you hate people?
Heidi: I hate people. That's my saying, 'I hate people'.
Drew: Do you?
Heidi: No.
Mike: I hate people.
Drew: You hate people?
Mike: I can't stand fucking people. When I was using my drugs everybody was ripping me off, EVERYBODY was ripping me off! I didn't know a person that wouldn't rip me off.
Bob: What it really is, is 'I'm scared of people'.
Mike Starr: That's right.

(Pinsky 2010)

This is a very important point that has developed since Heidi first discussed her love for birds in the previous group session and one-on-one with Dr. Drew were she discussed her lack of friends. Now, Heidi has disclosed that she hates people. Well, she states that she doesn't really hate people, that's just her saying. Mike, however, agrees with her and says he hates people too, giving the reason that people rip him off and ultimately violate his trust by lying to him. This betrayal is what is key for many of the celebrities featured on the show. Not only in their childhood have people betrayed them, but in adulthood as well. However, what is not discussed by Heidi or Mike is the role they played in being 'betrayed' by others. Often, addicts lie, steal and manipulate in pursuit of their addiction. What is more important than who betrayed who in this people vs. celebrity discussion is this now repeated statement of 'I hate people.' Bob states that *I hate people* should really be *I'm scared of people.* Dr. Drew concludes the group session with a very important message:

> What we've been talking about here is other people coming into our lives and being able to focus and having these interpersonal experiences. A key piece of recovery: we need other people, it's an interpersonal experience. Even if you're scared and you hate people, magically they start coming into focus in this environment and you start experiencing other people and that fills you and lets you experience yourself. You may not stay sober, but this will change you. *This will change you and it will lead you towards sobriety.*
> (Pinsky 2010)

Other people fill you and let you experience yourself. Dr. Drew's message is a powerful and important one: that of the importance of interpersonal connectedness. Bruce Alexander's dislocation theory of addiction coupled with Durkheim's concept of anomie help to explain this dynamic of hating people vs. being scared of people. The real issue here in terms of addiction and hating people is the fact that more and more, people today are dislocated from one another. We live under the illusion of connection. We are connected through our Facebook friends or Instagram followers but can't seem to stand talking to a stranger in the grocery store. As more and more aspects of our daily lives are focused on the bottom line, the quantity, price or cost, our humanity becomes a little bit further removed. We no longer see others as an end, the epitome of happiness. People are instead seen as tools or objects to get ahead and advance one's self.

Tom Sizemore: 'sick and tired'

Bruce Alexander expands upon Karl Polanyi's definition of dislocation in his work *The Globalization of Addiction* (Alexander 2008). He describes Polanyi's ideas about psychosocial integration as the human need 'to be free and still belong' and dislocation as the lack of psychosocial integration or 'the psychological and social separation of the individual from society' (2008: 59). This is closely related to Marx's ideas about alienation and Durkheim's concept of anomie. All of these important concepts point us to the understanding that as human beings we often lose sight of the importance of our relationships with others. When one focuses too much on one's individual autonomy, disaster can follow in the form of dislocation, anomie, addiction, narcissism and alienation. Individuals today are attempting to adapt to a society without moral regulation. The economy, which touches so many aspects of our lives, is unrestricted and free.

> It is not possible for a social function to exist without moral discipline. Otherwise, nothing remains but individual appetites, and since they are

> by nature boundless and insatiable, if there is nothing to control them they will not be able to control themselves.
>
> (Durkheim 1957: 10–11)

What is addiction? Uncontrolled behavior? Over-indulgence in drugs or alcohol? An obsession? Even in the face of regulation and consequences one still chooses to indulge. Moral discipline and regulation is important in so many aspects of our daily lives: the family, the school, the work place. Rules, laws and limits are put forth to control our natural hedonism in all aspects of society – except in the economic realm. And now, all aspects of our life are ruled by the economy.

> If we put forward this anarchic competition as an ideal we should adhere to – one that should even be put into practice more radically than it is today – then we should be confusing sickness with a condition of good health.
>
> (Durkheim 1957: 121)

Tom Sizemore is one such individual who is not only struggling with addiction but is suffering from this societal disorder. Dr. Drew is concerned about Tom's girlfriend Monroe, as she is also struggling with an addiction. Drew decides to have a one-on-one session with Tom to discuss the possibility of Monroe entering treatment.

> Drew: Do you think she's up for it?
>
> Tom: You know it's life threatening for me now.
>
> Drew: That's right. It's a very serious concern for me. If we can get her sober: excellent [thumbs up]. If we can't then I'm really worried about both of you. I mean let's face it.
>
> Tom: You know I'm sick and tired of this whole business. I'm sick and tired of being in trouble. I'm sick and tired of not making any money. I'm sick and tired.
>
> (Pinsky 2010) (see Figure 6.3)

Many of the celebrities featured on this show are indeed 'sick and tired' of their addiction. The new narcissus is also a condition affecting many members of our society today and is worthy of being addressed. The new narcissus is also sick and tired of exploiting others for their own personal gain to the point of destroying all meaningful relationships. For both addicts and the new narcissus, the struggle is recognizing how one's behaviors are the cause of their state of being sick and tired. Unfortunately, individuals are not entirely to blame for their condition. Yes, one can make a choice to use drugs or alcohol or to use others for one's own selfish gains; however, society also plays a role in instilling these dark lessons in the minds of its members. The dark lessons of consumerism are seeping into our personal lives and relationships.

Figure 6.3 Tom Sizemore, 'sick and tired'

Instead of seeing others as objects or a source of attention and admiration, a dramatic shift must occur for us to begin to recognize that people are important and valuable – period.

> Tom: Do you want to come in here?
> [looks at Monroe and smiles]
> [Monroe laughs]
> Drew: What's that?
> Tom: I wanted to know if she wants to come in here.
> [looks back at Monroe]
> Drew: Well it'd be good for you.
> Tom: I wanna go home.
> Drew: Right now?
> Tom: Yeah.
> Drew: So you're going to leave treatment and go home?
> Tom (to Monroe): Yeah, I want you to take me home.
>
> (Pinsky 2010)

Prior to the meeting Dr. Drew, in a voiceover, informs the audience that he is concerned that Monroe might be a trigger for Tom to want to go use. Tom continues to tell Monroe that he wants her to take him home. As Dr. Drew rightly points out, 'I gotta go is always I gotta use.' For addicts and the new narcissus, confronting their sickness is often so painful that one cannot bear facing the truth. The truth can be the person one has become, the loss one has suffered in life or coming to terms with one's treatment of oneself and others. Rather than face one's authentic, raw, true self, the new narcissus often wants to flee, run away and avoid having to face reality. Tom says

> I've never given sobriety a real shot since this last slip in 2003 and it's been a six year nightmare. I've got a chance now to make it better and I don't wanna be like this anymore [laughs]. I wanna feel better. I wanna do better.

Tom decides to stay in treatment and not go home with Monroe.

This is the difficult aspect of addiction and the new narcissus; the sickness engulfing the individual serves as a way to function in our society today. Individuals are responsible for their own choices and actions, but society also plays a role in shaping its members. If the dark message of society is the quantification of everything and the pursuit of an infinite goal then many are doomed to adapt in an unhealthy way too. Many who read this may argue that without regulation and without restriction, individuals are free to be innovative. While this may true, the unhealthy aspect of infinite goals that can never truly be reached will always inflict damage. Durkheim's vision of confusing sickness with a state of good health has already become reality. So many people fervently believe in the pursuit of wealth and a consumer based society where even human beings are quantified and seen as objects to be bought and sold. The ease with which so many people overlook the dark, deadly and destructive aspects of consumerism, speaks to how devoted and how blindly members of our society adhere to their faith in consumerism. Faith that money will bring happiness. Faith that quantifying everything provides value and faith that seeing people as objects is just 'the way things are'. Many recognize the illness but feel powerless to even begin to find a cure.

The new narcissus, however, can be stopped with an understanding of how our society is structured and where the encouragement to be false exists. Heidi Fleiss, who once dated Tom Sizemore, is now meeting with Dr. Drew in a one-on-one session. Drew expresses concern about Tom and Heidi interacting with one another.

> Heidi: Because the truth is look, I couldn't give a fuck if he was hit by a car outside here or he made a billion dollars, I would have the exact same emotion towards it …
> Drew: None.
> Heidi: None.
>
> (Pinsky 2010)

The new narcissus is quick to shuttle away any emotions or feelings that might jeopardize the deep down, true self that is hidden away and so carefully protected. Often, the new narcissus seems cold or emotionless when in reality they are allowing their false self to block any emotions and feelings from reaching the fragile, true self. Drew tries to probe Heidi more for her feelings towards Tom. Eventually she shuts down and stares back at Drew with a dazed look.

Figure 6.4 Heidi 'I can't care'

Drew asks Heidi if she would like to call Tom out for any of his past behavior towards her and she responds in a pleading manner: 'I don't care. You know I can't care, Dr. Drew. If I cared it would make me really weak' (see Figure 6.4). Heidi's fear of being vulnerable and facing her feelings and emotions is not only scary but it may be seen as a threat to one's source of comfort: the artifice. The new narcissus will stop at nothing to conceal and protect their true self. If the false self was to be exposed or even banished, the true, 'weak' self would have to face others and the new narcissus would have to face their true self. This is unacceptable to the new narcissus. The artifice that has been created is absolutely essential for survival and when that artifice is called in to question, or asked to be stripped away, the instant reaction for the new narcissus is avoidance.

Immediately after Heidi's one-on-one session with Dr. Drew she goes outside and sits next to Tom by the pool.

> Heidi: I came here because I'm too lonely. I get high alone.
> Tom: Me too, I'm the same way.
> Heidi: I'm too lonely.
>
> (Pinsky 2010)

Heidi's impression of apathy is really a front and means of protection. Instead of facing one's true feelings and emotions, it seems easier to tell everyone else that everything's fine. Vulnerability and weakness are natural steps in any person's life. The new narcissus promises the modern individual that they will never have to be vulnerable or weak again as long as the artifice continues. By constantly lying and manipulating and deceiving others through this artifice, the new narcissus begins to suffer disastrous consequences. The new narcissus often suffers from loneliness and struggles to maintain close relationships with others. The loss of friends and family can then push the new narcissus to use drugs and alcohol as a way to cope with the constant projection of falseness.

Mike Starr: the dislocated addict

At the start of Episode 7, Shelley, a counselor at the Pasadena Recovery Center, is seen turning on the lights in patients' rooms with a boisterous 'Its 7 a.m.! Good morning!' Dr. Drew Pinsky, in a voiceover, speaks to this important aspect of avoidance in a patient's treatment process.

> It's Day 15 and while the patients are doing well with the treatment process, in less than a week they're going to be leaving the safety of the treatment environment. I'm still concerned that Mike Starr hasn't really faced some of the painful trauma from his past, including his dismissal from Alice in Chains and the overdose death of the lead singer and his best friend Layne Staley.
>
> (Pinsky 2010)

Here is that moment where one must peel away the artifice to really expose one's true self and the true causes of one's pain and ultimately, one's addition. Mike Starr is shown relaxing on a couch with headphones on and his feet up. Shelley is standing in a nearby medical nook sipping her coffee. Mike tells her, '[N]ow, if I don't answer you, its because I've got my headphones on. I'm working out heavily.' Shelley asks Mike what he is listening to. Mike immediately makes a face as though he's insulted and exclaims 'myself!' The conversation continues:

> Mike: My singer. Put it that way.
> Shelley: How many times have you listened to that record?
> Mike: 50 million 700, about a million times.
> Shelley: I mean after you record a record and you've heard it, you know, every piece and like …
> Mike: And then my singer dies.
> [Shelly looks shocked]
> Mike: And then my singer dies and the only way I can hear him is through this.
> Shelley: Mhmm.
> Mike: Yeah. That's why I listen to it.
>
> (Pinsky 2010)

Mike's startling statement 'and then my singer dies' is shocking and concerning but distracts from the initial response of 'myself' when asked whom he was listening to. Mike was listening to the band he was an initial member of (Alice in Chains), not just himself. He quickly corrects his statement to say he was listening to his singer. Mike is then shown in an interview: 'It takes me back to when Layne was alive and uh, I'm lucky. I got to play with him for as long as I did, a decade, so what a great time that was for me.' Mike implies that this decade was a great time because he played bass with Layne, but it could also be a longing for what once was. The new narcissus, as witnessed in *Hoarders*, relishes their past, their youth, agility and beauty.

For the new narcissus, who they once were often stirs up memories of a time when narcissistic supply was available in droves. Drew asks Mike how old he was when Alice in Chains formed and if he was using during that time. Mike says he was casually using but 'the day they kicked me out I was like [motions to arm] "Cobain, shoot me up," because we were playing with Nirvana and the Chili Peppers down in South America'. Mike goes on to claim that he died that same night:

> Dead for 11 minutes, Layne said. I woke up I was all wet and I was in a different room. I was in the bathroom. I just remember somebody punching me in the face crying and uh, I let him die too. And he saved my life. Isn't that terrible?

What is so somber about this interaction is how emotionless Mike seems even though his words communicate such pain and suffering. There is no pausing between words when Mike speaks and the viewer cannot help but think of how difficult sobriety must be for him. Drew observes that 'Mike Starr is clearly haunted by very intense feelings surrounding the death of his friend Layne Staley. These feelings remain a threat to his sobriety and we must continue to address them in treatment.' Even more so, when Drew tells Mike he doesn't want to lose another person to addiction, Mike flatly responds 'Ok.' Drew then tells Mike that he has 'to want to get better though' to which Mike does not respond and is shown staring off to the right as though he knows he cannot respond correctly (see Figure 6.5). This chilling and sad moment in the first few minutes of Episode 7 are even more unnerving if one knows that Mike Starr will pass away in March 2011, just a little over a year after completing Season 2 of a spin-off entitled *Sober House*. Many celebrities featured on this reality television show over the years have succumbed to their addiction. Joanie 'Chyna' Laurer, who was featured in Season 1; Jeff Conaway, featured in Seasons 1 and 2; Rodney King from Season 2; and Mindy McCready, Mike Starr, and Joey Kavar – all would pass away in the years following their appearance on the show.

Lessons on the artifice, constant reflections

When a person 'reflects' on something, what is it that they are truly doing? Thinking back? Contemplating ways to adjust their behavior accordingly

Figure 6.5 Mike in session

for similar future interactions? Dr. Drew's message of the importance of interpersonal relationships is an exceptionally difficult lesson to learn for the celebrities featured on this reality television show. They have been enamored with the new narcissus' reflection for too long, their gaze at what appears to be their own reflection looking back at them. Relationships with others have only hurt them or, in turn, they have hurt others. Arguably, for celebrities, the extent to which the new narcissus manipulates and uses others for his/her own selfish pursuits is magnified as a result of achieving one of the ultimate forms of success in our world: fame. The more famous one becomes, the more sources of narcissistic supply. The new narcissus is enamored with their own reflection but also the reflection of others. The new narcissus is willing to alter themselves, in whatever way necessary, in order to be well liked and admired by others. Interestingly enough, the new narcissus will often lie, manipulate and betray others in pursuit of narcissistic supply. The new narcissus is only interested in associating with others that are equally beautiful, talented and successful; if the new narcissus is as widespread as predicted, then narcissists will be surrounded by other narcissists who engage in the same lying, manipulative behavior that can ultimately lead to betrayal. At the beginning of Episode 4, Tom Sizemore has checked into rehab and joined the rest of the group. At a morning group session, Shelley, one of the counselors, asks the group if anyone has experience with honesty.

Heidi: Yes. You have to be honest every day of your life because what does one lie cost you? The truth.
Mindy: I agree.
Shelly: Ok.
Heidi: I just hate liars. I hate liars.
Mindy: Yeah.
Mike: I find when I lie I don't feel too good about myself.

(Pinsky 2010)

Mackenzie: the relentless cycle of betrayal

At the beginning of the morning session the patients are reflecting on their experiences with honesty. For the new narcissus, lying to others is key in order to not only maintain the delicately constructed artifice but also a way to obtain more attention and admiration from others. Addiction and the new narcissus are both sicknesses yet even when an individual is suffering from this sickness they continue down the path of unhealthiness. Here, during this morning session on honesty and truthfulness, all of the patients seem to be in agreement that lying and liars are bad, even hated. This is the scariest aspect of the new narcissus, even when an understanding of the sickness exists, individuals will continue engaging in the same behavior that hurts others and hurts themselves.

Mackenzie: My father sat me down once and he said 'Listen kid, uh, its pretty much always better to tell a lie than to tell the truth.'
[Heidi laughs]
Mackenzie: That's what my dad said.
Heidi: No way.
Mackenzie: I swear on my life that's what my dad said.
Heidi: That is so evil.
Mackenzie: I'm telling you that this is the way …
Mindy: Did you believe him?
Mackenzie: For a long time, absolutely. He's your dad, you know? He was my dad. My outlook on life was shaped by a very sick person but I have like a real part in what happened to me. I was present and I made choices that were bad based on my life experience up to that point.
Heidi: Yeah, but you can't blame yourself.
Mackenzie: No he was, he was definitely a bad guy. He was a really bad guy.
Heidi: Yeah but you can't think you're a bad girl.

(Pinsky 2010)

Through the process of socialization, the family, and more importantly, one's parents, are central to the development of the individual. If one of the most influential forces in your life informs you that lying is better than telling the truth, in a sense, you are learning that lying is a good skill to have. Through the experience of lying, a child or young adult may learn about the benefits that come with successfully lying to others. Many of the patients on *Celebrity Rehab* have suffered some sort of betrayal from influential and important people in their life. For many, this betrayal and the dark lessons of idolizing the new narcissus, begin in childhood.

> Heidi: Can I ask you a question? What did your dad think about your getting high?
> Mackenzie: We got high together.
> Mindy: Her dad stuck her first needle in her arm.
> Mackenzie: My dad shot me up when I was a teenager with coke.
> Heidi: And he was like 'cool, my daughter and I are partying'?
> Mackenzie: Oh yeah, he used to say 'got any drugs for yer ol' dad?'
> Heidi: If my dad said that to me I don't know what I would do. I'm so sorry Mac.
> Mackenzie: Thank you.

Mackenzie Phillips was first exposed to intravenous drug use by her own father and now that she is more mature and struggling with an addiction she is beginning to realize the 'sick' state that her father was in and the 'sick' lessons that she learned and internalized from his influence. Later, Mackenzie will reveal that she was involved in a consensual sexual relationship with her father beginning in her late teens and lasting a decade. Mackenzie would state in an Oprah Winfrey interview, shortly after filming *Celebrity Rehab*, that after one night of doing drugs, she woke up to her father having sex with her. She went on to say:

> I adored my father. I waited for him over and over again. I was constantly trying to get his attention and this deep visceral need to get his attention [...] Cover it with heroin, cocaine, alcohol, marijuana, barbiturates, everything you can think of. Over time your perception of things and as they should be, the world as it is, the rules of society become warped and twisted.
>
> (Pinsky 2010)

Many scholars of narcissism speak of the traumas of childhood leading to narcissism in adulthood. For Mackenzie, lack of attention from her father may have pushed her into drug use to fill that need. Drug use may have even been normalized growing up in an environment of drug users. Beginning to use drugs at the age of 11 and intravenous cocaine use by the age of 17, along with the rape and eventual consensual affair with her father, arguable 'warped' Mackenzie's sense of reality. A voiceover of Dr. Drew begins at the end of the morning session on honesty.

> While the details of their trauma may differ, there's one thing that all these patients have in common. That's that they've all been betrayed by people close to them. If the deep consequences of the helplessness caused by this betrayal is not addressed the anger and more importantly, the resentment, will lead to more drug use.
>
> (Pinsky 2010)

The new narcissus often develops as a result of these misguided feelings of helplessness. If one's natural state (i.e. true self) experiences betrayal, trauma and/or abuse, then one may attempt to protect one's true self by hiding it away. The presentation of a false, artificially constructed self, can then serve to protect one's true self. Any abuse, trauma or betrayal experienced by the individual is deflected by the artificially constructed self and therefore not experienced by the true self. Even more, this feeling of helplessness is false and arguably an excuse for the new narcissus' subsequent behavior. This is an important aspect missing from Dr. Drew's analysis. The once experienced feeling of helplessness in childhood has now morphed into a denial of responsibility for that same infliction of abuse on others in adulthood. The new narcissus often engages in the same behavior as their abuser. In life, an individual adjusts their behavior and actions accordingly when they suffer consequences to their actions. The new narcissus, in the face of consequences, only tries harder to not get caught. The pattern of lies and manipulation the new narcissus projects, in order to accumulate the most important drug of attention, is an intentional abuse. The new narcissus is aware of all their actions because they are constantly calculating their next move.

The new narcissus is the purest form of the individual becoming one with the economy, free from moral discipline with an extreme focus on the self, always in pursuit of unchecked appetites and the unbridled pursuit of attention and admiration from others. The new narcissus has won and must continue to do so, winning being the purest form of success within a consumer society. The self is the ultimate object and must be desired and remain in the highest category of economic viability in order to survive. For what happens to a business or product when it is not no longer viable? Discontinued, out-of-business or no longer in commission. Shame was once experienced but now the new narcissus, my false self, protects me. I no longer choose to experience shame.

Addiction is merely a means by which the new narcissus attempts to avoid facing their actions and abusive behaviors. *Avoid those feelings of guilt and shame and 'smoke more drugs'*. Addicts, like the new narcissus, are constantly faced with the consequences of their actions. Tom Sizemore lost his house and his wealth and arguably his 'star power' and A-list status in Hollywood. Many others ended up in jail and lost the companionship of friends and family. Medical professionals and rehabilitation specialists often say that these consequences result from the addict's state of powerlessness. From this perspective, the addict has become a slave to their addiction and has therefore lost the power to make appropriate choices regarding their behavior and actions. Herein lies an important aspect of addiction and the new narcissus: constant reflection and choice. We are choosing our very own enslavement to the reflection gazing back at us. Is that the new narcissus or is that me? The new narcissus is similar to other addicted individuals in that they may use and abuse drugs as a coping mechanism for past trauma or as a means of escape from current trauma in their daily life. Many causes of addiction are explained by the structure of society and the experience of the individual within that structure. The new narcissus' unique response to the current structure of society is to deny responsibility and avoid being held accountable for their deceptive ways. Remember, the new narcissus is convinced that they are unique and special and therefore should only receive unique and special treatment. The anomic state of society (characterized by a lack of regulation) influences the formation of an individual who also wants to be free from regulation. All behaviors, even lying, manipulative, abusive behaviors, are accepted forms of obtaining the most attention and admiration. This results from the fact that this behavior often goes unchecked and worse yet, is often rewarded. Falseness is rewarded in our world today. When that falseness is discovered and shared with the world, in most cases the new narcissus will deny responsibility for their actions and avoid being held accountable.

Reward the illusion: the child beauty queen grows up

The new narcissus is a result of life in an increasingly anomic world. Kari Ann Penache exemplifies an important life lesson that too many young people are learning today: falseness, if performed in a way to appear as greatness, will result in the same rewards as someone who is truly great. Kari Ann Penache was formerly Miss Teen United States, a title she won at the age of 19, before it was stripped from her due to her appearance in *Playboy* magazine. She originally appeared on *Celebrity Rehab* for a sex addiction in a previous season but Dr. Drew reveals that he didn't realize her sex addiction was also coupled with an addiction to methamphetamines.

Kari Ann joins the group a little late and therefore is assigned to her own room, whereas all the other celebrities are sharing a room with one other person. During one particular group session Dr. Drew explains how the patients are entering the second half of rehab: 'With all addicts there's some level of denial about the disease. As these patients face the second half of treatment it's important that they fully understand the cunning nature of addiction and how it effects each of them.' This important aspect of denial is witnessed in the chapter on *Hoarders*, reiterating to the viewer that hoarding, like addiction, is a disease.

Dr. Drew opens up the group session fumbling over his words a bit as he tries to broach this topic with the patients. 'You know I just want to re-enforce you know what this thing is, that is addiction. Addiction is the only disease that you have to convince people they have. The only one. Why is that? Why do we have to convince people ...' Unfortunately, addiction isn't the only disease you have to convince people they have. Many 'mental' disorders go undiagnosed or individuals that suffer from mental health issues are often unaware that their behavior exemplifies certain psychiatric conditions. Many diseases today are not simply the result of biology or genealogy but instead result from an increasingly anomic state of societal affairs. While certain individuals may be more prone to addiction or hoarding or other mental health disorders because of their biology or genealogy, some individuals may suffer from these 'diseases' purely because of their interaction with the social world. Addiction has existed throughout history. Any individual, regardless of the historical period, can develop one of these 'diseases' because of lessons taught and expectations placed upon the individual. The expectation is not to be addicted, however, and the unique lesson in our modern era is to never be satisfied.

Dr. Drew continues his opening to the group session:

> [w]hat's difficult, what's difficult for people to get their head around is you can control your relationships with the substances, and then all of a sudden you can't control it anymore. Is it a different disease? When you were controlling it? Is it a different disorder?

It even seems Dr. Drew may be unsure of the solution and asks these questions in hope of discovering the answers. Here, issues of control and denial of the disease are important focus points for Dr. Drew. However, these are also important in understanding the relationship between addiction, celebrity status and the new narcissus. For many of these celebrities, they have been able to live a life where consumer desires and aspirations are easily met. The ability to now 'lose control' when it comes to the purchase of these goods is now unparalleled when one reaches a celebrity status. Often, an individual is not prepared for the seemingly endless amount of wealth that accompanies fame. Just as material possessions provide a temporary satisfaction for the modern individual, so too does drug use. Is it really surprising when someone squanders their newly acquired fortune, given they have not been provided with the necessary skills to understand how to keep that fortune? Too often, people are quick to criticize celebrities and others who lose their fortune just as quickly as they acquired it. The encouragement to spend, spend, spend, is everywhere and once someone is presented with a seemingly infinite supply of cash it can be very difficult to control and maintain. Is it any less surprising for individuals who have access to a seemingly infinite supply of drugs that also supply them with those same moments of satisfaction, to then squander their lives in pursuit of more drugs? Dr. Drew looks to Bob to continue the discussion. Forrester states:

> Well actually the thing I was gonna talk about is when I was a drug addict full on, all I saw [in my] exchanges with people was: what can they do for me? What can I get? What's the angle here? It's the mindset of the

> drug addict and alcoholic, and if the mindset is 'what can this person do for me' or 'what are they trying to get from me', then you're always gonna get let down. And you're going to build a chest cavity full of resentment and mistrust.
>
> (Pinsky 2010)

This is the symptom of the new narcissus, using others in order to gain an advantage for one's self. The new narcissus may have been abused or mistreated in childhood but as an adult, the new narcissus chooses to engage in that same behavior in order to please the desires of their falsely created self that seems to protect the true and damaged self. For drug addicts, one's drug supply is important, but for the new narcissus, while that may be important for some narcissists, others are still after priority number one: narcissistic supply. This mindset that Bob speaks of is the mindset of our anomic world: 'What can this person do for me?' Using others in order to achieve one's own selfish pursuits or advancement. People today are constantly 'let down' because our goals, dreams and aspirations are misguided. If the collective goal is material success then 99 per cent of individuals today will be let down because there will always be some material possession that is better than the one the individual just obtained. In 1897, Emile Durkheim warned of the effects of living in a world with infinite goals: eternal dissatisfaction and suicide. Instead of escaping from the world permanently, through suicide, the modern individual can escape the world in short bursts through continuous drug and substance abuse. The worst of all possible fates is that suffered by narcissus – suicide from addiction to the appearance of one's self.

Kari Ann responds to Bob's revelation of using others for selfish pursuits by talking about her lack of trust in other people. She says that when 'I first meet you. I trust you. I'll tell you everything. I'll do anything, right? And then all of a sudden I put up this wall and I don't trust you anymore.' Mackenzie responds to this and says that she feels Kari Ann doesn't trust any of the other patients and that she wishes she would engage with the group and be more open.

> Mackenzie: You go in there and you close the door and we don't see you for hours.
>
> Kari Ann: Well I'm tired. I'm tired.
>
> Mackenzie: But you're not too tired to like put on makeup and change clothes four times a day.
>
> Kari Ann: So you're making fun of me getting dressed and getting ready? I have problems …
>
> Mackenzie: That wasn't the …
>
> Kari Ann (forcefully): I don't like to come out if I'm not dressed and ready to.
>
> Drew: Ok, you're in attacking mode now.
>
> Kari Ann: Because I feel very attacked.

Drew: No. They're asking you to join them.

Kari Ann (to Mackenzie): I will join them! But like don't make comments about me getting dressed. I don't make comments about you NOT getting dressed.

Mackenzie (mouth drops open): Wow. I didn't deserve that. All I said was …

Kari Ann: I didn't deserve that either.

Mackenzie: That wasn't an attack. That's a soft spot for you because you are overreacting to what I said.

Kari Ann: Ok doctor!

(Pinsky 2010)

Kari Ann is very concerned about her appearance, so much so that she isolates herself in her room for hours at a time and changes what she is wearing several times a day. This obsession with appearance is of the utmost importance for the new narcissus. How one appears to others offers the first opportunity to achieve narcissistic supply. Dr. Drew asks Mindy McCready if she has something to say to Kari Ann.

Mindy: You know I see a lot of things and a lot of pain in her that you know, I kind of understand. You know the whole not being able to leave the room without getting dressed …

Drew: Was that you?

Mindy: No. It was somebody else in my life that had that same issue. That will not leave the house, will not leave the bathroom without being absolutely perfect.

[waves hand in front of her face]

And they think that they have to be perfect all the time. And they think they're hiding something by being perfect. They think that if they come out and every eyelash is just so, that they're not gonna know how messed up you are inside.

[Kari Ann is beginning to cry]

… and I am on the receiving end of that person, knowing how messed up they are.

Drew: So it triggers all your stuff?

Mindy: It triggers all kinds of things.

(Pinsky 2010)

Mindy McCready alludes to the mistreatment she experienced from someone in her life that taught her an important lesson on perfection: always be perfect on the *outside*. While Goffman's concept of the mask draws upon the importance of appearance, it is incorrect to assume the modern individual plays multiple roles. For the new narcissus, there is only one role one must master: perfection (often through artificiality). Dr. Drew encourages Mindy to address Kari Ann's behavior and how it triggers her past experiences.

Mindy: Well, I mean, I, in my own personal experience as a young person dealing with someone that wouldn't leave the bathroom before they got dressed which I'm talking about my [bleeped out]. Um, she was, um, abusive and selfish and she only cared about one thing and that was whatever her agenda was that moment and I see all those, those kinds of traits in you. I see that selfishness in you.

Kari: Everything that you grew up with I grew up with too. The same 'everything has to be perfect on the outside'. You couldn't touch the couches because they're white. Um, [crying] you don't go into the grocery store without your lipstick on because you never know if you're gonna run into, you know, Mr. Right, um …

Mindy: Aren't you scared you're going to turn into that?

Kari: Um. [sniffling] I'm having a hard time being in here.

[grabs her pack of cigarettes]

Drew: But you're doing a good job.

(Pinsky 2010)

Instantly, when Kari Ann is confronted with this internalized lesson she has mastered so well, her response is to run away. The extreme focus on appearance and even more so, the 'perfect' appearance, led to traumatic consequences for a young Mindy and Kari Ann. 'Growing up' with a narcissist often teaches children the disturbing message that deceit, manipulation, and an extreme focus on the self are traits to be emulated. Today, when faced with the lure of the new narcissist, individuals can chose to indulge in the perceived rewards that come with a presentation of falseness or alter the path laid by those before them and not be selfish, manipulative and conceited to the point of abusing others. Kari Ann does not want to face the choice she has made and wants to leave the group session.

Kari: Can I please leave? Just for a minute.

Drew: Do yall want to say anything to Kari Ann? To encourage her, make her feel ok, feel safe. Mindy do you want to say something?

Mindy: I just want her to toughen up and be present with us and not want to go smoke a cigarette and not cry tears so that she can go smoke cigarettes.

Kari Ann: Fuck!

[gets up to leave]

Mackenzie: Kari Ann! Kari Ann! Don't!

Kari: Why? You guys are fucking nasty people.

Mackenzie: Kari Ann don't do this.

Kari: No, no, no, no.

Mackenzie: Come back! Come back! You were there. Don't leave! Don't leave, man.

(Pinsky 2010)

Kari Ann leaves the group session. It's too late. She has left and can no longer confront herself. She retreats to her room and Mackenzie quickly follows after her, to find her standing in front of the long mirror in her room blotting away her tears and running makeup (see Figure 6.6). Mackenzie encourages her to come back to the group but Kari Ann simply replies 'Does it look like I fucking want to go back to group right now?' Even this sharp, biting response is indicative of the internalized message she so desperately clings to: *what it looks like*. Her tears have washed her appearance away and now she must re-apply the artifice. She cannot confront the exposed self that has been revealed beneath, for it is too painful a truth to confront. Kari Ann was a pageant queen. She desperately needs the artificially constructed self in order to continue earning the Ultimate Grand Supreme title in all things in life. The dictionary tells us that vanity is 'inflated pride in one's self or one's appearance' or 'something that is empty, valueless'. Interesting to think about vanity in relation to the new narcissus. One must continue to gaze at the reflection looking back at one: ensure that the perfection is maintained and properly presented at all time.

Kari Ann is a wounded soul and this revelation begs for a moment of reflection. Audience members may view her behavior as childish, defensive or simply an over-reaction to an accusation. However, as a victim of abuse, she is retreating from the source of that abuse: a lifestyle that she is now fully

Figure 6.6 Kari Ann adjusting her appearance in the mirror

engaged in. The new narcissus not only lies to others, they lie to themselves too. This is how the true self is protected and tricked into believing the artifice will always protect them. The artifice is the cause of their pain and suffering and the artifice must be peeled away and the raw, damaged flesh of the new narcissus' true self must be exposed before one can begin to heal. Dr. Pinsky and his staff understand that addiction can cause an individual to isolate themselves and deny the source and cause of their addiction. Patients often deny that they suffer from an addiction. An understanding of this deeper issue reflected in the new narcissus, falseness, is really what needs to be addressed. The socialization experience of the addict, or of any modern individual who learns the dark lesson of the new narcissus, means that person will be liable to repeat the same pattern of abuse in their interactions with others. How many individuals today have suffered growing up with an adult who encouraged this artificiality, this lesson that what matters most is how you *appear* on the outside and how you *appear* to others? *Keep focusing on the reflection.*

Near the end of the season, the show chronicles a weekend where friends and family members can come visit. Dr. Drew informs the audience that the group will organize a dinner for their family members as a way of doing service to others (one of the central tenets of recovery). All the cast members are shopping in a store for decorations for the dinner party. Kari Ann seems to be in a frenzy as she tries to buy some of the most expensive items in the store

> Kari Ann: Oh we need a dragon! Can we get a dragon?
> Event Planner: No.
> Kari Ann: I want one. I want a dragon.
>
> (Pinsky 2010)

Kari Ann repeats over and over again, 'I want it. I want it. I want it.' And then when she is told no for what seems to be the final time, she declares 'I don't like this store anymore.' This seemingly childish and spoiled behavior is typical of the new narcissus: the eternal child who refuses to grow up. Many scholars have noted that narcissists tend to act like children. The new narcissus is stuck forever in a child-like state where the most important goal is to obtain the most attention and admiration from others. From birth we are socialized to understand the importance and value of *things*. Similar to the individuals we saw suffering in *Hoarders*, the patients like Kari Ann in *Celebrity Rehab* are suffering from the same issue: an unquenchable thirst for objects, attention, drugs, sexual partners, vacations, experiences, etc. Hedonism 'is a doctrine that pleasure or happiness is the sole or chief good in life'. Consumerism is indoctrinating individuals with the motto of hedonism. The new narcissus is a symptom of a society whose primary value is distracting the individual with an unobtainable goal and deceptive satisfaction. The new narcissus is really the result of Durkheim's foretelling of an anomic society. Think what the world would be like if values were different from a young age: to be grateful for all things and to be satisfied when our thirst is quenched.

The young girls in *Toddlers and Tiaras* were told that if they have the best personality they will win even though they are ultimately competing in a beauty pageant. It's not called a Young Personality Pageant because this is the illusion. The new narcissus learns the message of falseness and the importance of projecting the right kind of image to others yet even when one follows these rules they still can't win. Kari Ann is now struggling with an addiction yet most of her behavior is indicative of the chronic abuse of the wrong value: infinite goals and a lack of regulation. Her exclamation and subsequent repetition of 'I want it, I want it, I want it' reflects this dark lesson of the new narcissus. The dragon head and her spoiled behavior merely exemplifies how the individual today constantly struggles with the limitless goal of achieving material wealth. Even more so, once it is acquired that same desire and thirst is there, if not stronger than before. If Kari Ann can't use her drugs to numb this thirst then surely the dragon head will.

Avoidance till the end

At the beginning of Episode 8, Kari Ann Peniche jumps in bed with Tom Sizemore and asks him to come paint bikinis with her and Mike Starr outside. She leaves his room and goes outside to where Mike is painting on a canvas.

> Mike: So can you hang out with me and be my friend?
> Kari Ann: Yeah. I like to make the boys happy.
> Mike: Yeah.
> Kari Ann: And if a little boobies makes 'em happy …
> Mike: Yeah.
> Kari Ann: What the fuck? A little boobies never hurt anybody.
> (Pinsky 2010)

Tom joins the two of them outside. Kari Ann then proceeds to encourage both Mike and Tom to paint a bikini on her. Mike is ready but Tom shows apprehension. Kari Ann then removes her top and lies down so that they can begin painting. Tom, afraid of getting in trouble and being kicked out of rehab, refuses to paint and walks away. Mike begins painting on Kari Ann. It is not long before Loesha, a staff member, comes outside and catches them, telling Kari Ann to put her top back on and come inside. Loesha and other residents then confront Kari Ann, who claims she does not understand how her behavior is a problem.

> Loesha: You were naked.
> Kari Ann: I wasn't naked.
> Loesha: Yeah, you had your shirt off.
> Kari Ann: We were painting a bikini top.
> Loesha: How is that appropriate in any way?
> Kari Ann: There's parties all the time that …

Loesha: This isn't a party.
[Kari Ann stares back at her]
Don't act like you don't know.
Kari Ann: No I really didn't know that it was against the rules.
Loesha: You didn't know that taking your top off in front of the other male patients here is not ok?
Kari Ann: I didn't really know that it was against the rules.

(Pinsky 2010)

Loesha instructs her to go to her room and clean herself up. Once she's gone another cast member says that earlier in the day Kari Ann 'told all of us that she wasn't wearing her underwear' and that she 'flashed all the boys'. The staff member then goes and confronts Kari Ann about this. At first Kari Ann denies flashing the male residents. Then, after more questioning by the staff member she says that she didn't flash the male patients on purpose. When questioned again about whether or not the exposure was purposeful or not she says angrily 'I only did it once as a joke [...] I was bored'.

Kari Ann is bored because the new narcissus' satisfaction can never be quenched. There are never enough drugs, sexual partners, attention or possessions. The new narcissus is always seeking out more. Young girls and women learn from a young age that their sexuality is a valuable way to obtain success or any of the aforementioned items. Kari Ann not only participated in pageants, she won the ultimate title: Miss Teen United States. Many of the patients of *Celebrity Rehab* have obtained the ultimate title in their particular field: acting, professional sports, pageants, singing, modeling and even procuring. Now, life seems a bit boring and dull. The attention and adoration is slim to none and the drugs are the only thing left that seem to hold a limitless supply. Once the modern individual reaches the highest form of success in their profession, satisfaction and happiness is supposed to result. After all, this is the lesson and the expectation. The attention that seemed unrelenting when these celebrities were at the peak of their career is now slim to none and that high that was once achieved from all that attention must be achieved through some other means. Drugs can serve as a solution to one's unrelenting thirst. For the individuals in *Hoarders* the solution is their material possessions; for the *Sister Wives* it's the accumulation of spouses and children; for the *Real Housewives* it's a lifestyle of extravagance, for the young people in *Catfish* it's dating partners. All of these individuals in seemingly different reality shows are seeking to quench this same unquenchable thirst. All things are equated with a price, even people, and there is no limit to the wealth and things/objects/people one can buy. Until this message is reversed the new narcissus will become more prevalent, manipulating all, deceiving all and destroying all, simply for the benefit of personal gain.

The next morning the staff and Dr. Pinsky discuss what is going to happen to Kari Ann and Mike for violating the contract that stated no sexual contact (of any kind) with other residents. While the staff and Dr. Pinsky discuss the situation we also see Mackenzie, Mindy and Lisa discussing what happened. Mindy believes that Kari Ann knew what she was doing and manipulated the guys into the situation. Mackenzie and Lisa are in agreement and Lisa states that Kari Ann knew what she was doing. The staff and Dr. Pinsky believe that 24-hour room restriction will be the consequence of their behavior and neither will be 'kicked out' of rehab.

A-void-ance. A void. Something is missing within us; an emptiness and loneliness overwhelms us. Too many people are lost in their artifice. They have lost sight of their true self. When confronted with reality and the falseness it encompasses, one often refuses to face the void for fear of the pain it might engender. If one continues with the artifice and denies its existence than the true self, deep down inside, will be protected, free from pain and suffering. Kari Ann's inappropriate behavior is a way to avoid dealing with her issues of pain and addiction. The morning following the incident with Mike Starr, all the patients have a group process session with Drew and Bob. Tom says that he is glad that Mike and Kari Ann didn't get kicked out. Mackenzie says 'Drew, you're the first to tell us that behavior has consequences […] but I think the integrity of this program is being diluted by the lack of consequences'. This lack of consequences is an important aspect of the falseness of the new narcissus. Often consequences do not result when one fakes or lies about who they really are. Joey speaks up following this important point about consequences.

> Joey: I agree with you. I got two things to say though: 1) […] wouldn't you agree that people have been letting her get away with a lot of shit? You'd agree, right?
>
> Mackenzie: Absolutely.
>
> Joey: Then wouldn't you agree also that if you're an addict and you're as sick as she is … No offense [towards Kari Ann]. If you keep seeing that people are letting you get away with things: you're going to keep doing it?
>
> (Pinsky 2010)

When the most costly crime to society (elite and white collar crime) also happens to be the least punished, what does this say about the state of our world? Similarly, when someone can be rewarded for faking it as opposed to authenticity then that individual can continue engaging in the same deceit, manipulation and destruction of others. Joey goes on to say that if Kari Ann and Mike were kicked out of the program the first thing he (Mike) would want to do is go use. Kari Ann's behavior is indicative of the new narcissus' tendency to avoid. At the conclusion of the parents and family weekend Kari may have felt overwhelmed with feelings and emotions stemming from her connection to what is most important: her relationship with others. This disruptive and inappropriate behavior may have been an attempt to get kicked out of rehab so that she can go use again but it could also be an attempt to avoid facing those stirred up feelings and emotions. Bob Forrester states:

> What you're feeling usually in rehab is emptiness. We experience it as we get more sober. That has to go away so the easiest way to [make it] go away is to start fucking somebody else or start obsessing about a peer and really what I believe Heidi is doing right now is making that emptiness go away with crystal meth, right? Don't you think that Heidi started caring about you guys, right? She was starting to care about you guys and that was unacceptable to Heidi Fleiss.
>
> (Pinsky 2010)

Dr. Drew states that this is often how patients behave near the end of treatment: they begin to demean the treatment process and say that it doesn't work. Tom Sizemore follows up with 'There's something about being clean and sober that works.' There's something about being clean, sober and authentic that works. Falseness only works for a period of time before the façade is exposed. The new narcissus often refuses to face and confront this constructed falseness and will avoid, run away or retreat from the pain that comes with an understanding of that falseness. For example, Kari Ann has avoided any real consequences of her inappropriate behavior and would likely repeat the same behavior if tempted again. The new narcissus will also continue the vicious cycle of manipulating and using others for their own selfish pursuits if they are repeatedly given the opportunity to do so without any real consequences. 'When one is no longer checked one becomes unable to check one's self.' The proliferation of the new narcissus will continue to spread and grow unless the overwhelming presence of falseness and artificiality is removed from our society, and more importantly, there is a dramatic shift in perspective from pursuing infinite goals without regulation to pursuing goals that have some form of regulation and moral discipline.

> For the most part Dr. Drew, when I go to meetings it seems like they're all a bunch of losers and everyone wants something from me. They want a job. They want money. They want this. They want that. It just seems like a group of losers to me. It made me want to use really bad.
>
> (Pinsky 2010)

Heidi Fleiss revealed her above sentiments in her very first meeting with Dr. Drew. Many of the celebrities featured in this reality television program refuse to not only face their responsibility for the consequences of their addiction but they also see their own reflection looking back at them through their interaction with other addicts, and see that same behavior as deplorable, disgusting and indicative of a 'loser'. The new narcissus refuses to accept the reflection of themselves. Like Heidi and Kari Ann, Dennis Rodman has also avoided facing up to his addiction. Drew even orders a brain scan so that he can provide Dennis with concrete evidence of alcoholism and that alcohol induced dementia is a real possibility for Dennis' future if he does not stop drinking. Dennis simply responds that 'it doesn't matter'. Many who read this book might say that it 'doesn't matter'. On one occasion, previous patients and cast members of *Celebrity Rehab* come back to the treatment facility to talk with the current patients. Amber Smith speaks to the group about her experience while in the recovery center.

> I felt nothing when I was in here the first time. I listened but I had no emotions, just numb. It's so difficult. I know the pain. It's slow. It's building up your self-esteem and being with people and it hurts to be with people all the time because I really like to isolate.
>
> (Pinsky 2010)

Rewarding the void deep within us and continuing our fixated gaze upon the new narcissus, upon ourselves. Isolation and avoidance are the final stage in the endless cycle of the new narcissus. For Dennis Rodman, he is not only isolating himself but he also avoids facing his behavior and ultimately his struggle with alcoholism. Interpersonal relationships cannot be maintained when you use others for your own selfish pursuits. For many addicts, the deceit and pain they have inflicted on others will be difficult, if not impossible, to forgive. This painful realization can cause some individuals to try and change their deceitful ways, but for many, the new narcissus whispers softly in their ear to simply work a bit harder at creating a *better* artifice. One that will be more successful at tricking others in to believing the artifice is the real thing. *Maintain your gaze.* Even when Bridgette Nielson talks with Dennis Rodman one-on-one, he claims that 'the hardest part about this whole thing here is that it would be different if I was a fucked up mother fucker like most people here but you know what? I'm a lot stronger than these fuckers here'. Rodman, much like Fleiss, not only refuses to believe he suffers from addiction but he also believes he is better and stronger than everyone else. The new narcissus is fervently convinced that they are the most amazing, awesome person and often no one can convince them otherwise.

Dr. Drew attempts to help the patients on this reality television show but seems to miss the connection to narcissism and how this impacts treatment. Many of these addicted celebrities may also be suffering from narcissism and there appears to be zero shame involved in terms of the exploitation of their experiences in treatment. Dr. Drew is making a profit and gaining notoriety and attention for his efforts on the show. We, as audience members, may also be guilty of feeding the monster that is called the new narcissus. Tuning in to their treatment sessions, outlandish behavior and ultimate downfall and disgrace is malicious on the audience's part. An audience member is not helping them but they are enjoying watching the struggle. This is the dark side of reality television: choosing to watch. Future analysis will hopefully uncover audience motivation and reception but for now, the dark warning of the new narcissus is revealed for all to see.

7 The new narcissus goes global

The Real Housewives

Beginning in the United States in 2006, *The Real Housewives of Orange County* began what was to become an international, highly watched reality television franchise. By 2008 Bravo had expanded it to include *The Real Housewives of New York City* and *The Real Housewives of Atlanta.* The show has also held locations in New Jersey, Washington D.C., Beverly Hills, Miami, Potomac and Dallas. Internationally, the first premiere abroad was the *Real Housewives of Athens* in 2011, followed by Vancouver in 2012 and *Les Vraies Housewives* in 2013 which featured French women living in the Los Angeles area. In 2014, *The Real Housewives of Melbourne* premiered in Australia and in 2015 *The Real Housewives of Cheshire* premiered in the United Kingdom. This chapter will examine a variety of scenes from *The Real Housewives of D.C.*, *The Real Housewives of Cheshire* and *The Real Housewives of Melbourne,* to draw comparisons between the US, UK, and Australia, and to take a deeper look at some of the most striking examples of the new narcissus.

Understanding the game

The very first episode of *The Real Housewives of Cheshire* begins with a voiceover describing Cheshire as the 'land of the rich and famous' and claiming that you can either move up or out and that life in Cheshire is all about being apart of the in crowd. The voiceover ends with 'play the game right and you'll really make it big' (Dunlop et al. 2015a). Each housewife has her own introduction in which she is shown wearing a formal gown. As the women pose against a glamorous backdrop, a voiceover of each woman delivers her unique tagline. This is the supposed embodiment of Cheshire society: rich, famous, exclusive, and with great importance attached to 'playing the game right'. Every *Housewives* series is focused on the participants' success, lifestyle, consumerism and the presentation of their best self. As a housewife participant, you have a tagline, a brand, a personality that you must sell to the audience. You want to receive the most attention regardless of whether or not you are well received by that same audience: what matters is to gain the viewers' attention.

Lauren: 'It's all about me'

'I'm a domestic goddess. I don't listen to anything anyone tells me. It's all about me' (Dunlop et al. 2015a). In the *Real Housewives of Cheshire* the audience is first introduced to Lauren. Focus on your self. YOU are what is most important. Lauren is depicted as a 'domestic goddess' in her perfectly decorated mansion with not an item out of place. Lauren discusses her love for shopping as the camera flashes to images of fine jewelry with high price tags. 'Everything has value. You just have to learn how to exploit it.' Lauren is then shown meeting with a jeweler and purchasing a very expensive pair of diamond earrings. She quickly informs the viewer that there is a certain form of value in Cheshire society and that exploitation and manipulation are a means by which you can obtain such value. Later, Lauren's husband comes home and she confesses her purchase:

> Lauren: I've got the most beautiful dress and I've got no jewellery to go with it. You don't look really happy about it.
> Paul: Go on.
> [Lauren pulls out earrings]
> Paul: What are they?
> Lauren: They're earrings!
> Paul: That's one earring?
> Lauren: Yeah. Do you like it?
> Paul: Really?
> Lauren: It looks amazing on.
> Lauren (in an interview setting): Our marriage is a game. And I have to play the game correctly to get the diamonds. And it's all about getting the diamonds.
> [switch back to Paul and Lauren]
> Paul: You can't just go out buying stuff. It's not fair.
> Lauren: I just thought that you'd actually want to buy me a little present.
> Paul: I want to buy you stuff.
> Lauren: Well you just have!
> [laughter and they embrace and kiss]
> Lauren (in interview setting): Paul has always fancied me and he still does. It's a bit like sleeping with the enemy but there's only so many blowjobs I can give [laughs].
>
> (Dunlop et al. 2015a)

Within the first 10 minutes of the first episode of the *Real Housewives of Cheshire* the viewer has been told what defines Cheshire and what the housewife Lauren values: expensive material items, looking beautiful and using her sexuality as a way to properly 'play the game' (i.e. get expensive material items). Lauren also likens her marriage to that of a game. She must successfully use herself as a sexual object through which she can obtain more diamonds. For Lauren, life is about 'getting the diamonds'.

In all the *Real Housewives* series, material possessions are valued by the women and by those whom they interact with. These possessions serve as a symbol of value and are a representation of success in the modern world. Every housewife draws attention to her nice things. They are always concerned to look their best at all times. They are often shown having their hair and makeup done or shopping for expensive clothing and jewelry. Each season the housewives take a vacation together as a group. This is always an important time, with several episodes devoted to chronicling the trip. This is also a prime opportunity for the housewives to look as good as possible with the right hair, makeup and the most stylish fashion selections. The vacations are always at very expensive hotels and resorts at some of the most expensive destinations around the world. Vacations on the *Real Housewives* reality show are always luxurious, booze-filled and full of drama. Remember, the goal is the same for reality television as it is for all other television shows: viewers. Therefore, it is extremely important to understand what the viewer is consuming when engaging with reality television.

One way to allegedly present your best self at all times, in addition to constantly having one's hair and makeup done by professionals, is through plastic surgery. Many *Housewives* episodes will show the women having botox parties or undergoing some form of cosmetic surgery. In the first episode of *The Real Housewives of Cheshire*, Tanya, whose tagline is 'I have the dream body, dream man, career – I've got it all', discusses her husband, children and how she enjoys shopping. The she talks of her love of plastic surgery: 'I do think that I need to grow up. Just being naughty and stuff, it just sort of gives me a bit of a [makes funny face] I love cosmetic surgery. Well I say that, I'm gonna have my boobs done' (Dunlop et al. 2015a). At the beginning of Episode 3, Tanya, Ampika and Leanne go as a group to have botox injections. The obsession with looking young is not a unique aspect of the new narcissus. Uniqueness for the new narcissus comes from an adaptation to obsessing over material objects: becoming the epitome of self-objectification. Seeing one's self as the ultimate object allows the new narcissus to shape and create one's body and face in a way that will garner the most narcissistic supply. The modern individual can now have cosmetic surgery in order for their body to fit the ideal vision they have of themselves. Plastic surgery procedures are not cheap. Be your best self or better yet be your best-created self. One is encouraged to accept the idea of radically altering one's face or body in order to reach some understanding of greatness. The 'real' housewives are often artificially constructed in the strictest sense, their faces and bodies adjusted accordingly.

What is important in understanding the pressures faced by the modern individual and the development of the new narcissus is self-objectification. For all the *Real Housewives* examined in this chapter, capitalism is the dominant form of the economy, where wealth and material objects are considered a reward for achieving success. For the new narcissus, the self becomes the ultimate object to be worked on, created, packaged and sold for consumption. In the case of the *Real Housewives* franchise, one must sell one's lifestyle and one's best (artificially constructed) self. The venue of the reality show is a means by which each housewife can project this *thing* of which they are the most proud: themselves. Even more telling of our modern era is the normalized aspect of plastic surgery. The new narcissus is merely the sad outcome of altering ourselves, even via torturous procedures, in order to fulfill the expectations of a consumer society.

Creating the artifice: 'It's so hot!'

The reader has witnessed Lauren from the *The Real Housewives of Cheshire* declare her love for diamonds and that through her sexuality she can obtain more diamonds. 'The consumer object produces distinction(s), produces status stratification' (Baudrillard 1998: 86). Plastic surgery allows (mostly) modern women to alter their body in order to present a more desired self, the ultimate consumer object. Through surgery women can maintain their beauty and presentation of youth, a highly desired commodity within our world. The *Housewives* embody the highest level of status stratification that Jean Baudrillard alludes to in his work *The Consumer Society.*

Pettifleur

The Real Housewives presents the viewer with the lifestyles of rich and sometimes famous housewives. Pettifleur Berenger, from the *Real Housewives of Melbourne*, demonstrates how valuable the artifice has become for the new narcissus. She is on a shopping excursion in Dubai with three other housewives. Pettifleur and Suzy have tried on some dresses and have come out of the fitting room to show Lydia and Gina. Pettifleur is completely enamored with her reflection in the store mirror.

> Lydia (in interview): The funny thing is that Pettifleur wouldn't take it off.
> Lydia: Pettifleur, you're such a show off. You are. Seriously.
> Lydia (in interview): I think she was more interested in looking at herself and prancing around in it. It was very, very funny.
> Lydia: It's way too big.
> Pettifleur: I love it, though.
> Pettifleur (in interview): It's massive on me but I just needed to see what my body looked like in that dress. And I liked what I saw.
> Gina (in interview): The whole vibe. She's just got such an inflated idea about her beauty.
> Gina: I've seen enough of your ass can you go put it away now?
> [snaps the top of Pettifleur's underwear that is showing]
> Pettifleur (in interview): I have never been shy when it comes to flaunting my body. When you've got it, flaunt it.
>
> (Washington 2016a)

The new narcissus is absolutely obsessed with the 'self' they have created. Through plastic surgery, extensive workout and diet regimens, the proper attire, hair and makeup … the entire *package* is now glorified. Lydia and Gina immediately point out Pettifleur's inability to pull herself away from looking at herself in the store mirror. They smile and laugh about her fixation on her own image; however, I believe this is a serious matter. People today often seem to shrug off the flamboyant and outlandish behavior of the new narcissus. Pettifleur even states in her interview that it wasn't the dress she was fixated on it was *her body*. 'I have never been shy when it comes to flaunting my body. When you've got it, flaunt it.' The narcissus sees the body as the ultimate project to be worked on. The women begin to appear annoyed with Pettifleur and her fixation upon the mirror.

> Gina: Have you had a good look?
> Pettifleur: No.
> Gina: Ok, keep looking.
> Gina (in interview): You know most women when they dress up want to inspire love, admiration, all those things but Pettifleur wants all that plus that element of jealousy so there's a bit of a little twist at the end and you can feel it.
>
> (Washington 2016a)

Gina calls Pettifleur out on her inability to part ways with the mirror and believes that not only is Pettifleur enamored with herself but she also wants the other women to be jealous of her looks. Sam Vaknin states that

> Women [narcissists] concentrate on their body […] they flaunt and exploit their physical charms, their sexuality, and their socially and culturally determined 'femininity'. They secure their Narcissistic Supply [attention, admiration, adoration] through their more traditional gender role: the home, children, suitable careers, their husbands, their feminine traits.
>
> (Vaknin 2001: 118)

Pettifleur, similar to many other housewives, is extremely preoccupied with her appearance, her 'look'. We shouldn't forget that Narcissus was fixated upon his reflection in a pond. The new narcissus needs not only their own reflection but to also see themselves reflected back through others. Are they beautiful enough to attract attention? What else must be altered in order to garner more stares and adulation from others? Pettifleur then tries on some sunglasses and proceeds to talk to herself as the other three girls are looking at a dress together.

> Pettifleur: No, these are flat aren't they?
> Gina: Who are you talking to love?
> Pettifleur: I'm just talking to myself.

[all three of the other women laugh]
Pettifleur (in interview): Yeah! When I'm trying to buy something I ask myself
[intentional pause and smile]
because I get the honest answer
[intentional pause and smile]
from myself.

(Washington 2016a)

Pettifleur believes that she is the best. She believes that she looks beautiful and attractive. She enjoys admiring her own beauty, her own creation, her own perfected self reflected back at her. 'The narcissist learns that the only person [s]he can trust to always and reliably be available, the only person [s]he can love without being abandoned or hurt – is [her]self' (Vaknin 2001: 32). The artifice is created as a result of living in a modern world that is not only accepting of falseness but at times, encourages it. Pettifleur relies on her 'self', this place of perceived comfort and security. Retreating too much inside one's self, as Durkheim warned, causes one to become too egotistical. Pettifleur now has a purse on her shoulder and she is back in front of the large store mirror (see Figure 7.1).

Pettifleur: You can see this honey, coming down the street. Look at that. It's hot. So hot.
Suzy (in interview): This is a new experience for me. Someone that shops like that, that just spends their entire time just looking at their reflection in the mirror.
[pretends to be Pettifleur in front of the mirror].

Figure 7.1 Pettifleur: 'That's so hot!'

Although Suzy believes Pettifleur's behavior is unusual, this is still a reflection of many modern individuals. People may not say their thoughts and feelings out loud, but the encouragement to glorify one's own body is prolific. Pettifleur appears to be the embodiment of an advertisement come to life. 'Look at that. It's hot. So hot.' *Don't you want to buy it?* Or maybe you'd be willing to pay me a little attention instead? Attention, admiration, adulation, adoration: the ultimate form of currency. Reality television is an advertisement for *real* life.

For a new show to secure viewers and profit, the premise and 'characters' must be unique, appealing, attractive, outlandish, dramatic, extreme and entertaining. This is why spotting the new narcissus within seemingly different reality television shows is not difficult. Regardless of content and plot, all reality shows must have unique personalities as the stars of the show. Reality television is fairly inexpensive to make, although as many reality shows become popular the main characters begin demanding very high fees. Some housewives have made up to seven figures each season, with many making at least $100,000 per season.

A few minutes of this particular episode are then devoted to showing the other housewives shopping before returning to Pettifleur, Suzy, Lydia and Gina.

> Pettifleur: I think I like this. Do you think that its too big for me?
> Suzy: They take too much of your face.
> Lydia: No, no.
> Pettifleur: Really?
> Gina: They're maybe a fraction too big.
> Lydia: They are a lot too big.
> Pettifleur: Are you girls jealous and you think I rock it so much?
> Lydia: Oh my gosh …
> Pettifleur: I'm only kidding! Take a bloody joke for Christ's sake.
> Lydia: No. Oh my God, I've never seen someone so … um, checked herself out so much. Hurry up!
> [slaps Pettifleur on her butt]
>
> (Washington 2016)

Pettifleur is seeking admiration from the other ladies in a confrontational manner that is later excused through the proclamation that it was simply a joke. 'The more he fails to secure the attention of the target group – the more daring, eccentric and outlandish he becomes' (Vaknin 2001: 125). Pettifleur's behavior may be an attempt to become the focus of this season's episodes. Her seemingly outlandish behavior and over the top rudeness to the other housewives causes reactive drama amongst the women and Pettifleur benefits. People are watching her. People are loving and admiring her. Pettifleur is typical of someone who has mastered the artifice but still has moments of desperate cries for attention. When narcissistic supply runs low, the new narcissus resorts to outbursts of insults in order to obtain the attention required.

Michaele Salahi: 'Every little girl wants to be Cinderella'

The viewer is first introduced to Michaele Salahi. She is in the process of having her makeup put on by professionals. A voiceover begins and then the camera switches to Michaele in an interview setting '[T]he new D.C. is colorful fashion, beautiful clothes [camera cuts away to Michaele in a hotel suite surrounded by other women as she looks at different dresses on a bed] so I spend a lot of time just trying to look good. I love to just make an entrance' (Gallagher and Greensfelder 2010). The camera then switches back to Michaele in a salon getting her hair done. There are two additional individuals observing Michaele and they appear to be listening hard to everything she has to say. Michaele proceeds to talk about how she did an event for President Barack Obama.

Michaele has summarized the city she lives in as 'colorful fashion, beautiful clothes'. So one's appearance is what is most important. Michaele even states that looking good is what she spends a lot of her time doing. In fact, this is how she has been introduced to the viewer. As a woman is who concerned about her appearance, looking good and wearing beautiful and likely expensive clothes. Georg Simmel's 1904 essay *Fashion* discusses the delineation of value in the modern world: 'fashion on the one hand signifies union with those in the same class […] and, *uno actu*, the exclusion of all other groups' (Simmel 1904: 102). The viewer must not forget that these women are members of an exclusive club and this show is a but a glimpse of their 'fabulous' lives, their carefully constructed and painstakingly presented lives. Reality television now serves as a new and powerful part of society that communicates who is a member of the elite group while simultaneously perpetuating the unachievable goal of satisfaction. Being beautiful. Looking good. Being distinct and elite. Are these the ideals of the modern woman? The reader has already witnessed the gendered messages about inclusion in today's social world in Chapter 2 with the exploration of the reality show *Toddlers and Tiaras.* The *Real Housewives* of today's modern world are the little girls in *Toddlers and Tiaras* all grown up.

> [In interview] When you first look at me you think 'God, she has no substance'. After I talk with them a little bit they see that I have a heart of gold and there is a whole lot of substance here. I was the average normal girl. I did modeling. When I met Tareq he exposed me to a whole different world. You know, I'd go to Paris for the night for dinner. He just wowed me. [camera shows Michaele and Tareq at dinner and he has given her a diamond bracelet] Every little girl wants to be Cinderella or have that fantasy prince and I definitely have mine. I was like wow, is this too good to be true?
>
> (Gallagher and Greensfelder 2010)

Michaele goes on to discuss that they live in Virginia's wine country and that Tareq owns Oasis Vineyard and is the President of the US Polo Cup. She states that they go into D.C. every day and that they often stay in hotels.

Many little girls are socialized through Disney films and there are important lessons to be learned by the young, impressionable viewer. In Disney films, the female leads often aspire to find love and a husband. Many are 'damsels in distress' needing to be rescued by their Prince Charming. There's a moral to many Disney stories: love is most important and can be obtained through one's beauty. Always look your best. *The Real Housewives* are Disney Princesses all grown up and come to life. Michaele is equating herself to Cinderella, whose beauty captured the heart of her very own Prince Charming: Tareq Salahi. Disney movies also teach the important lesson to men that their role is to woo women and ultimately strive to obtain the most beautiful woman you can find as your prize.

Today, child beauty pageants are a way for little girls to play princess for a day. The moral lessons of Disney have come to life with constant competition in the form of little girls dressing up in false appearances and housewives competing to be the most admired, the ultimate message being: the little girl/housewife with the best false appearance wins. Remember, the little princess that wins is increasing her chances of someday winning the prize of Prince Charming. Miss Ultimate Grand Supreme is the fairest of them all and one shot closer at stealing the heart of her very own Prince Charming. This prince will provide for your every need (material possessions) and the price is that you 'look good'. You can no longer be that *average* girl. Be an example of beauty, in fact, society's definition of beauty: 'material representation or embodiment of an ideal' (Merriam-Webster Online n.d.). Be the ideal that sells whatever adorns your body. The important role for a woman in a consumer world is how you look. Modeling and pageants have the same message for today's men and women: focus on your look … if it is appealing enough, it will transport you to a different world. *Paris. Diamonds.* If necessary, the best artificially constructed appearance wins above all. If you aren't naturally beautiful, there are a number of consumer remedies that will help you achieve the best artificially constructed appearance (makeup, pills, surgery). I mean, this all sounds too good to be true, doesn't it? Having created this perfect package. This perfected, beautifully falsified self that sells the best look.

Michaele was once that average girl and now she has succeeded in obtaining the prize of her Prince Charming; and in order to remain a success the modern housewife must be able to maintain their artifice. They must have their hair and makeup done often in order to continue presenting the best self, the one with wealth, status and privilege. For the new narcissus, having an audience, having others perform these menial tasks, is essential because applying one's own makeup or doing one's own hair is simply beneath them. After all, they've won haven't they? The ultimate life prize for the modern individual: monetary success, status and recognition. Regardless of whether or not individuals of today's society know the *Housewives*, their status is still solidified. The repeated message is that you, as viewer, can also improve your social position through your *look*.

What is not unique to housewife Michaele Salahi is her tendency to exaggerate in regards to her status and position within the elite class. In fact, Michaele and her husbands' tactics had previously been witnessed in *the Real Housewives of NYC* with Alex McCord and her husband Simon. Both women exemplify what is commonly referred to as a social climber, one who works too hard to be one of the most exclusive group. Even at the very top, individuals still experience the bottom. Both Alex and Michaele (and their husbands) often exaggerate their skills and accomplishments. It's ironic that social climbers are chastised when amongst the most elite, considering the climbers are merely attempting to emulate exactly the same things all elite individuals do. Maybe it's that they don't like being reminded of the reflection, of the artifice. It's just a little too in your face – tone it back a bit and just *be real*. Michaele, in her introduction, reveals that she put on event for the president of the United States and that her husband owns a vineyard and is the president of the U.S. Polo Cup. In reality, Tareq and Michaele *sponsored* an event called America's Polo Cup from 2007 to 2010. However, the title 'President' of a seemingly authentic national team, the U.S. Polo Cup, is how Michaele portrays her husbands' status and company rather than for what it is: a charity polo match. The new narcissus is extremely crafty in their ability to take seemingly trivial details and morph reality into one that matches their artifice.

Pettifleur: 'Give me some attention here'

This is Pettifleur Berenger's second season on *The Real Housewives of Melbourne* and the third season of the show. All of the housewives have arrived in Dubai for a vacation arranged by Chyka. After arriving at the hotel, the ladies have all met down by the pool for cocktails. Lydia and Pettifleur are the last to join the group. 'The girls are all chatting. The attention was drawn to Lydia, however, I've arrived in my very sheer skirt showing half my ass and my very sheer top. You know, give me some attention here!' Pettifleur is upset because she feels that no one gave her enough attention on arrival. Even more, Pettifleur wants attention for her appearance: sheer skirt, sheer top, showing lots of skin. In fact, Pettifleur is so upset by the lack of narcissistic supply she begins crying. Lydia notices and asks her what is wrong.

> Pettifleur (to Lydia as all the girls are having a drink): Nothing against you, but just then no one made eye contact with me. It was all like 'hello, hello, hello, to you'. It was like I didn't even exist. Fucking hurts. It really does. I'm pretty upset.
>
> (Washington 2016b)

Nothing against you but you prevented me from obtaining my means of survival. My supply of attention and adoration and admiration is never enough. *You* stopped me from receiving it but *nothing against you*. Lydia thinks that Pettifleur is upset with the girls when in reality Pettifleur is upset with everyone and there is no limit to the amount of manipulation she will inflict whenever her supply is jeopardized. All are guilty of the crime and she is the victim. The other women have now picked up on the fact that Pettifleur is crying:

> Lydia: When we both walked in. I said 'Hi Hi Hi' and everyone forgot about her.
> Chyka: Are you upset, really?
> [sounding concerned]
> I didn't know that anything had happened.
> Gina: Did no one say hello?
> Lydia: She felt that.
> [Lots of the women: 'Oh.']
> Janet: Oh, they never say hello to me either.
> Chkya: Don't let that upset you.
> Pettifleur (crying): *The whole attention was just like'hi …'*
> Gamble: You're taking things too seriously darling.
> Gina: Sorry.
> Chyka: Sorry, Pettifleur, we don't want you to start off like this.
> Pettifleur: It's ok. I'm used to it.
> Chyka: No. Don't be like that.
> Jackie: Let's do a tequila shot. Come on.
> [Chyka and Janet to each other]
> Janet: It doesn't matter how much attention.
> Chyka: It's not enough.
> Janet: No.
> Gina (in interview about this situation): This is where Pettifleur becomes hard work because she's ultra sensitive when it comes to her and completely lacks sensitivity when it comes to other people.
>
> (Washington 2016b)

Pettifleur says 'the whole attention was just like "Hi"' The new narcissus gets upset when a routine source of narcissistic supply (in this example, arriving to a social occasion) suddenly becomes an occasion where the narcissistic supply is inaccessible, or worse yet, the new narcissus loses out to someone else on the supply. The other women are confused as to why Pettifleur is crying because she didn't receive enough attention.

> The narcissist's answer is simple: because he is entitled to it. He feels that he deserves whatever he *succeeds* to extract from others and much more. Actually, he feels betrayed, discriminated against and underprivileged because he believes that he is not being treated fairly, that he should get more than he does.
>
> (Vaknin 2001: 29)

The other women are aware of Pettifleur's insatiable need for attention and adulation. Janet and Chyka both recognize this and Gina even points to the fact that giving Pettifleur all the attention she needs is 'hard work'. The new narcissus exploits others as though they are consumer objects to be used until they are no longer of any value (or until a newer, better version comes along). The new narcissus has self-objectified and in the process objectifies all others too. Other people are seen as objects to be consumed and then tossed aside once they are no longer deemed viable.

What's more is that these extravagant vacations are witnessed on every *Real Housewives* show. One wife usually hosts the trip and arranges all the activities. It is a ripe opportunity for narcissistic supply. The women look their best and compete for the most attention. What are you wearing? Who did your hair? Sell your best self and the most watched lifestyle. But don't be a phoney. We need you to master your best self and really commit to being *her*. No one wants to buy a fake; at least, they want the projection of authenticity … you know, as long as it plays the part well.

Sell your (false) greatness to others

Tareq and Michaele Salahi: sneaking in

During the fourth episode, Michaele and Tareq have invited all the other housewives to Oasis Vineyard for a grape stomp. As the housewives are on the way to the vineyard in a limo, Stacie receives a voicemail from Tareq saying that his mother has tried to cause trouble and that there is extra security present at the vineyard. Tareq, in an interview, informs the audience that his Mom sued to end his ownership of the vineyard. In an interview, Mary says 'My main motivation to going out to that grape stomp is to see what the actual truth is out there. What is going on out there?'

Jason Backe (celebrity hair colorist): The first time that I, and I'm interested to hear what they said about this night. The Black Congressional Caucus dinner. We got there …

Stacie: I saw the pictures it looked fabulous. It seemed like you guys had a great time.

Celebrity Colorist: We had a great time. It was amazing after we snuck in and had no tickets.

Stacie: What do you mean snuck in?

Jason: You, snuck in to the congressional black caucus dinner?

Celebrity Colorist: Snuck in.

Jason: Wow.

Stacie: Why would you sneak in?

Celebrity Colorist: Nobody had tickets. And there was this whole story going on about our friends were supposed to meet us here. They have the tickets. They're on their way. And everything was happening very,

> very quickly and we like saw a bus boy coming out from a side door and we snuck in the side door.
>
> (Gallagher and Greensfelder 2010)

Tareq and Michaele wanted to be known as invited guests to the Congressional Black Caucus dinner. They wanted the prestige and more importantly, the attention that comes with being on the guest list of such an exclusive event. Exclusivity is of utmost importance for the new narcissus. Stacie and her husband Jason are in complete and utter shock at this revelation that has just occurred in the limo on the way to Michaele and Tareq's alleged winery. Stacie proceeds to call Tareq out of concern that the group is going to be walking into something questionable. After all, she has just learned that they snuck in a side door in order to go to the Congressional Black Caucus Dinner. Stacie asks Tareq what the situation is with his mother to which Tareq replies 'Well, you know, she's up to her games.' The phone call is cut short after Cat asks if it's safe for the group go to the winery.

As the group arrives at the vineyard Michaele and Tareq are acting oblivious to the strange circumstance of security all over the vineyard. Cat decides to call them out:

> Cat: Its very bizarre to have security here in the middle of nowhere. I mean, what's going on?
> Michaele: We're excited you're here. We're happy to have that behind us.
> Cat: Well you know it was only 15 minutes ago for us so its not that far behind.
> Michaele: Oh.
> Cat: Anyway …
> Mary: Can I have a little more please?
> [holds out her wine glass]
> [everyone laughs].
>
> (Gallagher and Greensfelder 2010)

Instantly, Michaele tries to avoid the negative questioning. Avoid the attempted sabotage of narcissistic supply. *I need everyone to pay attention to our beautiful winery. We are going to have such an amazingly fun day today!* Think of going to a car dealer and asking questions about a car you are considering purchasing. If you point out a flaw how does the salesmen react? Turn that frown upside down! Sure, there may be this negative quality but have you seen these five other great features? Same here for the new narcissus, you must truly master the projection of the artifice. Michaele and her husband are dedicated to the story that they are the owners of Oasis Winery. Owning a vineyard communicates success and power to others, and all the while Tareq and Michaele gloss over the litigation they have been involved in.

As the grape stomping event continues, Cat becomes more annoyed with the story. She points out to Mary that the grapes the women are stomping on are supermarket grapes. Cat leaves the event with Jason, the celebrity stylist, shortly after this. Many of the housewives speak about the outlandish behavior and extravagant ways of Tareq and Michaele Salahi. Cat is annoyed with the behavior. In fact, she can't stand it. Not all housewives are narcissistic, but they do embody an ideal: to always present your best self even if that self is false.

Later in the season Michaele proclaims that she used to be an NFL cheerleader. 'I'm a former Washington Redskins cheerleader for the NFL. I did the cheering through the 80s and we've been getting ready for a great halftime show for the Redskins' first home game and love our Redskins! Go Redskins!' The viewer then follows Michaele from her hotel suite with Tareq where she twirled her pompoms around to a practice being held in a stadium parking lot. Michaele looks the part, she is dressed in a black top and black pants with black dance shoes. She also has the correct pompoms. When the alumni begin to perform their dance Michaele is noticeably lost. One cheerleader even asks her 'do you know the whole routine?' To which Michaele responds with a smile (see Figure 7.2). *Smile, keep trying*. Michaele proceeds to run around to different alumni cheerleaders, giving them hugs and saying 'Oh, Hi! Hey you!' Later it is revealed in article published in 2009 by Paul Farhi of the *Washington Post* that Michaele was never a cheerleader for the Washington Redskins: 'The group's president, Terri Lamb, said Wednesday, "We have no record that she ever was a Redskins cheerleader. She was listed on our 1991 roster at Ms. Salahi's request and based on her misrepresentation to us."' Michaele is an expert at misrepresentation. She has become an expert at the artifice. *Keep smiling*. There's always a way to more prestige, notoriety, exclusiveness and attention.

Figure 7.2 Michaele practicing her performance

The new narcissus comes to the state dinner

Hair Stylist: So what are we doing today? What's the big event?

Michaele: Tonight is a really big night. It's a special dinner and um, it's really important. It's confidential and it's the state dinner.

Hair Stylist: Ooo!

Michaele: The president will be there and I can't wait. Being in that room with the prime minister and Mr. Tau-Tau and his wife and the ambassador of India. Its funny because I used to go to the White House. I was a makeup artist and I used to go and work with the Vice President and First Ladies. Its great to go back now as a guest. You know, you see it from both sides.

Hair Stylist: So how did you get the invitation? When did you get the invitation?

Michaele: Well it just came. That's the thing. The first way it came was through a phone call.

Michaele (voiceover): For me, the most important part of the invitation was getting the phone call. That was the biggest high that day when I found out that we were going to be invited.

(Gallagher and Greensfelder 2010)

Michaele is so excited to be attending the White House state dinner, especially now that she has worked her way up in her social world. She once was an employee doing the makeup of these important people and now *she* is an important person. *She* is a guest at the White House state dinner. Her elite status and prestige is so highly rewarding for her artificially constructed self. Notice that Michaele says 'that was the biggest high that day when I found out that we were going to be invited'. Instantly, the thought of a personal invitation to the White House is so satisfying, like a drug, which provides a high for the new narcissus.

But when prompted to show the invitation Michaele cannot find it. Michaele asks Tareq and seems concerned that the invitation is missing. Tareq assures her that they don't need an invitation. Tareq states in an interview: 'An invitation to the White House is really a formality. It's something that you keep. Possibly frame with pictures that you took when you went to the White House. You do not need the actual invitation in order to go to the White House'. After getting dressed, Michaele and Tareq proceed in a limousine to the dinner. The film crew follows as the couple approaches a checkpoint. Security cannot find the Salahi's name on the list. Michaele makes a joke that they always spell her name wrong and the checkpoint officer laughs. Security then tells the Salahis to proceed to the event. Near the end of Episode 8, which concludes with herself and Tareq heading into the state dinner, Michaele says 'you work hard and you give a lot of love; you end up at the White House'. Michaele fervently believes in her greatness, even though it may be a complete falsehood.

Two days after the White House dinner on Thanksgiving Thursday, the *Washington Post* ran a story revealing that Tareq and Michaele Salahi had crashed the event. As one former White House senior staffer stated when asked how this could have happened,

> A savvy pair of crashers, dressed to the nines, might arrive on foot at the visitors' entrance, announce their names – then express shock and concern when the security detail at the gate failed to find them on the guest list. On a rainy night like Tuesday, with a crowd of 300-plus arriving, security might have lost track of or granted a modicum of sympathy to a pair who *certainly looked as though they belonged there.*
>
> (Argetsinger 2009, my italics)

Michaele and Tareq Salahi know how to play the part very well and are always prepared for it by looking as though they belong where they are. They have become experts at the new narcissus and they know how to sell their fake status very well. At the beginning of Episode 9 viewers witnessed the pair reviewing photos from the event at the White House. Michaele exclaims: 'the dinner was really exciting and I was quite a buzz in the room. I definitely love to meet people and that night I was having such a great time and I had a chance to talk with Vice President Joe Biden at length and that was a huge high for me' (Gallagher and Greensfelder 2010). Michaele immediately points to the fact that she was a 'buzz in the room', that is, people loved her. Michaele loves to meet new people because she excels at meeting new people. Smile and they'll all love you. This is the second time the viewer hears Michaele describe her experience of the White House dinner as a 'high'. For the new narcissus, the attention garnered from 300 of some of the most powerful people in the United States is absolutely unparalled. Narcissists love to receive their drug, narcissistic supply, from important and powerful people. Tareq states in an interview:

> Being at the White House for the State Dinner was very surreal. It just was incredible, we couldn't sleep for uh, hours after we got back home just because we were so excited about the evening. It was just such a wonderful moment that we're gonna treasure forever.

The experience was so wonderful that both Tareq and Michaele were buzzing off the high. In the chapter on *Celebrity Rehab* we have already explored the parallels between the new narcissus' quest for attention and celebrities who suffer from addiction.

Both Tareq and Michaele have huge grins when discussing their time at the White House dinner. Tareq then mentions that there is a story in the *Washington Post* about them. As he speaks he is smiling the entire time.

> The gossip columnist in the *Washington Post* suggested that Michaele and I may have snuck in, oh come on its so crazy, ridiculous to even

> suggest that. I mean it's actually disrespectful to, really to the Secret Service and to the White House, but of course that would never happen at the White House.
>
> (Gallagher and Greensfelder 2010)

Tareq is totally enthralled by the fact that he has a story written about him in the *Washington Post*. As Vaknin says, '[t]here is almost nothing that the narcissist refrains from doing, almost no borders that he hesitates to cross to achieve renown. To him, there is no such thing as 'bad publicity' – what is important is to be in the public eye' (Vaknin 2001: 124). Michaele and Tareq received some of the best narcissistic supply they will ever achieve: attention from some of the most powerful people in America. To them, anything that happens as a result of them faking their way into the event is a reminder of that ultimate high. Bad publicity and public shaming do not seem to effect Tareq and Michaele. In fact, they were called before a House of Representatives Committee on Homeland Security, where they were questioned about their crashing the event (see Figure 7.3).

Both Michaele and Tareq plead the Fifth Amendment and refuse to answer any questions. Remember, there is no such thing as bad publicity so they keep smiling. At times, they stop and whisper with their lawyer before again repeating the Fifth Amendment. Stacie and her husband Jason are shown

Figure 7.3 Tareq and Michaele before the House Committee

reacting to the story in the *Washington Post*. Stacie calls the story to her husband's attention.

> Jason: Something is not making sense here. You can't just like get in, I mean we're not talking about a club we are talking about the White House. We've been to the White House before and there's no way.
> Stacie: There's no way.
> Jason: That you can crash a White House party.
> Stacie: You know what? It really is scary because the President could have been in danger. I mean you never know.
> Jason: You never know and that's why it's really terrible for them.
> Stacie: The fact that they got in is …
> Jason: Is an issue, is a serious problem.
> Stacie: Oh my god. It said that they posted photos of themselves with VIPs at the elite gather! Oh, on Facebook!
>
> (Gallagher and Greensfelder 2010)

Jason says the fact they were able to successfully sneak in to the White House dinner is 'a serious problem'. He may be referring to the breach of security and how it could have been an opportunity for someone else to put the president's life in danger. However, this event in American history may be reflective of a deeper issue and problem within the United States: the proliferation of the new narcissus. If you can successfully sell your (false) greatness to others then that's just as good as actually being great.

Maintaining the image is exhausting

What happens when people discover the artifice or the new narcissus is criticized for being false? Unfortunately, the new narcissus will do whatever it takes to avoid facing reality. This is the irony of reality television. Everyone knows its 'not real' yet it projects the impression of authenticity. For the new narcissus to remain successful they have to master their ability to avoid the truth (reality) and maintain the illusion.

Following the traumatic experience of testifying before the House Committee and two months after the White House state dinner, Stacie invites Tareq and Michaele over to have dinner and drinks. Cat is in attendance, but Mary and Linda refuse to attend. Cat is mostly quiet during the exchange and does not say hello to Tareq or Michaele. In an interview Cat states 'I just couldn't believe they walked in there in their plastic, fake, superficial way, talking about how lovely the décor was and this and that and la, la, la' (Gallagher and Greensfelder 2010). Finally, Cat gets up and retrieves her jacket and then addresses Tareq and Michaele: 'I just want to say before I go that I think the both of you are two of the most artificial, fake people I have ever met in my entire life. Thank God I got to the age of 38 before having ever to associate myself with anybody like you. You're a disgrace to America and you are a disgrace to. And at this point, Michaele stands up to leave the room, saying 'Cat, I won't take your abuse.' Cat continues to criticize Michaele's behavior as she retreats as far back in the house as she can.

This is the important final stage of the new narcissus: avoidance. Michaele and Tareq avoided the questions of the House Committee by pleading the Fifth Amendment. Now, when confronted again with their deceit, Michaele refuses to face the truth. She only wants the narcissistic supply. Remember Bryan, a.k.a. Skylar, from the reality show *Catfish*? This whole 'fake' performance is just a means to obtain more narcissistic supply. Cat leaves, and Stacie informs Michaele that Cat's invitation to the White House Christmas Party has been revoked because of the Salahi's connection to the show.

> Stacie: We don't want to prosecute you like everyone else has.
> Michaele: We can't even go there so I have to sign off. Signing off!
> Tareq: We actually have to leave.
> Michaele: We're not allowed to talk about that.
> Stacie: We're not talking about that but it would be bizarre to not.
> Michaele: I can't. We love you guys but we can't talk about that. I'm sure you understand that.
> Stacie: The reality is nobody could like be in a room with you after that and not ask like 'what's goin' on? What happened? How do you feel?' All of those normal questions that everybody would want to know. That's unrealistic.
> Michaele: The good thing is that the people that really know us can be in a room with us. And talk about happy things: their families, the day, what's productive.
>
> (Gallagher and Greensfelder 2010)

As soon as Michaele and Tareq are confronted with the reality that they are being called out for crashing the White House state dinner they instantly shut down the conversation. Michaele is focused on obtaining narcissistic supply; she does not want to face the artifice. She only wants to be with people who provide attention and admiration, not criticism. Stacie and her husband Jason are not only enabling Michaele and Tareq, they're anxiously awaiting their performance. By watching, by consuming we feed the new narcissus more and more.

> Jason: We really enjoyed hanging out with you guys and its hard for us quite honestly because the Tareq and Michaele that is read about in the newspaper and seen on TV, that is not the Michaele and Tareq that, that we know. [...] Whether you realize it or not, you guys are wearing a scarlet letter right now and we really hope that you guys are able to remove that shame from the Salahi name. Your parents worked hard, you guys worked hard.

Tareq: Yeah, no, there's no shame.
Michaele: I think we're talking about it again. I think it's time to go.
(Gallagher and Greensfelder 2010)

Avoid being confronted with your falseness. Avoid the consequences of your falseness. Tareq is so committed to the new narcissus that he doesn't even recognize the shame associated with his artificial self. Sam Vaknin warned that children who experience deep shame growing up will then attempt to eliminate any further experiences of shame in adulthood. Tareq is caught in his lie yet refuses to be ashamed in an attempt to compensate for possible shame experienced in childhood. *Keep it moving. Keep the image in focus.*

The mirror's reflection is 'devastating to us'

There was another occasion when the Salahis avoided being confronted with the behaviors of the new narcissus. At the grape stomp, following Cat and Jason's departure, Mary, Stacie and Jason had food and wine with Michaele and Tareq in a room with wine barrels. In the last few minutes of Episode 4, Tareq announces to the group that he has something to say. Mary, in an interview, alludes to the fact that she had no idea what Tareq was about to do. The first few minutes of Episode 5 pick up at the wine dinner. Tareq has just informed the group that a car was stolen in connection with his US Polo Team.

Tareq: All that gear got stolen.
Mary: Aww.
Tareq: And I mean the boots, the jerseys. I mean, no no.
Stacie: By who?
Tareq: No no. You know what? We're the most forgiving people …
Mary: Get to the point please.
Tareq: This agency came to us and they said your daughter, unfortunately, was on Facebook admitting 'did we enjoy that joy ride in that car we took from the America's Polo Cup'. And they were all wearing my jacket, my jersey and my polo mallet.
Stacie: But who did it? Are you saying that her daughter did it?
[Tareq nods yes]
Michaele: Well she was a part of it.
Mary: So you are directly implicating my daughter?
Tareq: And the FBI had been investigating this.
Jason: The FBI?
Tareq: And they were monitoring for the last 6 months every email, every conversation.
Jason: Tareq are you honestly telling me that the FBI is monitoring polo theft, I mean?

Tareq: When it comes to a $90,000 car, $25,000 gear.
Mary: These are big accusations.
Tareq: It's quite serious.

(Gallagher and Greensfelder 2010)

So Tareq has accused Mary's daughter Lolly of being involved in the theft of his vehicle and polo gear. He has also announced that the FBI has been investigating Lolly and her friends for six months, and then almost instantly claimed that he and Michaele are 'the most forgiving people'. However, this last claim might merely be a strategy in their relentless pursuit of narcissistic supply rearing its ugly head at the end of this dinner.

Stacie: This is her daughter. The mere fact that her name has been thrown out connected with …
Michaele: It's devastating to us!
Stacie: It's devastating and I can only imagine how she feels. What are the accusations that they are making so that she can deal with that.

(Gallagher and Greensfelder 2010)

Michaele is unable to empathize with Mary at all during this moment. The narcissist is unable to empathize with other individuals. Instead, Michaele is only focused on how she is affected by the car and gear being stolen. It's 'devastating to us!' She believes the devastation is not for Mary (whose daughter has just been accused of theft) but for herself and her husband! As the conversation continues, she begins to harp about the charity and how the real issue is how the charity has been affected. It's almost as if Michaele feels that being concerned about theft from their charity is somehow better than her being concerned only about herself. She is attempting to shift focus from her in-your-face narcissism to the more noble concern for the charity.

Tareq: Look, look. You know what I care about? I care about what happened to that gear.
Jason: Tareq, with all due respect, you know we cool, but are we really talking about polo gear?
Stacie: We're not talking about gear. How does this affect Mary and her child.
Michaele: We've already seen that her name is attached so we need to wait and see exactly how …
Stacie: No we don't need to wait and see anything.

(Gallagher and Greensfelder 2010)

Stacie and Jason are very concerned over the allegations Tareq and Michaele are bringing up against Mary's daughter Lolly. In fact, they appear to be somewhat shocked that they are even doing this. 'The narcissist's tales are so patently absurd that he often catches people off-guard' (Vaknin 2001:

102). This is the subtle outlandishness of the new narcissus. Tareq has exclaimed that they only thing he cares about is 'what happened to that gear'. The material possessions are what Tareq cares about and just as important, the damage this theft has done to him. Any perceived damage to the narcissus is blown out of proportion. Later, in an interview, Tareq says 'I didn't understand why Jason and Stacie were so upset. Because you know, a crime was committed against Michaele and I. We're the victims here. We're the ones that had all our car stolen and all our gear stolen. It's not about poor Lolly.' Tareq claims that he and Michaele are the victims. By becoming the victim, or at least playing that part, the new narcissus obtains narcissistic supply. Attention, admiration and adoration all come to someone who claims to have been victimized. The conversation carries on a few more moments before Mary leaves the table and everyone else follows. Stacie, Jason and Mary talk in the limo about how shocking the evening was after such a lovely day.

Later Stacie tells Cat and Linda what happened at the vineyard. She discusses how she was so shocked after spending time with them in Paris and then the nice day at the vineyard to suddenly witness Tareq and Michaele behave in such a drastically different manner. 'You're living a farce. What kind of people are you?' As Sam Vaknin states:

> The narcissist needs an audience to applaud, affirm, recoil, approve, admire, adore, fear, or even detest him. He craves the attention and depends on the Narcissistic Supply only others can provide. The narcissist derives sustenance only from the outside – his emotional innards are hollow and moribund.
>
> (Vaknin 2001: 88)

The Salahis are concerned with one thing and one thing only: securing narcissistic supply. Any attention will do, even negative attention. If playing the victim is what is required in order to receive their narcissistic supply then the new narcissus will gladly oblige. What is unique about the new narcissus and victimization is that often the new narcissus is the cause of their own victimization. The new narcissus has no moral barrier to prevent them from hurting and exploiting others in order to achieve their own selfish desires. Only when Stacie and Jason expressed such shock at the couple's behavior did Tareq and Michaele suddenly act defensively regarding the accusations they made against Mary's daughter Lolly. The entire accusation was an attempt to obtain narcissistic supply and when Stacie and her husband admonished Tareq and Michaele for their behavior the pair went into defense mode.

The new narcissus is a 'mean girl'

Similarly, another very clear example of the final stage of avoidance concerns Pettifleur from *The Real Housewives of Melbourne*. Earlier in the chapter it was mentioned that the housewives had ventured to Dubai for a vacation hosted by Chyka, and that Pettifleur had not started off the vacation on a very positive note, claiming to have been ignored by the other women when she arrived for drinks by the pool. Pettifleur successfully played the victim in order to secure the attention she so desperately needed. Later on in the trip, Jackie learns that Pettifleur has been calling her a 'mean girl' behind her back, so Jackie confronts her and demands to know what is supposed to make her a 'mean girl'.

> Pettifleur: You say things about me like 'you're annoying' but tell me why I'm annoying.
> Jackie: Well I'll tell you why you're annoying. You have a beautiful girl over here named Chyka that you told looked too frumpy in a white dress. That says she needs to change her lipstick and make it darker. Now that's a mean girl.
> [Pettifleur looks confused]
> Jackie: You. You're the mean girl. Not me.
> Pettifleur: Ok.
> Jackie: You call her the black widow. Do you know how mean girl that is? You actually said to her 'why should I come to your wedding?' That is mean girl.
> Gamble (in interview): Pettifleur's not mean, she's a bitch.
> Jackie: I have never talked about the way you dress to people. I have never bitched behind your back to people and I certainly haven't discussed what you do even though I see it as annoying and crude and ignorant and how you degrade people.
> Pettifleur: I degrade people?
> Jackie: You do.
> Jackie (in interview): I've seen her be rude to clothing assistants, shop assistants. Why? Because all of a sudden she lives somewhere in the top of the penthouse in the city? It's like 'no, girlfriend'.
>
> (Washington 2016b)

Jackie is very adept at criticizing Pettifleur's hypocritical behavior. When she learns that Pettifleur has been calling her a mean girl it sends her over the edge because she feels that the real mean girl in the group is Pettifleur. Interviews with other housewives that are shown during this segment indicate that the other housewives agree.

> Jackie: I used to clean windows. I used to vacuum floors. I used to clean toilets.
> Pettifleur: That's fine, good for you.
> Jackie: And I said I remember where I come from. You don't. You think you're King shit. When we were at the beach and you started crying. Boo-hoo! What? Because nobody said you look fucking fabulous?
> [camera cuts to Gina in an interview setting]

Gina (in interview): I have never come across a woman who is so self-absorbed as Pettifleur. She should actually employ a motivational speaker, just to be in her ear all day.
Gina (talking to Pettifleur): You do have a way of rubbing people the wrong way. Its like with Chyka, you've insulted her. Maybe it's the way you're saying it.
Pettifleur: Are you my friend?
Gina: Don't give me that bullshit.
Pettifleur: Give me some supportive shit.
Gina: I'm trying to help you! Ok so let me …
Pettifleur: I didn't know talking about lipstick could be so … kindergarten fighting …

(Washington 2016b)

Jackie sees the new narcissus and is not afraid to call attention to the artifice. Pettifleur has acted extremely full of herself the entire trip and her incessant need for attention is overwhelming for many of the housewives. Pettifleur is not afraid to be outrageous, self-righteous and even rude in her behavior towards the other housewives as long as she receives the narcissistic supply she so desperately needs.

Pettifleur: Oh, come on!
Gina: They all care about you.
Pettifleur (with tears in her eyes): Really?!
Gina: They feel that you actually care more about yourself than them.
Pettifleur: I do.
Suzy: How are we supposed to be your friend Pettifleur?! When you've got that attitude?

Pettifleur, similar to Tareq and Michaele in *The Real Housewives of D.C.*, is not ashamed to admit that all she cares about is herself. 'The narcissist begins to believe his own lies. He makes himself to be what he wants to be and not what he really is' (Vaknin 2001: 42). When confronted with lies, manipulation and abuse, the new narcissus will not only avoid the confrontation but they will then adjust themselves accordingly in order to improve their presentation of the artifice. Remember, the self is always a project to be worked on. One may even be so engrossed in one's 'storyline' that one no longer knows what is real and what is false.

Pettifleur: ARE YOU KIDDING ME?!? Are you kidding? All of you have yelled. Chyka has upset me because I was complimenting her.
Janet: You never complimented her …
Chyka: Pettifleur, am I not allowed to get upset? You were not complimenting me.

Chyka (in interview): I never talk to you like that. I never ever say negative things to you. I'm only ever saying nice things to you. Why do you feel it's ok to do it to me?

Pettifleur (yelling): Come on Chyka! You are a grown woman!

(Washington 2016b)

Pettifleur attempts to claim that she complimented Chyka by saying she looked frumpy in a white dress and needed to change her lipstick because it wasn't the right lipstick color for the dress she had on. Clearly, Pettifleur insulted Chyka, she did not compliment her. However, Pettifleur is thoroughly convinced of her rightness. She may not be aware of her behavior towards others, but the reality is she insulted Chyka and now she sees this insult as giving a compliment, and that she is the one who is being attacked by the group. When criticized, the new narcissus will not only avoid facing the facts, they will also attempt to turn the confrontation into an opportunity to receive more narcissistic supply. Again, just as we witnessed in *The Real Housewives of D.C.* when the Salahis were called out for bad behavior, almost instantaneously the new narcissus, in this case Pettifleur, uses criticism as an opportunity to play the victim.

Gina (in interview): She's a victim. It's actually driving me mad. It's enough. Snap the fuck out of it.

Gina: It's absolute bullshit. You're not playing the victim card. Fuck you! I'm not putting up with that shit. You call her a black fucking widow and what do you want? You tell me to walk out the door and hope the door doesn't slap you on the ass on the way out. And then you think there's a friendship?

Pettifleur (in interview): I will change my behavior if I think I need to change my behavior. I didn't listen to a word she was saying … so. I'm fine as I am.

[Pettifleur then proceeds to lie down next to the table]

Gina: Friendship is about how you make the people around you feel. That's it. It's as simple as that. If you're making them feel like shit. You're not going to have friendship. Ok? Jesus.

(Washington 2016b)

Gina jumped at the chance to support Jackie's condemnation of Pettifleur. The new narcissus often pushes people to the point where they can no longer contain their feelings. The new narcissus is always convinced of their righteousness and elevated status, even though their position has been obtained through the projection of an artifice. The new narcissus does not want to face their deep down, true self. Pettifleur has begun to alienate the other housewives through her rude and callous behavior. However, she fails to accept responsibility for her actions. Instead, she proceeds to lie down next to the table instead of hearing what some of the housewives have to say.

'[A]ny sign of disapproval, disagreement criticism, or remonstrance – reduce[s] him to a state of insulted, sulking agitation' (Vaknin 2001: 210). Pettifleur must now play the role of martyr in order to continue receiving narcissistic supply.

The reflection is a misrepresentation of reality

Many of the housewives begin to distance tehmselves from Pettifleur as a result of her behavior. In fact, the following night at dinner, Janet tells her:

> For four or five days I decided I loved you and I actually really worked on it because I was very interested to have a relationship with you. After about four or five days it didn't matter how much I loved you it was a bottomless pit. It was never enough for you. It never filled the void. You still were *about you*. You didn't really give a shit about me except for what I could do for you.
>
> (Washington 2016b)

Herein lies the epitome of the new narcissus. The modern individual is living in an anomic world where one is socialized to believe that participation in consumerism is the route to personal happiness. Modern individuals are encouraged to see themselves as an object to be 'worked on' and created.

> Unlimited desires are insatiable by definition and insatiability is rightly considered a sign of morbidity. Being unlimited, they constantly and infinitely surpass the means at their command; they cannot be quenched. Inextinguishable thirst is constantly renewed torture.
>
> (Durkheim 1951: 256).

This is the state of our modern world, socialized to pursue an insatiable goal: material possessions and wealth. No matter how much wealth or material objects one obtains the void within one's self will never be filled. That is the illusion, the misrepresentation of reality. Janet described Pettifleur as a 'bottomless pit' and said that there was never enough love to satisfy her. The new narcissus has developed as an adaption to our modern world. The new narcissus, lacking any real sense of self-confidence or self-esteem, develops an artificial self as a means through which to receive the most attention, admiration and adoration from others, in order to achieve a success that does not seem possible through their genuine self. The new narcissus is dependent on narcissistic supply in order to thrive in the modern world.

> The narcissist is forced to use other people in order to feel that he exists. It is through their eyes and through their behavior that he obtains proof of his uniqueness and grandeur.
>
> (Vaknin 2001: 29)

Often, the new narcissus is a successful individual who may be envied and loved by many people. When the artifice, and the manipulation the new narcissus has inflicted on others, is exposed then avoidance is the solution. Pettifleur wants to avoid Janet's accusations. She does not want to admit to her behavior, accept responsibility or face up to the artifice she has created.

> Pettifleur (in interview): I could see that she was asking me for some sort of apology …
> Pettifleur: To me Janet, if that's how you're feeling. I'm really sorry. I don't mean to make you feel that way.
> Pettifleur (in interview): I'm like ok, I'll shut the bitch up and I gave it to her.
> Chyka: That's all she wanted to hear.
> Janet: That's all I wanted to hear. Pettifleur, let's go on from here you and I.
> [Pettifleur gets up and goes around the table to give Janet a hug.
> Gamble rolls her eyes]
> Gamble (in interview): I find this so ungenuine.
>
> (Washington 2016b)

Pettifleur shuts down the conversation with Janet by 'shut[ting] the bitch up'. She issues a fake apology to Janet in order to secure her as a source of narcissistic supply (see Figure 7.4). Pettifleur, possibly recognizing her vulnerable position following the previous night's disastrous dinner, may find herself desperate to retain the friendship – i.e. narcissistic supply – of any of the housewives. More importantly, her place on the show may be in jeopardy, so she must attempt to mend as many relationships as possible. Gamble, a fellow housewife, sees this for what it is: a charade.

Figure 7.4 'I'll shut the bitch up!'

> To a certain degree, we all exploit each other. But, the narcissist abuses people. He misleads them into believing that they mean something to him, that they are special and dear to him, and that he cares about them. When they discover that it was all a charade, they are likely to respond much more forcefully than usual [...] It is a vicious cycle: the narcissist alienates people and they leave him. This, in turn, convinces him that he was always right in thinking that people are selfish and will always prefer their self-interest to his welfare. His off putting behavior is, thus, enhanced, leading to yet more serious emotional ruptures with his nearest and dearest.
>
> (Vaknin 2001: 65)

The new narcissus is doomed to this endless cycle of self-objectification and avoidance. When some aspect of the constructed self fails the new narcissus avoids facing their responsibility in the creation of that falseness and their focus turns to modifying and improving the artifice. Pettifleur, upon further reflection into her projection of self, quickly retreats and performs the obligatory apology even when she admits in an interview setting that she doesn't really mean it. This is a clear articulation of the importance of projecting an artifice and avoiding, retreating and then repeating that artifice when in danger of losing one's supply. It's like the directions on a shampoo bottle: wash, rinse and repeat. Project an artifice, deny and avoid when confronted with your lie and then modify the artifice as quickly as possible in order to resume the production. That is always the goal for the new narcissus: to maintain one's supply of validation.

There are so many other 'Real Housewives' who exemplify the characteristics of the new narcissus and who have not been discussed in this chapter. One important connection to conclude with is that many of these women are the little girls in *Toddlers and Tiaras* all grown up. Being a 'Real Housewife' is similar to having the status of Ultimate Grand Supreme. You may win the title one year but you may not be asked back for next year's season. The hard lessons for the little girls of *Toddlers and Tiaras* still exist for the grown women of *The Real Housewives*: self-objectification, the importance of your 'look', being the most extravagant in order to win, selling yourself, and realizing just how exhausting maintaining the image can be. Very few will win but all want the top prize: to be recognized as the best (Ultimate Grand Supreme title or the most talked about housewife). One important distinction that develops over the life course for the housewives is the realization that being the bad girl can get you the same rewards as being the good girl. There are no rewards for being the 'best' housewife, unless 'best' means the most talked about on blogs, social media, and even national news, because that status will not only result in more narcissistic supply but more money and material possessions, the ultimate form of happiness. For grown ups, the well-developed new narcissus has learned that sometimes an individual can obtain the same rewards through being amoral. The new narcissus is a symptom of our society, an adaptation of the gravest kind to living in a consumer environment. The lesson that artificial can be just as good as the real thing is profuse within our society and the new narcissus is the sad outcome of the modern individual who is excelling in the classroom of life.

8 Entranced by the new narcissus' reflection gazing back at us

The preceding exploration of six reality television shows uncovered the message and ultimately the consequences of media socialization. What emerges in this analysis of our experiences today is the idea of the false self, the new narcissus. An extreme focus on the individual, concern with material possessions, limitless aspirations, obsession with success and notoriety – all contribute to the development of a false self all while losing sight of our true, distinct and unique individual nature. The new narcissus takes over, showing that individual how easy it is to fake it and they better they fake it, more success, possessions and notoriety are sure to follow. Christopher Lasch warned of the dangers of narcissism in the late 1970s. Today, with the growth of reality television, individuals are internalizing the message of narcissism.

By examining the individuals taking part in these six reality television programs the new narcissus emerges as a result of experiences, experiences which are vital to the human condition. Should one's experiences speak to lessons of falseness and trauma then the new narcissus begins to appear. This process through which the false self begins to gaze back when we look into our reflection, occurs as a result of a consumer-structured society. Lasch wrote of how an increasingly bureaucratic environment (a symptom of a consumer society) leads individuals to focus more upon themselves even to the point of damaging their social relationships with others. This study of reality television aims to shed light on our culture's new story of narcissism that can be witnessed and *experienced* within reality television.

Anomic adaptation

Modern individuals live in a society ruled by the pursuit of the accumulation of material goods. '[T]he humans of the age of affluence are surrounded not so much by other human beings, as they were in all previous ages, but by objects' (Baudrillard 1998: 25). The industrial revolution of the mid-nineteenth century saw an increase in the exchange of goods and services. Individuals were more able to consume and purchase objects that surpassed their basic needs. Consumerism as we understand and experience it today increased at a drastic rate following World War II with the introduction of credit. The Great

Depression had ended in the US and in other industrialized nations. Gradually, individuals were becoming more economically secure. After the economic war machine that was World War II, the US economy emerged stable and ready for even more profit accumulation. The rest of the world economy was in a much more dire economic situation as much of Europe's infrastructure had been destroyed along with two generations of young men. The 1980s, 1990s and early 2000s saw the gradual elimination of economic restraint. All social life must be subject to control, balance and regulation, that is the purpose of a society: to regulate human behavior through a stable and secure social structure. The economic realm has become free from all that.

What was once purely economic (the pursuit of profit) has now reached many avenues of our daily lives, even that of religion. Durkheim once wrote of the importance religion held for individuals within a society. 'Religious beliefs proper are always shared by a definite group that professes them and that practices the corresponding rites. [...] The individuals who comprise the group feel joined to one another by the fact of common faith' (Durkheim 1995: 41). The social solidarity, or sense of belonging, that religion once supplied has slowly shifted to a faith in the economy. Even more individuals are heavily socialized by the morals and values communicated by the media rather than religion. That which was once profane has now become sacred. As Durkheim stated, '[b]elief creates reality itself' (1983: 23). Our reality is the idea that consuming can bring the modern individual comfort, security and happiness. However, consuming often does just the opposite, providing a state of discomfort, insecurity and unhappiness.

Our modern world has morphed into an environment of limitless aspirations, goals and pursuits causing a state of unrest and insecurity for the individual. Durkheim foreshadowed that 'religion seems destined to transform itself rather than disappear' (1995: 432). Religion once supplied individuals with rules, regulations, morals, values and most importantly a structure that could shape and guide their life. Fast-forward to today where religious organizations have an extreme focus on profit and consumerism. What religious ceremony will attract the most consumers? A false, mechanized charisma that attracts memberships in the tens of thousands? Ultimately we are concerned with the profit that comes with individuals consuming the religion rather than purely internalizing the message religion can offer in and of itself. With increased knowledge of what appeals to individuals, one can learn to manipulate others for their own personal benefit. Corporate churches now exist with memberships in the tens of thousands. Pastors of these mega-churches are worth millions of dollars. Religion, which once encouraged humility and charity, now preaches individualism and the pursuit of material wealth. God wants you to be wealthy; he wants all people to be wealthy.

Hoarding is viewed as a mental disorder. However, this disorder could also be a reflection of a societal disorder; of a society that advocates narcissism with a focus on consumption. Anxiety as a result of having too many choices is a clear consequence of such societal characteristics. Hoarding may reflect an inability to cope with the plurality of choices presented to individuals and the inability to come to terms with one's sense of self. A focus on individualism and the advocating of narcissistic tendencies pushes individuals to a state of anxiety and shame, leaving room for the false self to take over. Consumption helps define the individual, so by consuming as much as possible one becomes a super-individual, as unique and original as possible, completely different from all others. Sound a bit narcissistic? Viewing material possessions as definitive in one's life leads to hoarding.

Loyalty and authenticity are slowly diminishing in our society. We live in a world of excess, entitlement issues and falseness. Are individuals humbled today? The experience of modesty and subservience were at one point necessary for individuals in order to be respectful of others and grateful for their status in life. An unhealthy level of focus on autonomy can lead to entitlement and narcissism for the individual. Reality television regularly presents individuals who achieve fame through deliberate disregard for how their actions impact others. In many instances their behavior is rewarded merely by providing them the attention that comes with a media audience (see, e.g. Chapter 6 on *Celebrity Rehab*). Vaknin points out that the narcissist 'direct[s] their love at other people's impressions of them [… b]ut the most important characteristic of the narcissist's projected image is its lovability' (Vaknin 2001: 195). There is so much focus on appearances and the way we present ourselves to others that we have begun to lose sight of our true self. There is little quality to our relationships because we care less about the people in our lives and more about how they think of us: 'the other-directed person is, in a sense, at home everywhere and nowhere, capable of a rapid, if sometimes superficial intimacy with and response to everyone' (Riesman et al. 1950: 334). There is a focus on being the best, the coolest, the brightest, the most popular; and less on how our actions affect others and how the decisions we make may have lasting repercussions.

We have shifted from a face-to-face environment for social interaction to that of mediated experiences and cyber-interaction. Primary groups, as discussed in sociology, provide the individual with expressive needs (intimacy, companionship and emotional support), whereas secondary groups provide the individual with instrumental needs (task-oriented, seen as a means to an end). Primary groups are long-lasting, typically consisting of family and one's closest friends, whereas secondary groups are rather short-lived and could be likened to a study group or classmates in a semester-long course. Secondary groups are now masquerading as primary groups. Can intimacy, companionship and emotional support be solely provided through online interaction? The reality show *Catfish* warns us of what can happen when the modern individual forms a relationship online under this illusion. Any relationship founded on artificiality causes disastrous results for the individual.

In a world focused on consumerism, Baudrillard warns '[a]ffluence does not exist, but it only has to make us believe it exists to be an effective myth' (Baudrillard 1998: 193). Americans today do believe. Their consumerism is comparable to religious belief. '[Consumerism] is a class logic which imposes salvation by objects' (Baudrillard 1998: 60). The message is consistent and constant and results in a fervent faith and steadfast belief in the idea that one can be saved by consuming. If all aspects of our society are now based on the pursuit of profit than this shall begin to affect the individual. Americans today seek salvation from their state of unhappiness through objects and things. The modern individual is overwhelmed, confused, agitated by the absence of that fulfillment which was promised them by the consumer society. As a result, individuals attempt to achieve this fulfillment by consuming even more. There is a momentary satisfaction gained from accumulating material possessions or purchasing exhilarating life experiences; however, there is no limit placed upon the amount of possessions or experiences one can obtain. The modern individual must submit to this never-ending goal and promise of fulfillment that will never be met. Maybe, just maybe, if they have faith in consumerism, if they believe that it will one day provide the ultimate satisfaction than the structure of the consumer society will actually fulfill its task and promise.

Where do individuals develop a faith in consumerism? 'Consumption is an active, collective behavior; it is something enforced, a morality, an institution. [...] The consumer society is also the society of learning to consume, of social training in consumption' (Baudrillard 1998: 81). One learns to consume from a young age. Think of a young child who is taught how to save their allowance – in order to what? Learn the importance of saving what one earns? Or is there an alternative goal in mind: to save for a consumer object? Surely, this endless goal would produce a state of discomfort and suffering from never being satisfied with what one has. 'Pleasure always means not to think about anything, to forget suffering even where it is shown. Basically it is helplessness. [...] The liberation which amusement promises is freedom from thought and from negation' (Horkheimer and Adorno 2002: 144). In a consumer society members endlessly seek out things, experiences, amusements and entertainment. When these objects fail to provide relief, comfort, security and happiness the individual may begin to feel helpless in this consumer world. Learning to consume in order to feel happy, yet happiness is but brief and momentary. A helpless state resulting from this suffering is commonly a consequence for many in a consumer society. However, similar to religious beliefs, one cannot know happiness without suffering. Suffering is justified in the consumer society in order to push individuals to seek out more entertainment, amusement and happiness in objects and things. The modern individual must now adapt to the consumer society.

Individuals desire to be unique and special because with each passing day differences are disappearing. This world is increasingly becoming a disenchanting one.

> The spread of American and indigenous fast food causes less and less diversity from one setting to another. In the process, the human craving

> for new and diverse experiences is being limited, if not progressively destroyed. It is being supplanted by the desire for uniformity and predictability.
>
> (Ritzer 2004: 147)

Is this truly the desire of the modern individual: uniformity and predictability? When one goes to a McDonalds in Dallas, TX or a McDonalds in New York City or Melbourne or London, one expects to receive the same food and the same experience. This experience, after all, is what they are paying for. Happy moments must now be staged, choreographed, rehearsed and ready for the close up of the camera's gaze. *They* will be watching: your peers and friends. Are you ready for your presentation of self? Spontaneity is the exact opposite of uniformity and predictability and this is escaping from our existence today. To repeatedly focus on, plan and execute the same behaviors and experiences over and over again we are losing sight of the experiences that provide the utmost value for the individual. The focus shifts to being *on point*, ready to present the artifice at any given moment. Be uniform and predictable just like your social structure.

This is the contradictory promise of a consumer society: be different, but really be the same. Individuals in our society are encouraged to buy consumer goods in the hopes of defining who they are as a person. Recent research has discussed the importance and consequences of material objects and consumption patterns in defining one's identity.[1] What are the right products to buy and more importantly how can the individual distinguish one's self?

> [T]he conformism of the buyers and the effrontery of the producers who supply them prevail. The result is a constant reproduction of the same thing [...] What is new about the phase of mass culture compared with the late liberal stage is the exclusion of the new.
>
> (Horkheimer and Adorno 2002: 134)

A reproduction of that which has already existed: the ultimate consumer product. An example of this cult of difference and exclusion of the new in today's world would be that of ProHealth Toothpaste. For quite some time, I was intrigued, as a consumer, by this new, innovative toothpaste that promised a concern for and improvement of my dental health. Then, new varieties of the toothpaste were released: ProHealth Cavity Protection, ProHealth Enamel Shield and ProHealth Plaque Control. Well now, I was confused as to which product would be best for me. So I turned to the ingredients. All ProHealth toothpaste varieties, all ten of them, contain the exact same active ingredient: Stannous fluoride 0.454% (0.16% w/v fluoride ion). A promise of difference and exclusivity, when in reality they're all the same. '[F]reedom to choose an ideology – since ideology always reflects economic coercion – everywhere proves to be freedom to choose what is always the same' (Horkheimer and Adorno 2002: 166–167). This cult of difference is really an oxymoron. Much of what exists in the consumer society is not new and improved but the same with a shiny, new package to conceal that sameness. The individual, must in turn, present a shiny, new package (artifice) to all others in order to conceal their hollow, empty and extremely fragile self.

In *Toddlers and Tiaras* viewers may be perturbed by the behavior of the parents, who seemingly push their daughters into beauty competitions before they are able to clearly understand what they are participating in. However, this program provides insight into the exact same characteristics of our society that result in the hoarding disorder: narcissism, consumerism and the encouragement of the false self. 'Narcissists tend to breed narcissists' (Vaknin 2001: 208). Spoiling a child can lead to unrealistic expectations of what the world should provide that individual once they are grown up. Some insight gained from examining *The Real Housewives* shows (Chapter 7) might help clarify what these little girls are to become. Encouraging young girls to present an artificial appearance that ultimately determines whether or not they are 'successful' at the beauty pageant, yet telling them that they are being judged on their personality is ludicrous and just another illusion. This is a harsh message to learn and internalize at such a young age: you must present an illusion of the real.

Individuals are encouraged to focus on themselves even to the point of objectifying one's self. There is constantly a dichotomy between the real and the false, illusion and reality: this illusion of difference/uniqueness. If the modern individual is surrounded by deceptive practices, promises and satisfaction, will they not eventually begin to reflect these same principles? Our goals, dreams, aspirations and desires are misguided from the start. The modern individual merely tries to adapt. The new narcissus appears in times of trouble with a promise … one needs to only buy into the illusion.

Artifice

In *Sister Wives*, individuals seek out narcissistic supply from many sources, even those closest to them: the family. Selfish pursuits and interests can be devastating not only for the individual who lacks exposure to the value of human interaction and relationships but worse yet, they may encourage this same behavior in their offspring. The limitless pursuit of wealth has even entered into the realm of family where you can potentially have as many wives as you please while disregarding or even refusing to acknowledge the emotional toll this can take on them. The narcissistic husband is able to pursue limitless pleasure and satisfaction from his multiple wives yet they are free to suffer and repress feelings of jealousy and inadequacy.

Individuals must now balance the dichotomy of illusion vs. reality in both their social and individual existence. Durkheim warned that the economic aspect of society that threatened to impact all facets of daily life would have drastic effects on the individual. 'The obstacle, for example, against which the victim of insatiable desires dashes may cause him to fall back upon himself and seek an outlet for his disappointed passions in an inner life' (Durkheim 1951: 288). The women chronicled in *Sister Wives* struggled with issues of jealousy yet masked their true feelings and emotions with a smile. *Hoarders* reflects the dangers of falling back upon one's self when the promises of the new narcissus and society only seem to offer relentless disappointment. In *Celebrity Rehab*, the patients at one time emulated society's definition of success, so how could they possibly succumb to addiction? What's so bad about their success? It is a success that promises limitless pursuits and an unrelenting quest for satisfaction that never comes.

An increased focus on this reflection looking back at you reminds you of the importance of your appearance to others. The new narcissus' grasp is strong and so very promising. The artifice need only be projected. '[B]ureaucratic institutions, which put a premium on the manipulation of interpersonal relations, discourage the formation of deep personal attachments, and at the same time provide the narcissist with the approval he needs in order to validate his self-esteem' (Lasch 1978: 44). False friendliness and an upbeat personality are encouraged, if not required, in most workplaces.[2] One cannot be sad, angry or irritable in the modern bureaucratic environment. Often, individuals are taught to use the company to achieve a certain position in the workplace and in turn, the company uses individuals. Examples of loyalty to a company that is reciprocated by that company's loyalty to its employees, are few and far between. Everyone is replaceable by the newer, younger more attractive commodity: the individual. The mechanized aspect and repetitive nature of most jobs are taking their toll on the individual. Individuals see people getting ahead, promoted and rewarded for stepping on others or using others for their own selfish goals. Loyalty and respect have diminished, if not completely disappeared from most work places.

Social media, bureaucracies and increasing pressure to focus on the self are drastically impacting individuals and our personal relationships. Modern individuals are 'chronically bored, restlessly in search of instantaneous intimacy – of emotional titillation without involvement and dependence' (Lasch 1978: 40). Technology has provided even more opportunities to extract instantaneous gratification from others. Meaningful, long-lasting relationships may be difficult to maintain amidst our absorption in social media and brief communication. *Catfish: The TV Show*, portrays the opportunities individuals now have available to them through social media and the Internet to portray their false self to others in the pursuit of attention, admiration and success. We now have avenues through which we can mask our true identity in order to pursue this attention while unashamedly damaging other individuals emotionally.

There are benefits of illusion, of artifice. 'Narcissism appears realistically to represent the best way of coping with the tensions and anxieties of modern life, and the prevailing social conditions therefore tend to bring out narcissistic traits that are present, in varying degrees, in everyone' (Lasch 1978: 50). Tension and anxiety are ever present in the modern world with the pressure to achieve economic success. Technology further complicates these feelings with a shift towards instant gratification and brief interactions with others. Often times our interactions are purely for the sake of achieving an end. Rarely are there interactions where the relationship alone is seen as an end in and or itself. *What can you do for me?* This 'imperative of competition and upward social mobility and [...] imperative to maximalize their pleasures. Under so many opposing constraints, the individual comes apart' (Baudrillard 1998: 182). The pursuit of a limitless goal causes anxiety and tension for the individual. The new narcissus gazes back at us with a promise of providing the means by which to cope. Focus on yourself, better yourself, you are the only one that matters in the world that is so willing to overlook you – unless of course you can project the right image. Then the world will lavish you with the attention, adulation, adoration and admiration (narcissistic supply) you so rightly deserve. There are so few who can promise such things to you when you are merely your true self. Give in. Give in to the illusion.

> Doomed to our own image, our own identity, our own 'look', and having become our own object of care, desire and suffering, we have grown indifferent to everything else. And secretly desperate at that indifference, and envious of every form of passion, originality and destiny.
>
> (Baudrillard 1996: 131)

Baudrillard warns that a world of illusion and artificiality obsessed with the accumulation of material objects will result in the individual viewing themselves as an object. The individual as the ultimate object that can be altered, manufactured and presented in such a way as to receive not only the most attention but hopefully, economic success too. 'Narcissism emerges as the typical form of character structure in a society that has lost interest in the future' (Lasch 1978: 211). The pressure to achieve pushes individuals to become neurotic, chronically anxious about their ability to achieve economic success. The new narcissus allows the individual to focus, first and foremost, on the creation of their most desired self. By altering yourself, in order to better your social status, the creation of an artificial self will benefit you.

Our world is surrounded by illusions. Individuals are airbrushed or they starve themselves to the brink of death in order to achieve a standard of perceived beauty and perceived perfection. In many avenues, professions and social interactions there are similar standards of exceptionality that many individuals strive for. This is a difficult balance to maintain: having the bar set high in order to encourage innovation and true talent, yet allowing some level of fulfillment of one's endeavors. Pursuit of limitless goals can have devastating effects upon the individual, and these consequences are the focus of this research. If an individual cannot achieve and obtain these infinite goals through the presentation of their true self then they may resort to creating an artificial self through what they observe around them. Individuals are immersed in the media today (television, radio, film, Facebook, Twitter,

Instagram, Snapchat, blogs, YouTube, video games, etc.) that present 'successful' individuals and disseminate the message that self-objectification is important. Too much focus on the self, coupled with constant immersion in the media, the mirror, our reflection, encourages individuals to alter their self in an artificial way in order to hopefully achieve success.

Avoidance

If the modern individual has been forced to adapt to a consumer society by presenting an artificial self, then when others recognize this artifice it will put that individual in the worst possible state. They will not only have to admit that they are presenting an artifice to others but will also be forced to admit that their faith in a consumer society and the promises of satisfaction are flawed, just like their false self. Instead, the individual that has recognized the benefits of presenting an artifice will attempt to protect that artificiality at all costs, i.e., they will avoid any challenges or confrontations concerning their true identity. Accountability is absolutely out of the question and avoidance is necessary in order to keep the artifice alive and well. '[T]he whole process of consumption is governed by the production of artificially diversified models' (Baudrillard 1998: 88–89). Artificiality rules the consumer society: false representations of meaningful interactions, false enchantment in places to help cope with dehumanization and deceptive satisfaction with the promise of eternal happiness. 'We have to beware of interpreting this gigantic enterprise of production of the artificial and the cosmetic, of pseudo-objects and pseudo-events, which is invading our daily existence, as a denaturing or falsifying of an "authentic" content' (Baudrillard 1998: 126). The removal of meaning and authenticity is a tragic consequence of a consumer society.

Having predictability, calculability and efficiency at every avenue encourages a false persona for many individuals in their daily interactions with others.[3] An increase in the amount of falsified interactions is encouraging the individual to also be false. 'We are surrounded by waves of fake spontaneity, "personalized" language, orchestrated emotions and personal relations. "Keep smiling"' (Baudrillard 1998: 161). Individuals in a consumer society must maintain this artificiality even at the cost of their own authenticity. Stjepan Mestrovic warns:

> [I]n today's post-emotional society, this 'natural' relationship between emotion and action has been permanently severed. Emotions serve no appreciable purpose as such, and the more useless one's emotions are, the more one demonstrates to the peer group that one has attained the level of prestige that makes the owning of emotions a luxury that one can afford. (1997: 55)

Even our feelings for others can be falsified and made mechanical. If modern individuals now have faith in the illusion that the consumer society provides, at what point do we begin to believe the illusion we put forth to others and deny the real?

Manuel Castells discusses how advances in technology are altering the landscape of consumerism.

> [T]he ultimate subversion of the life-cycle is accomplished, and life becomes this false landscape punctuated by chosen moments of high and low experiences, in the endless boutique of customized feelings. So when death does happen it is simply an additional blip on the screen of distracted spectators.
>
> (1996: 481)

A grim portrait of existence: to live in a world with customized feelings with an added pressure to have the latest and greatest technology. This results in confusion, anxiety and dissatisfaction. Emotions that invoke sadness or grief must be replaced with ones that invoke happiness and elation. The new narcissus must be kept alive and your gaze is the only way. Will you continue to look back, giving the new narcissus all the power? 'The peculiarity of the self is a monopoly commodity determined by society; it is falsely represented as natural' (Horkheimer and Adorno 2002: 154). Scripted interactions and false friendliness are 'natural'. Everyone must participate. Those are the conditions of a consumer society.

> While the mechanism is to all appearances planned by those who serve up the data of experience, that is, by the culture industry, it is in fact forced upon the latter by the power of society, which remains irrational, however we may try to rationalize it; and this inescapable force is processed by commercial agencies so that they give an artificial impression of being in command.
>
> (Horkheimer and Adorno 2002: 125)

Who is truly in control in the consumer society? The driving force in consumerism is the economy, which has been freed from regulation. The pursuit of profit is limitless and has run out of control. Artificiality is at the forefront of this runaway character of the economy. Conformity can only be guaranteed under the guise of control and security, even when individuals feel the anxiety and insecurity that comes from an anomic state. Individuals attempt to adapt to this irrational structure of society by rationalizing its limitless goals and false promises of satisfaction. An artificially created self begins to gaze back at us as we look in the mirror, promising attention and success. Just as individuals have adapted to the structure of a consumer society, rationalizing irrational goals and pursuits; so too has the individual created an artifice. This artificial self is a product of living in a world full of artificiality, false promises, false presentations and unobtainable goals and pursuits. When an individual has maintained a lie or artifice for some period of time it is a difficult psychological state for any individual when confronted with the truth. No one wants to hear that the reflection looking back at them in the mirror is a false one. I can see myself and I know that what I see is *real*.

All of these reality television programs share the revelation of artificiality and the resulting avoidance that occurs on behalf of the individuals portrayed. This is the endless cycle that results from the hostile takeover of the new narcissus. First, an adaptation to a consumer environment: a belief and faith in the consumer structure to the point of denying the false promises. Then, amidst this illusory environment of false promises and artificiality the individual sees the benefits and rewards offered for successfully altering themselves and presenting an artifice to others. The new narcissus that stares back at us is alluring. All must continue faith in the belief that the structure works so when that faith or those promises or even the artificiality is called into question all must avoid and deny the criticisms, the truth. The new narcissus must survive at all costs and the falseness must be maintained.

Fake enchantment: illusion becomes our reality

The new narcissus is a new sociological problem that results from fake enchantment. As this book has illustrated, many social theorists insist that we are living in an increasingly *dis*enchanted world. Some may believe these illusions in a consumer society, whether it be in advertising, or online, in the workplace or the media, as attempts to *re*-enchant a disenchanted world. Bureaucracies, rigid social structures and a focus on consuming can be exhausting and draining for the modern individual. The Internet and media and reality television can provide solace and comfort and even satisfaction. Are we, through media and other illusory experiences, truly enjoying an *enchanting* experience? An experience of comfort and security from these illusory experiences is lacking, further propelling an environment of artificiality in both social interactions and individuals' presentation of self. This is the question that remains: Are we attempting to re-enchant a disenchanted world or are we participating in fake enchantment? The new narcissus is a fraud, a phoney, a fake. We appear to accept the illusion, the artificiality, the falseness, even when we know it exists. Is an experience of fake enchantment truly satisfying?

> The media give substance to and thus intensify narcissistic dreams of fame and glory, encouraging the common man to identify himself with the stars and hate the 'herd' [...] making it more and more difficult for him to accept the banality of everyday existence.
>
> (Lasch 1978: 21)

An extreme focus on being the greatest, best, most admired, most esteemed, most successful individual does not result in a happy existence. Unconditional love, respect, loyalty and trustworthiness as well as a raw, flawed, real human interaction is what is needed today. We are humans and we are not perfect.

We need to wake up and recognize the reality we are creating for ourselves. Reality television may be produced, altered, falsified or even scripted. However, that does not remove the message that is transmitted to viewers. These messages are still reflecting beliefs, behaviors and trends within our current existence. That is why this analysis is crucial to understanding the changes that are occurring within the modern individual.

Reality television may even be a way to cope with the banality of our current existence. The more the structure of our society becomes consumed by the pursuit of profit at all costs, with blatant disregard for human feeling and emotion, the more individuals will see themselves as objects. If we continue to objectify everything then at some point individualism will reach such an extreme that the essential ingredients of compassion and empathy within human relationships and social interaction will disappear.

> The tired pupil is the one who passively goes along with what the teacher says. The tired worker or bureaucrat is the one who has had all responsibility taken from him in his work. Political 'indifference' [...] is the indifference of the individual deprived of any decision-making powers and left only with the sop of universal suffrage.
>
> (Baudrillard 1998: 183)

There are people everywhere who experience a lack of autonomy and freedom in their jobs and are instead forced to fulfill the wishes, dreams and desires of their narcissistic co-workers and bosses. This indifference is already a societal symptom of extreme individualism and artificiality. There is too much emphasis on success, fortune and fame that is only obtainable by a few yet presented as obtainable for many. The message is: avoid disagreement, project fakeness. Even more, an extreme focus and pursuit of this societal value of achieving economic success serves what purpose for the betterment of humanity? At one point, wealth may have sought to improve the lives of the members of society through improvements in medicine, science and technology, but now, is this still the end goal for wealth accumulation? Isn't the end goal instead: what can this money do for *me*?

Producers of reality television programs may encourage the participants to exemplify certain aspects of their personality, even if that is not the 'real' them and how they normally behave.

> [T]he sign that the world is becoming opaque, that our acts are getting out of our control and, at that point, we have no perspective on ourselves. Without that guarantee, no identity is possible any longer: I become another to myself; I am alienated.
>
> (Baudrillard 1998: 188)

The individuals portrayed in these reality shows may be alienated from their true sense of self. Individuals adapt by creating a false self: one that can shield them from shame, hurt and other feelings that prevent economic success. Pay attention to *others* for cues as to how to best behave and present yourself in the hopes of being the most successful, most admired individual. Pay attention to what you see on reality television. Audience reception of the texts of these reality television shows may be ambivalent; however, might we be looking at a reflection of ourselves in consuming reality television? As an audience, are we alienated from social interaction by consuming reality television? Reality television, again, may be a coping mechanism in order to adapt to a consumer society's lack of moral regulation and limitless goals. The result is an alienated audience, leading to not only disastrous consequences for the individual but for our relationships with others as well. There has always been a curiosity about how 'the other half lives' and a certain fascination with celebrities. 'It is always the excessiveness of their lives, the potential for outrageous expenditure that is exalted' (Baudrillard 1998: 46). In a consumer society where possibilities are limitless, being bombarded with celebrities and their lifestyles is like showing an addict his drug of choice and saying 'You can look, but don't touch!' 'The psychological and social pressures of mobility of status and competition at all levels (income, prestige, culture, etc.) are becoming burdensome for everyone' (Baudrillard 1998: 40). Designer everything. Design your house. Design your car. Design your baby. Will the future allow the possibility to alter the genetic makeup of human beings so that they reflect what has been deemed socially desirable and beautiful? Durkheim's concept of anomie as a result of the dangerous, runaway, amoral character of economic life is devastating for so many individuals in our society that just cannot come to terms with these limitless aspirations.

We have become immune to the illusions that surround us, whether they are products, television or individuals, and we brush this falsity off as being only a few bad apples or the unusual behavior of a few. Fake enchantment ultimately feels real, so who cares if it's actually fake? However, this is a concern as it is an overarching reflection of our society. The new narcissus is consuming many. 'These dispositions are so inbred that society has grown to accept them and is accustomed to think them normal' (Durkheim 1951: 257). Constantly seeking out narcissistic supply coupled with a desire to surround ourselves with better and more important people leads to the belief that our status is exemplified by association. Relationships no longer have a true value, instead there is this focus on presenting an artifice of what is deemed desirable by others.

Voyeurism is merely a means through which an individual 'keeps up' with what is desired by others and is used as a way to maintain one's own artifice. Or think of the Facebook phenomenon. Facebook is all about appearances and glorifying one's self. Do you have the best pictures of yourself? Do you have the most friends? Are more people commenting on your status updates? How many people are commenting on your posts and posting things on your wall? How many 'likes' are you receiving in a day? Whether or not an individual chooses to focus on these dimensions of Facebook is not what is important. What is important is the fact that it is the *structure* of Facebook:

to be more liked, admired, esteemed, followed, envied, ultimately equating an individual's sense of self to how successful they are in that medium. Customize your profile. Customize yourself. We aren't even truly interacting with other individuals. The interaction is detached and removed from real, meaningful interactions with other human beings. 'The person as a determining instance disappears and is replaced by personalization' (Baudrillard 1998: 170). Facebook is the perfect example of our obsession with appearances and projections of ourselves. But worse yet, it is an opportunity to present a false self, in order to become more popular, more liked, to have more friends, more attention.

I am not saying that people who do extraordinary, wonderful, unique and memorable things do not deserve to be exemplified and appreciated by many. However, when someone fakes greatness, that is when we have a problem. When we are encouraged to fake it when we don't physically possess those skills or attributes, then it is a problem. When the focus is put on material possessions in defining who we are as individuals, we have a problem. When we are encouraged to go with the rule that lacks a rule (limitless pursuit of wealth) because if you do not you will lose your job, or your friends, or anything, then we have a problem. If, instead, we are encouraged to recognize the traits that we truly possess as unique and genuine and great then we do not have a problem. If, instead, we value our relationships with others for the genuine security, happiness, comfort and love they can provide rather than selfish pursuits, then we do not have a problem. We have genuine recognition for true greatness and unique individuals. We are all unique and special and that needs to be recognized. 'Belief creates reality itself' (Durkheim 1983: 23). We are not unique and special when we put on fake hair, teeth, makeup, and above all a fake personality on in order to be viewed as such. We are not exceptional or worthy of emulation when we deny our true feelings and casually go along with an irrational consumer structure the promises satisfaction through infinite desires. Replacing meaningful interactions and human relationships with material objects to the point of obsession with those objects is focusing on this artificial belief that money is a valuable life goal and pursuit. Why isn't our collective goal the betterment of humanity?

The question still remains how audiences truly view such programs as *Hoarders*, *Toddlers and Tiaras*, *Sister Wives*, *Catfish: The TV Show*, *Celebrity Rehab* and *The Real Housewives*. Do they view these behaviors and lifestyles as deviations from normal behavior, mere pathologies or exclusions? Further research might examine the reception of audience members to such examples of reality television. For the time being, it seems that our individualistic society may simply be enjoying the role of voyeur, entertained by these seemingly odd behaviors of unusual and different members of our society. 'Normal' people do not behave and think in these ways … right? Unfortunately, we do indeed behave in very similar ways to all of the people in these television shows. Sure, our behavior and thought processes may not be as extreme as those portrayed but we cannot avoid the nature of our society's ideology. People may not even be aware of the push to be narcissistic, focused on our own biographies and self-promotion, but it is necessary in so many avenues of our daily life, and if we do not possess these skills and qualities we are encouraged to just fake it. Individuals may routinely immerse themselves in watching reality television in order to help cope with the learned helplessness that comes from the realization that our social structure is flawed. It may contribute to why many Americans spend countless hours in front of the television, separating themselves from this anomic society, or worse yet, immersing themselves in it and the messages that continue to portray the benefits of limitless pursuits, fame, fortune, success and notoriety that are achieved through artificiality. The new narcissus' reflection back at us is strong and enticing, the more fixated our gaze the less we become. Losing sight of ourselves means we are losing sight of our humanity, what separates us from the animals. Just as the tale as old as time (well, at least a tale that's over 2,000 years old) warns that an extreme love of the self has two outcomes: death or suicide. As individuals and as a society we should aspire to neither.

Notes

1 For more on consumerism and identity see Bullen 2009, Pecora 2002, Philips 2005, Rose 1992 and Tudor 2009.
2 David Riesman also discusses the idea of false personalization in his book *The Lonely Crowd: A Study of the Changing American Character*. Riesman articulates the changes occurring in the modern workplace and this emergence of impersonality alongside automation: '[t]his new sensitivity […] makes it difficult for people to extricate themselves from chains of false personalization by wearing a completely alien work mask' (Riesman et al. 1950: 305).
3 See *McDonaldization of Society* by George Ritzer (2004).

Bibliography

Alexander, Bruce K. (2008) *The Globalisation of Addiction: A Study in Poverty of the Spirit*. New York and Oxford: Oxford University Press.

American Psychiatric Association. (2013) *Diagnostic and Statistical Manual of Mental Disorders: DSM-5*. Washington, DC: American Psychiatric Association.

Andrejevic, Mark. (2002) 'The Kindler, Gentler Gaze of Big Brother: Reality TV in the Era of Digital Capitalism'. *New Media and Society* 4: 251–270.

Argetsinger, Amy and Roxanne Roberts. (2009). 'Reliable Source: Tareq and Michaele Salahi Crash Obamas' State Dinner for India'. *The Washington Post*, 26 November. Retrieved from www.washingtonpost.com/wpdyn/content/article/2009/11/25/AR2009112504113.html?sid=ST2010061204459

Baudrillard, Jean. (1970) *The Consumer Society: Myths and Structures*. London: Sage.

Baudrillard, Jean. (1996) *The Perfect Crime*. New York: Verso.

Baudrillard, Jean. (1998) *The Consumer Society: Myths and Structures*. 2nd edn. London: Sage.

'Beauty'. (n.d.) *Merriam-Webster Online Dictionary*. Retrieved from https://www.merriam-webster.com/dictionary/beauty

Bullen, Elizabeth. (2009) 'Inside Story: Product Placement and Adolescent Consumer Identity in Young Adult Fiction'. *Media, Culture and Society* 31(3): 497–507.

Callero, Peter. (2003) 'The Sociology of the Self'. *Annual Review of Sociology* 29: 115–133.

Campbell, W. Keith, Joshua Miller and Thomas Widiger. (2010) 'Narcissistic Personality Disorder and the DSM-V'. *Journal of Abnormal Psychology* 119(4): 640–649.

Castells, Manuel. (1996) *The Rise of the Network Society*. Cambridge, MA: Blackwell.

Castells, Manuel. (2010) *The Rise of the Network Society*. 2nd edn. Oxford: Wiley/Blackwell.

Corben, Billy. (Director). (2012) *Broke*. Motion picture. Miami, FL: Rakontur.

Dunlop, Scott (Creator), Sarah Dillistone, David Granger, Daran Little and Sean Murphy (Executive producers). (2015a) 'Welcome to Cheshire'. *The Real Housewives of Cheshire*. Television series. London: ITV Network.

Dunlop, Scott (Creator), Sarah Dillistone, David Granger, Daran Little and Sean Murphy (Executive producers). (2015b) 'The Girl Who Got It All'. *The Real Housewives of Cheshire*. Television series. London: ITV Network.

Durkheim, Emile. (1951) *Suicide: A Study in Sociology*. Translated by John A. Spaulding and George Simpson. New York: Free Press of Glencoe.

Durkheim, Emile. (1957) *Professional Ethics and Civic Morals*. Translated by Cornelia Brookfield. London: Routledge and Kegan Paul.

Durkheim, Emile. (1983) *Pragmatism and Sociology.* Translated by J. C. Whitehouse. Cambridge: Cambridge University Press.

Durkheim, Emile. (1995) *The Elementary Forms of the Religious Life.* New York: Free Press.

Durkheim, Emile. (1997) *Division of Labor in Society.* New York: Free Press.

Farhi, Paul. (2009) 'Former Redskins Cheerleaders Doubt Michaele Salahi's Bona Fides'. *The Washington Post*, 3 December. Retrieved from www.washingtonpost.com/wpdyn/content/article/2009/12/02/AR2009120203781.html

Freud, Sigmund. (1914) 'On Narcissism: An Introduction'. In G. Albrecht (ed.), *Encyclopedia of Disability.* Thousand Oaks, CA: Sage.

Gallagher, Sean and Abby Greensfelder. (Executive producers). (2010) *The Real Housewives of D.C.* Television series. New York: Bravo.

Gibbons, Timothy, Bill Hayes, Christopher Poole and Kirk Streb (Executive producers). (2010) 'Meet Kody and the Wives'. *Sister Wives.* Television program. Silver Spring, UT: Discovery Communications.

Giddens, Anthony. (1991) *Modernity and Self-Identity.* Stanford, CA: Stanford University Press.

Gitlin, Todd. (2001) *Media Unlimited: How the Torrent of Images and Sounds Overwhelms Our Lives.* New York: Metropolitan Books.

Goffman, Erving. (1959) *The Presentation of Self in Everyday Life.* Garden City, NJ: Doubleday.

'Hedonism'. (n.d.) *Merriam-Webster Online Dictionary.* Retrieved from https://www.merriam-webster.com/dictionary/hedonism

Hirsch, Irwin and Cara Hirsch. (2000) 'A Look at Our Dark Side'. *Journal of Popular Television and Film* 28(3): 116–123.

Horkheimer, Max and Theodor Adorno. (2002) *Dialectic of Enlightenment.* Stanford, CA: Stanford University Press.

Keys, David. (2004) 'The Ugly End of Narcissus: Ancient Manuscript Sheds New Light on Enduring Myth'. *BBC History Magazine* no. 5: 9. Retrieved from www.papyrology.ox.ac.uk/POxy/news/narcissus.html

Lareau, Annette. (2003) *Unequal Childhoods: Class, Race and Family Life.* Berkeley, CA: University of California Press.

Lasch, Christopher. (1978) *Culture of Narcissism: American Life in an Age of Diminishing Expectations.* New York: Norton.

McRobbie, Angela. (2001) '"Everyone Is Creative": Artists as New Economic Pioneers?' Open Democracy. Retrieved from www.opendemocracy.net/node/652/pdf (consulted January 2010).

McRobbie, Angela. (2002) 'Fashion Culture: Creative Work, Female Individualization'. *Feminist Review* 71: 52–62.

Mestrovic, Stjepan. (1997) *Postemotional Society.* Thousand Oaks, CA: Sage.

Mills, C. Wright. (1959) *The Sociological Imagination.* New York: Oxford University Press.

Mussman, Jonathan (Executive producer in charge). (2013) 'Jen and Skylar'. *Catfish: The TV Show.* Television series. New York: MTV Networks Music & Logo Group.

'New Light on the Narcissus Myth'. (n.d.) *The Oxyrhynchus Papyri Collection Online.* Retrieved from www.papyrology.ox.ac.uk/POxy/papyri/4711.html

Ong, Jonathan. (2009) 'The Cosmopolitan Continuum'. *Media, Culture and Society* 31(3): 449–466.

Pecora, Vincent P. (2002) 'The Culture of Surveillance'. *Qualitative Sociology* 25(3): 345–358.

Philips, Deborah. (2005) 'Transformation Scenes: The Television Interior Makeover'. *International Journal of Culture Studies* 8(2): 213–229.

Pinsky, Drew (Executive producer). (2010) *Celebrity Rehab with Dr. Drew.* Television series. Los Angeles, CA: Irwin Entertainment.

Pinsky, Drew and Mark Young. (2009). *The Mirror Effect: How Celebrity Narcissism Is Seducing America.* New York: HarperCollins.

Riesman, David, Todd Gitlin, Reuel Denney and Nathan Glazer. (1950) *The Lonely Crowd: A Study of the Changing American Character.* New Haven, CT: Yale University Press.

Ritzer, George. (2004) *The McDonaldization of Society.* Thousand Oaks, CA: Pine Forge Press.

Rose, Nikolas. (1992) 'Governing the Enterprising Self'. In Paul Heelas and Paul Morris (eds), *The Values of the Enterprise Culture: The Moral Debate.* New York: Routledge, 141–164.

Sharenow, Robert and Andy Berg (Executive producers). (2010) 'Deborah and Jim'. *Hoarders.* Television series. New York: A&E Broadcasting Company.

Simmel, Georg. (1904). '*Fashion*'. In Peter Kivisto (ed.), *Social Theory: Roots and Branches* (101–105). New York: Oxford University Press.

Sims, Matt (Writer), Lauren Lexton and Tom Rogan (Executive producers). (2009) 'National Gold Coast'. *Toddlers and Tiaras.* Television series. Silver Spring, UT: Discovery Communications.

Tudor, Deborah. (2009) 'Who Counts? Who Is Being Counted? How Audience Measurement Embeds Neoliberalism into Urban Space'. *Media, Culture and Society* 31(5): 833–840.

Twenge, Jean M. and W. Keith Campbell. (2009) *The Narcissism Epidemic: Living in an Age of Entitlement.* New York: Free Press.

Vaknin, Sam. (2001) *Malignant Self-Love: Narcissism Revisited.* Skopje: Narcissus Publications.

'Vanity'. (n.d.) *Merriam-Webster Online Dictionary.* Retrieved from https://www.merriam-webster.com/dictionary/vanity

Washington, Kylie (Executive producer). (2016a) 'Do Buy'. *The Real Housewives of Melbourne.* Television series. Australia: Matchbox Entertainment.

Washington, Kylie (Executive producer). (2016b) 'Desert Storm'. *The Real Housewives of Melbourne.* Television series. Australia: Matchbox Entertainment.

Index

For Product Safety Concerns and Information please contact our EU
representative GPSR@taylorandfrancis.com
Taylor & Francis Verlag GmbH, Kaufingerstraße 24, 80331 München, Germany

www.ingramcontent.com/pod-product-compliance
Ingram Content Group UK Ltd.
Pitfield, Milton Keynes, MK11 3LW, UK
UKHW011016180926
475701UK00004B/772

* 9 7 8 0 3 6 7 3 3 2 9 5 2 *